THE SPEECH

THE SPEECH

RACE AND BARACK OBAMA'S
"A MORE PERFECT UNION"

EDITED BY

T. DENEAN SHARPLEY-WHITING

BLOOMSBURY

NEW YORK BERLIN LONDON

Published by Bloomsbury USA, New York

All papers used by Bloomsbury USA are natural, recyclable products made
from wood grown in well-managed forests. The manufacturing processes
conform to the environmental regulations of the country of origin.

LIBRARY OF CONGRESS CATALOGING-IN-PUBLICATION DATA

The speech : race and Barack Obama's "A more perfect union" / [edited by] T. Denean
Sharpley-Whiting.—1st U.S. ed.
p. cm.
Includes text of Barack Obama's "A more perfect union" speech, delivered
Mar. 18, 2008.
ISBN-13: 978-1-59691-667-8 (hardcover)
ISBN-10: 1-59691-667-2 (hardcover)
1. United States—Race relations. 2. United States—Social conditions—21st century.
3. Obama, Barack—Political and social views. 4. Obama, Barack—Oratory.
5. Speeches, addresses, etc., American. I. Sharpley-Whiting, T. Denean. II. Obama,
Barack. More perfect union.
E184.A1S698 2009
973.932092—dc22
2009006603

First U.S. Edition 2009

1 3 5 7 9 10 8 6 4 2

Designed by Sara E. Stemen

Typeset by Westchester Book Group
Printed in the United States of America by Quebecor World Fairfield

For Haviland, "Let's Get Free" (DP)

THE LAST FIRST

not the first heavyweight champion of the world,
    airline pilot, quarterback in the NFL, college graduate,
    doctor, teacher, big league baseball player, preacher-pastor,
    ceo, mountain climber, university president, entrepreneur,
    heart surgeon, inventor, governor or poet.
not the first mathematician, physicist, engineer, supreme court justice,
    fastest man alive, publisher, reporter, ambassador, entertainer,
    four-star general, best-selling author, executive chef, sergeant
        major,
    scientist, basketball hall-of-famer, economist, secretary of state,
    nobel prize winner, astronaut, law enforcer, chair of the joint
    chiefs, senator, first responder or state legislator.
not the best trumpet player alive, bank president, husband, father,
    organic farmer, rapper's rapper or coach's coach.
not an undefined question looking for an answer or
    hidden agenda claiming the authority of one.
not an exploiter of the commons.
    is the green hands nurturing fields, crops and rain forests.
    is the water, food, education, clean energy, preventive health
        and intellect required.
    is the humanitarian connecting music and economy, writing
        political notes

legible to professionals, novices, students and elders the world
over.
is the community organizer maneuvering citizens' campaigns
expecting to implant knowledge, consent and saneness on
impracticability
as renegade* and renaissance* expand the *can* in *we* and *yes*
at the early-light of this promising century
not the last, is the first
barack obama, president.

—HAKI R. MADHUBUTI
December 19, 2008

*Secret Service code names for president-elect Obama and Mrs. Obama

CONTENTS

CONTENTS

THE SPEECH

CHLOROFORM MORNING JOE!

Introduction by T. Denean Sharpley-Whiting

That's what the voice sputtered into the phone. Like in the movies, she imagined placing a handkerchief firmly over the nose and mouth of the Republican host of MSNBC's *Morning Joe*. It would not be the last time that this dear friend rang me up with all sorts of mischievous ranting proposals—red-hot pokers, woodsheds, and three-minute dirt naps—for how to rid us, temporarily at least, of the likes of the garrulous Joe Scarborough. In the days leading up to Barack Obama's historic speech on race, Scarborough brayed nonstop about the relationship between the Reverend Jeremiah Wright and the junior senator from Illinois. Fresh off twelve straight caucus and primary wins, having just clinched the lead in the delegate count over Hillary Clinton, who many had assumed would be the presumptive Democratic nominee for the presidency, Obama entered the six-week-long primary battle in Pennsylvania fending off questions about his pastor's fiery oratory.

The major news networks were wallpapered with Wright every day, all day. Barack Obama had some explaining to do to white America, though the call to do so was never articulated so plainly. Who was this seemingly affable, African American man who had lulled the white electorate by virtue of his tangled ancestry into believing that he too identified with them? Who was the Reverend Jeremiah Wright? What kind of church preached such hate? Was this how black people worshipped? How could Wright "damn" America? What did Obama know? Hear? Read? (As in the church's news bulletin, which had reprinted a *Los Angeles Times* editorial by a Hamas leader.) Was he in the pews on that day? How could he have attended the church of such a rabidly unpatriotic black racist for so many years? And this "wackadoodle," as Wright had been called by Maureen Dowd in one *New York Times* op-ed, had baptized the children, the children, for crying out loud! Scarborough was unloading, and my friend, a member of that "liberal professorial elite," shrieked at every one of his patently obtuse conclusions about race and racism in America.

We watched as Obama and his surrogates did the media rounds to stem the negative coverage. It was painful. It was awful. The "crazy uncle" meme was not playing well with the chattering classes, primarily because Jeremiah Wright is not crazy. Salty? Yes. Crazy? Not so much. Privately many black Americans did not think so either until he reemerged in April wilding out at the National Press Club. The media smelled a story with legs, long ones. By Friday, March 14, 2008, flipping from channel to channel, pundit to pundit, I had settled uncharacteristically on Fox. I listened as Geraldo Rivera, who owed his career resurgence in the 1990s to another redoubtable African American man—O. J. Simpson—pronounced after Obama's interview on Keith Olbermann's *Countdown* that something had gone out of the Illinois senator's eyes. That it was now over for him and Obama knew it. The pundits had already begun the postmortem on the Democratic front-runner's candidacy.

That Obama took the lead on our gnarled conversations about race in America by delivering the speech "A More Perfect Union" stunned his critics and supporters into nearly forty minutes of silence. The aftershocks of the "race speech," as "A More Perfect Union" would come to be commonly known, were swift. Some were quite emotive in their praise, others highly cynical in their criticisms. If it is true, as Dowd wrote, that only Barack Obama could have "alchemize[d] a nuanced 40-minute speech on race into must-see YouTube viewing for 20-year-olds," then it is also true that only Barack Obama could have had such a speech published immediately in France by Grasset in a slim, bilingual edition titled *De la race en Amérique*. It is also true that only Barack Obama's campaign could have sold "A More Perfect Union" as a DVD whose vinyl packaging sported the much-ballyhooed faux presidential seal and, further, offered copies of said speech in its headquarters across the country on an eight-and-a-half-by-fourteen-inch Obama-blue foldout.

And who can forget theocratic conservative Pat Buchanan's summing up the speech as a "shakedown" worthy of "black hustlers"? Or neoconservative Bill Kristol's "let's not and say we did" have a national conversation on race in his snarky *New York Times* op-ed on March 24?

But wherever the public and the punditocracy fell on the spectrum, what became clear was that Barack Obama was a man prepared to lead at decisive national moments, one who seemed to have an uncanny knack for landing on the right side of history. He had demonstrated such acuity early in his dramatic political rise when he delivered his first speech critical of the authorization for the U.S. invasion of Iraq. On October 2, 2002, at noon in Chicago's Federal Plaza, Obama delivered "Against Going to War with Iraq." The event was billed as an antiwar rally. Similar to Franklin D. Roosevelt in his 1936 "I Hate War" speech in Chautauqua, New York, in which he assuaged isolationists but allowed for the necessity of war to preserve peace, Obama, in following the political axiom "You got to dance with them what brung you," did a minuet with the antiwar faction, followed by a nifty dip and slide with respect to the *justness* of some wars.

To FDR's "We are not isolationists except insofar as we seek to isolate ourselves completely from war. Yet we must remember that so long as war exists on earth there will be some danger that even the nation which most ardently desires peace may be drawn into war. I have seen war . . . I hate war," Obama stated emphatically that he was against not all wars but "dumb" wars. He began this denunciation by drawing on the Civil War as an example of a just war, noting that it was bound up with the "hopes and dreams of slaves" desiring liberty and equality and with the willfulness of a president who demanded no less of the country and its free countrymen and -women than that they fully embrace and extend the nation's founding creed to all. He equally took up the cause of the Second Great War, which liberated a continent and a persecuted people from the evils of Nazism:

> Let me begin by saying that although this has been billed as an anti-war rally, I stand before you as someone who is not opposed to war in all circumstances.
>
> The Civil War was one of the bloodiest in history, and yet it was only through the crucible of the sword, the sacrifice of multitudes, that we could begin to perfect this union, and drive the scourge of slavery from our soil. I don't oppose all wars.
>
> My grandfather signed up for a war the day after Pearl Harbor was bombed, fought in Patton's army. He saw the dead and dying across the fields of Europe; he heard the stories of fellow troops who first entered Auschwitz and Treblinka. He fought in the name of a larger freedom, part of that arsenal of democracy that triumphed over evil, and he did not fight in vain.
>
> I don't oppose all wars.

The Iraq War, a "dumb war," did not qualify as an ennobling undertaking. The themes of patriotism, democracy, his grandfather's service to the country, and his pushback against the dogged political stereotype of the Democratic, war-averse dove would all be revisited in his ascent toward the presidency of the United States. His opposition to the Iraq invasion, articulated again in 2003 and 2004, was shared by only twenty-three sitting U.S. senators. It was a prescient and bold stance to take at the time, when Obama was an Illinois state senator. In response to those who later accused him of never opposing his party, he would point repeatedly to these moments. The 2002 speech as a political maneuver put Obama, given the dismal turn of events in Iraq, on the right side of the issue. In 2003, he announced his decision to run for the U.S. Senate.

By July 2004, Obama had been tapped to deliver the keynote address at the Democratic National Convention in Boston. Like the 2002 Iraq speech, his "The Audacity of Hope" address combined the ideas of patriotism, unity, and democracy. He began with a recitation of his own colorfully twined personal narrative of mixed-race identity, part African and part American, part black and part white. Despite its ending, the love story of the Kenyan international student Barack Hussein Obama Sr. and Stanley Ann Dunham, a Kansas native who had migrated with her parents to Hawaii, made for a reassuring symbol of America's overcoming its protracted struggles over race and racism. The junior Obama was the veritable fruit of racial harmony. His success was an American dream to which all could aspire. His was a story of hope and a changing America, he explained. And he tied that narrative to the resounding hope that the presidential candidacy of Senator John Kerry of Massachusetts was supposed to represent to the nation in the run-up to the general election as Kerry ran against President George W. Bush.

Barack Obama had indeed landed on the national political scene. In the immediate aftermath of his convention speech, PBS's Jim Lehrer, along with Mark Shields and David Brooks, sat gushing effusively about the forty-two-year-old Illinois state senator as possibly the next president of the United States. In January 2005, he was sworn in as only the second black representative from the state of Illinois in the U.S. Senate, and only the fifth African American in the Senate since Reconstruction. By 2007, the junior senator was among nine Democratic candidates who sought the nation's highest political office. He would go on to win it.

The themes and title of the 2004 Democratic Convention address and the title of Obama's second bestselling book, *The Audacity of Hope: Thoughts on Reclaiming the American Dream*, were drawn from a sermon by the well-respected pastor of a black church on Chicago's South Side. Ironically, Reverend Wright, pastor at Trinity United Church of Christ for over thirty years and Obama's pastor for twenty, found himself again at the inspirational center of one of the presidential hopeful's speeches, the most compelling one to date: "A More Perfect Union." Compared to Abraham Lincoln's "A House Divided" as well as his Gettysburg Address, John F. Kennedy's speech on religion, and Dr. Martin Luther King Jr.'s "I Have a Dream" speech, as each of these addresses reached for American unity in the face of Americans' racial, religious, and ideological differences, "A More Perfect Union" is "The Speech" that many say Obama always knew he would have to give someday in his run for the presidency. Despite his quasi–rock star status and numerous media-driven attempts to cast him as "post-racial" because of his DNA, a position he himself never claims, Barack Obama is a black man, and one who had in March 2008 gone further than any other black man who had sought the American presidency. He could not avoid addressing the perilous conundrums of race and racism in America, though he may have wished otherwise, for these are thorny thickets that require a scalpel rather than a hatchet in their dissection. One can never be too sure-footed when walking through them, treading lightly when assigning blame and offering empathy when parsing their complexities. And if nothing else, Obama also clearly understood that despite all attempts—academic, scientific, and otherwise—to render race a social construction with no biological relevance, Americans cling, desperately, irrationally even, to race making, or "racecraft," as Karen E. Fields brilliantly notes, as a way of navigating sociocultural and political realities and fictions.

Unlike the "Audacity of Hope" address, whose occasion was reserved for the extolling of Senator Kerry's worthiness to lead the nation, "A More Perfect Union" was tethered to Obama's own political ambitions. The stakes were much higher. The media's endless thirty-second looping of Reverend Wright's "greatest hits," characterized often as bombastic, unpatriotic, antiwhite sermonizing, had the potential to crater Obama's candidacy. Like former president Bill Clinton's much-decried racially tinged assessment of Obama's primary win in South Carolina, Wright's homiletics had the effect of coloring Obama in a bit too darkly; his damning of American racism and genocides at home and abroad diminished Obama's averred gift of "second sight" into both black and white worlds, marred his claim to authenticity and a new politics. As Obama campaign manager David Plouffe remarked in an interview with Condé Nast's Portfolio.com, "Reverend Wright was the most severe test we faced . . . We didn't think it would deny us the nomination, but we knew it would be a hit to the main engine." Jeremiah's jeremiads imperiled the currency of the "O" brand of politics, one that shunned partisan political attacks as well as dicing up the electorate into so many factions. "A More Perfect Union" restored the electorate's faith in that giftedness as it staunched the bloodletting in Obama's support and ultimately poll numbers.

The site and staging of the speech, delivered on March 18, 2008, at the Constitution Center in Philadelphia, were as critical as the words themselves. As Obama waxed on about patriotism, democracy, racial reconciliation and restoration, and the quest for an inclusive American identity, he was flanked to his left and right by a wave of flags in the hall of a museum dedicated to the U.S. Constitution and the story of "We, the people." Here, Barack Obama discussed his vision of America. Here, he contrasted this new America, one America indivisible, with the vision of our Founding Fathers. They were men who cherished freedom and democracy, but like Reverend Wright's, their American experiences were informed, and warped, by their time, he reminded us. Who could read the words of Thomas Jefferson's 1776 Declaration of Independence without genuine astonishment at the hope that springs forth regarding the political philosophy of his emergent nation, and yet who could not cringe in perplexity when reading Jefferson's 1781 *Notes on the State of Virginia*, where he is unbowed in his inane thesis that black women are preferred "uniformly" by the male "Oranootan" over females of "his own species."

In the minefield of race that was neither of his choosing nor of his making, Obama drew again upon what he knew best: his biography, his life as a black man of mixed-race ancestry reared in a white family, detailed in his bestselling memoir, *Dreams from My Father*.

The memoir's subtitle, *A Story of Race and Inheritance*, reveals conflicts of Du Boisian proportions. In 1897, the Massachusetts native and public intellectual of Dutch, French Huguenot, and African ancestry William Edward Burghardt Du Bois published "Strivings of the Negro People" in the *Atlantic Monthly*. He used the term *double consciousness* to explain how the American Negro, in the parlance of the time, reconciled "his twoness" as both "an American, a Negro; two souls, two thoughts, two unreconciled strivings; two warring ideals in one dark body . . . longing to merge his double self into a better and truer self." The first African American to graduate from Harvard University with a Ph.D. further explained that the "Negro is a sort of seventh son, born with a veil, and gifted with second sight in this American world."

Obama writes, "I was engaged in a fitful interior struggle. I was trying to be a black man in America, and beyond the given of my appearance, no one around me seemed to know exactly what that meant." His blackness, the propinquity of his ethnic Africanness and whiteness and Americanness and maleness, pushes the boundaries of Du Boisian double consciousness to a more expansive consciousness in which his *races*, nationalities, and gender vie for reconciliation and acceptance. Obama had read Du Bois, James

Baldwin, Richard Wright, and Ralph Ellison and found them want-
ing. He had hoped to find in them models for "reconciling the world
as I'd found it in terms of my birth." What he found in those pages
were black men who struggled to reinvent themselves in and against
the crucible of American racism and a web of stereotypes. They lost,
beating hasty retreats to Africa (Du Bois) or Europe (Wright and
Baldwin) or stalling in America, unable to produce another literary
masterpiece in the form of a novel (Ellison).

Like many post–civil rights, post–Black Power generation
blacks, Obama found in Malcolm X, with his willful "acts of self-
creation," an inspirational poster *man* (Malcolm would never have
countenanced the term *boy*, given its racially loaded history) for reconciled black maleness. It is, of course, no coincidence that Al Qaeda's senior deputy Ayman al-Zawahri would draw upon Malcolm X's
excoriating rhetorical flourishes to assail then-president-elect Obama
as a "house negro," denying him a place alongside "honorable black
Americans" like Malcolm. The obviously well-read Al Qaeda member clearly understood what Malcolm X's autobiography meant to
Obama as evidenced in *Dreams from My Father*; our U.S. media,
meanwhile, remember the man whose likeness stares out from a com-
memorative U.S. postage stamp as little more than a "polarizing"
figure. Interestingly, though, by the time of "Wright Redux" in April
and Obama's televised parting with his pastor, the media had shifted
into psychoanalytic mode, hatching a story line brimming with Oe-
dipal flavor: the epic father-son conflict, jealous mentor–ascendant
mentee. This potboiler, as it happened, mimed Malcolm X's highly
public break with his spiritual mentor and Nation of Islam leader,
Elijah Muhammad.

And why not *The Autobiography of Malcolm X*? From the promising child Malcolm Little to the thugged-out Detroit Red to the
doctrinaire Nation of Islam separatist Malcolm X to the expectant
El-Hajj Malik El-Shabazz/Malcolm X after his travels to Mecca,

Malcolm was a transformational and transformed figure before a torrent of bullets ended his life in 1965. As Alex Haley wrote in his introduction to *The Autobiography*,

> Malcolm . . . recognized the Negroes as an integral part of the American community—a far cry from Elijah Muhammed's [Nation of Islam] doctrine of racial separation. Malcolm had reached a midpoint in redefining his attitude to this country and the white-black relationship. He no longer inveighed against the United States but against a segment of the United States represented by overt white supremacists in the South and covert white supremacists in the North.

And in Malcolm's own words toward the end of *The Autobiography*,

> My pilgrimage broadened my scope. It blessed me with new insight . . . In the past, yes, I have made sweeping indictments of *all* white people. I will never be guilty of that again . . .
>
> I have given to this book so much of whatever time I have because I feel, and I hope, that if I honestly and fully tell my life's account, read objectively it might prove to be a testimony of some social value.
>
> I think that an objective reader may see how in the society to which I was exposed as a black youth here in America . . . when I heard "The white man is the devil," when I played back what had been my own experiences, it was inevitable that I would respond positively . . .
>
> I believe that it would be almost impossible to find anywhere in America a black man who has lived further down in the mud of human society than I have; or a black man who has been any more ignorant than I have been; or a black man who has suffered more anguish during his life than I have. But it is only after the deepest darkness that the greatest joy can come.

His story is an American story, complete with a redemptive spirit, uncompromising "discipline," and hope in spite of adversity; his resembles America's story, one of metamorphoses, of "repeated acts of self-creation," as Obama writes of Malcolm, "forged through sheer will of force"—from British oppression, Native American extirpation, and slavery to Civil War to civil rights, until the nation is wholly reconciled, indivisible.

Certainly, from my own dorm room and those of my peers in the late 1980s at the University of Rochester, Malcolm's edifying baritone could be heard floating down the corridors of Helenwood Hall. We exchanged tapes purchased at the only black bookstore in the city from a man named Chaka. Malcolm gave us permission to be black in ways that had nothing to do with whites. Whiteness did not consume us because we were thoroughly comfortable with ourselves. We were a post-movement generation though we were still political. Whites joined us, even outnumbered us, in the protests against apartheid in South Africa. We grappled intellectually and personally with the pernicious effects of racism, but never obsessed about race—we left that to whites. Though the mantra was that all *we* ever talked about was race, *they* were the ones, in point of fact, who had socially and culturally engineered the racial phantoms of welfare queens, undeserving affirmative action babies, and nothing but vicious, criminally minded, angry black men. While they were hand-wringing about their Frankensteins, we were pocketing undergraduate and advanced degrees, thinking about venture capital and start-ups, entering public service, academe, and corporate America.

Besides, many of us, like Obama, had miscegenated histories that were made from legal unions and post-emancipation coupling. We knew a lot of, and about, whites even if the vast majority of them didn't know us. My own French, African, Osage (Native American), Irish maternal grandmother was the product of my Irish great-grandfather and my great-grandmother, whose own belonging to one race or another was anybody's guess, phenotypically speaking.

Indeed, my grandmother and great-grandmother made an art of "passing" out of convenience before we, the browner brood, arrived on the scene. But they, like many others before and after them, cast their lot with blacks, for they loved their people, on the one hand, their will to survive, their creativity and dignity in the face of all and sundry obstacles, and on the other, America's one-drop rule of blackness had also codified and constrained their racially knotted lives. Between my grandmother and me, there were shades of difference, but we were both black. And Malcolm's self-possession, his possessive investment in blackness* and the articulation of his unequivocal claim to Americanness "without," in the words of writer Ta-Nehisi Coates, "explanation, [w]ithout self-consciousness, [w]ithout permission," further indelibly marked my generation, a generation of which Barack Obama is a part.

And yet, while Malcolm's hope and reconciled manly blackness may have offered a young Obama a salve of sorts as opposed to Du Bois's doubling paradigm, which he wrote about thirty-five years after the first Emancipation Proclamation was issued by Abraham Lincoln in 1862 and thirty-one years after the Thirteenth Amendment abolished slavery in the United States, Du Bois's insights on the "Negros'" gift of second sight continue to have salience. For Du Bois, the gift allows African Americans to see beyond the strictures, the myths, and the prejudices in America to hope. Obama verily uses this trope of second sightedness in "A More Perfect Union," methodically wrapping it around his biography, which in turn grants him authority. And we cede him that authority.

We allow that perhaps his second sight is a bit deeper, his insights more intimate than those provided by our "passing," near-white, and "whites who married into the family" kinship ties and

---

* Here I am playing on the title of scholar George Lipsitz's *Possessive Investment in Whiteness: How White People Profit from Identity* (2006).

histories could ever be. We understand that the lives of many Americans are ones circumscribed by de facto segregation, that most of us know one another from flash in the pan acquaintances, fictions—literary, cultural, and social—and the nightly news rather than as guests at one another's dinner tables. So when Barack Obama speaks knowingly of white anger and the anxieties of working-and middle-class white Americans, no matter how such frustrations may not square with or compare to the lived realities of working-and middle-class black folks, we have to know that he may be voicing his own white grandfather's disappointments and failures, the sacrifices of his white grandmother, of which he speaks compassionately in *Dreams from My Father*:

> Gramps had left the furniture business to become a life insurance agent, but as he was unable to convince himself that people needed what he was selling and was sensitive to rejection, the work went badly. Every Sunday I would watch him grow more and more irritable as he gathered his briefcase . . . I could hear the desperation creeping out of his voice, the stretch of silence that followed when the people on the other end explained why Thursday wasn't good and Tuesday not much better, and then Gramps's heavy sigh after he had hung up the phone, his hands fumbling through the files in his lap like those of a cardplayer who's deep in the hole . . . She would confide in me that she had never stopped dreaming of a house with a white picket fence, days spent baking or playing bridge or volunteering at the local library . . . was surprised by this admission, for she rarely mentioned hopes or regrets . . . but I came to understand that her career spanned a time when the work of a wife outside the home was nothing to brag about, for her or Gramps—that it represented only lost years, broken promises . . . That's how my grandparents had come to live . . . They had decided to cut their losses and settle for hanging on. They saw no more destinations to hope for.

Obama empathizes with the scattered dreams of his African father, the shattered dreams of his white grandfather, the righteous bitterness of Reverend Wright, and the stoicism of his white grandmother. At peace with his white and African inheritance, at home in his blackness, and thoroughly reconciled in his claim to Americanness, with "A More Perfect Union" he casts out his biography where seemingly disparate impossibilities are sublimely made whole into a bridge, an invitation, a suggestion, to cross.

Even as he demurs regarding the possibilities that his candidacy augurs, saying, "I have never been so naive as to believe that we can get beyond our racial divisions in a single election cycle, or with a single candidacy—particularly a candidacy as imperfect as my own," his hope is clear; indeed, his political future necessitated that at that moment we put cynicism aside and ponder his carefully crafted paean to "e pluribus unum" as a bridge on which to meet one another anew in order to perfect the union.

The Speech: Race and Barack Obama's "A More Perfect Union" highlights various aspects of "A More Perfect Union," including its themes, arc, and structure, and why it deserves a place in the history of American politics and race relations. The twelve essays in this volume examine more specifically the generational hangovers, the literary, political, social, and cultural threads taken up in the senator's address.

The volume also includes the text of the speech itself and a three-part journalistic account of the life of the speech in the public sphere: the buildup to its delivery, its initial reception, and its reverberations throughout the remainder of the 2008 presidential campaign. In effect, *The Speech* memorializes a moment in American history and also tells the story of race as an issue in that campaign. It is less a Festschrift than a critical engagement with a big thinker, our time, and the untidy past that informs that time. The collection's contributors—journalists, scholars, writers, and public intellectuals— do not all necessarily agree with the speech or the historical and political interpretations of the speech maker. But these fissures and ruptures, too, represent the diversity that is America. A hearing is what Barack Obama called for; a conversation on race is what "A More Perfect Union" was, secondarily, intended to engender. And that it has done.

RACE AND BARACK OBAMA'S "A MORE PERFECT UNION"

WRIGHT STUFF, WRONG TIME

PART I

Derrick Z. Jackson

Barack Obama would never have had to make his fabled speech on race—at least that particular speech—had it not been for his once mentor the Reverend Jeremiah Wright. Wright was Obama's window onto black frustrations the nation forever hid from itself with its rose-tinted textbooks, muted mass media, and exclamations of equality over exceptional individuals like Tiger Woods, Colin Powell, Michael Jordan, or Oprah Winfrey.

In January 2007, just before his February 10 announcement that he was running for president, Obama sat with Wright at their Trinity United Church of Christ for a book signing of Obama's *The Audacity of Hope*. The title came from a Wright sermon. In a January 21, 2007, story on Wright in the *Chicago Tribune*, Obama said, "What I value most about Pastor Wright is not his day-to-day political advice. He's much more of a sounding board for me to make sure that I am speaking as truthfully about what I believe as possible and that I'm not losing myself in some of the hype and hoopla and stress that's involved in national politics."

But conservatives were questioning the "unashamedly black" value system of Trinity and mining the words of Wright, which were then known to have included calling voters for President Bush "stupid." An *Investor's Business Daily* editorial that month warned that Obama was part of "a militantly Afrocentric movement."

Obama defended Trinity in a February 6 interview with the *Chicago Tribune*, saying of conservative critics, "I would be puzzled that they would object or quibble with the bulk of a document that basically espouses profoundly conservative values of self-reliance and self-help . . . If I say to anybody in Iowa—white, black, Hispanic or Asian—that my church believes in the African-American community strengthening families or adhering to the black work ethic or being committed to self-discipline and self-respect and not forgetting where you came from, I don't think that's something anybody would object to . . . I think I'd get a few amens."

But the Obama campaign and Obama saw that the objections were becoming a public relations quagmire heading to nightmare. On announcement day in Springfield, Illinois, Wright, according to the *New York Times*, prayed beforehand with Obama but did not give a planned invocation. Obama spokesman Bill Burton said, "Senator Obama is proud of his pastor and his church, but because of the type of attention it was receiving on blogs and conservative talk shows, he decided to avoid having statements and beliefs being used out of context and forcing the entire church to defend itself."

According to Wright, Obama told him the night before, "You can get kind of rough in the sermons, so what we've decided is that it's best for you not to be out there in public." Wright said that Obama cited to him a *Rolling Stone* article that quoted Wright in full throat in a sermon: "Racism is how this country was founded and how this country is still run!" Speaking of the United States as "we," Wright said in the sermon, "We are deeply involved in the importing of drugs, the exporting of guns, and the training of professional killers . . . We believe in white supremacy and black inferiority and believe it more than we believe in God . . . We conducted radiation experiments on our own people . . . We care nothing about human life if the ends justify the means! . . . GAWD! Has got! To be sick! Of this shit!"

The attention only increased, with Fox News at the forefront.

The Fox network is owned by conservative media mogul Rupert Murdoch (who also owns the *Wall Street Journal*) and run by Republican Roger Ailes, who was the campaign strategist for Presidents Richard Nixon, Ronald Reagan, and George H. W. Bush. Bush's 1988 campaign against Democrat Michael Dukakis was notorious for an ad featuring a furloughed black rapist named Willie Horton that successfully tarred the Massachusetts governor as soft on crime. Ailes boasted, "The only question is whether we depict Willie Horton with a knife in his hand or without it."

Fox twisted the knife in a March 1 interview with Wright by Sean Hannity. Utterly ignoring the segregated history of American churches, Hannity badgered Wright about Trinity's "black value system," saying, "Now, Reverend, if every time we said black, if there was a church and those words were white, wouldn't we call that church racist?"

The calls of reverse racism grew louder and louder until April 30, when a *New York Times* article on the relationship between Obama and Wright noted, "It is hard to imagine, though, how Mr. Obama can truly distance himself from Mr. Wright." That same day, MSNBC's Tucker Carlson called Wright a "full-blown hater" for saying that 9/11 was a wake-up call to white America. Carlson asked conservative commentator and former presidential candidate Pat Buchanan, "If there was a Republican presidential candidate who had a friend who was a member of the Klan or some skinhead group who was attacking black people, you would say it's a problem, no?"

Buchanan responded, "He has got to renounce him, sure."

That was still ten and a half months before the "race speech."

Keeping Wright offstage in February critically kept him from being center stage as the coverage turned to the general horse race, which included front-runner Hillary Clinton, and the jockeying over who least supported the Iraq War. However, Obama unashamedly referred to the unashamedly black Wright in a "special shout-out" in a June 5 speech at historically black Hampton University in

Virginia. Obama gave his most scathing racial critique of America in that speech, saying that the Bush administration was ignoring a "quiet riot" among African Americans that could erupt, as had happened in 1992 in Los Angeles after police officers were acquitted in the beating of Rodney King.

"If you had gone to any street corner in Chicago or Baton Rouge or Hampton, you would have found the same young men and women without hope, without miracles and without a sense of destiny other than life on the edge," Obama said. He noted that the government response to Hurricane Katrina "was colorblind in its incompetence," but that racial disparities revealed by the disaster were "a powerful metaphor for what's gone on in generations."

In January 2008, Obama stunned the world by winning Iowa. He was pulled back to earth by Hillary Clinton in New Hampshire. Then, just before the January 19 Nevada caucuses, Wright provided fresh red meat for the talk shows. Pooh-poohing feelings among African Americans that Clinton's husband, former president Bill Clinton, "was good to us," Wright said of Bill Clinton, "That's not true. He did the same thing to us that he did to Monica Lewinsky."

Obama released a statement saying, "As I've told Reverend Wright, personal attacks such as this have no place in this campaign or our politics." Still, Obama added, "That doesn't distract from my affection for Reverend Wright or appreciation for the good works he has done."

The distractions mounted. Obama was eking out a small but critical lead in delegates with his fifty-state, no-red-state-no-blue-state campaign. But voting patterns were revealing serious racial fissures among white Southern and Rust Belt working-class Democrats. Clinton was transforming herself into a white lunch-pail populist, knocking back whiskey shots in Indiana. The media that had once asked if the biracial Obama was black enough were now questioning his appeal to white Americans.

In a February 26 debate in Cleveland, the late Tim Russert of

NBC asked Obama about an endorsement from controversial Nation of Islam leader Minister Louis Farrakhan. "What do you do," Russert asked Obama, "to assure Jewish-Americans that, whether it's Farrakhan's support or the activities of Reverend Jeremiah Wright, your pastor [who had traveled with Farrakhan to Libya in 1984 to meet with Muammar Qaddafi], you are consistent with issues regarding Israel and not in any way suggesting that Farrakhan 'epitomizes greatness' [which Wright had said of Farrakhan]?"

Obama cited his Jewish support in Chicago. But Clinton tried to trip him up on semantics, saying that while Obama had denounced the endorsement, he needed to further reject it because "there's a difference between denouncing and rejecting." Obama said, "I have to say I don't see a difference between denouncing and rejecting . . . But if the word 'reject' Senator Clinton feels is stronger than the word 'denounce,' then I'm happy to concede the point and I would reject and denounce."

The audience laughed. It would be the last laughing matter involving Wright. Two weeks later, the most infamous slew of Wright sermon clips, purchased by Fox and ABC, flooded into American homes. In them, the pastor called America the "US of KKK-A" and said, "The government gives them the drugs, builds bigger prisons, passes a three-strike law and then wants us to sing 'God bless America.' No, no, no . . . God damn America for treating her citizens as less than human."

Obama issued more statements, such as to CNN's Anderson Cooper: "I can't be clear enough about the fact that these are not reflective of the views that I have." But with the talk shows saying that Obama's reflection in the mirror was that of Wright, he announced that he would give a major address. In a March 17 press conference, he said, "Part of what I'll do tomorrow is to talk a little bit about how some of these issues are perceived from within the black church community, for example, which I think views this very differently."

The candidate, who up to this point had walked a racial tightrope as no black man had ever walked one before, saw that he was about to be fatally shamed by his unashamedly black pastor. Successfully explaining the perspective of black anger while running a crossover campaign of hope would take nothing less than a miracle. Not a single word could be misspoken. He wanted to renounce the message without condemning the messenger. A sign of his knowing how thin the tightrope had become was the way he ended a campaign speech in Pennsylvania: "God bless you and God bless America!" It was something he had rarely said in prior closings. He knew he desperately needed America's blessing.

OBAMA AND THE
GENERATIONAL CHALLENGE

Omar H. Ali

I have asserted a firm conviction . . . that working together we can
move beyond some of our old racial wounds . . . to continue on the
path of a more perfect union . . . Let us find that common stake we all
have in one another, and let our politics reflect that spirit as well.
—SENATOR BARACK OBAMA, "A More Perfect Union," 2008

Delivered at the Constitutional Center in Philadelphia on March
18, 2008, Barack Obama's "speech on race" may be considered,
among other interpretations, as a challenge to the concept of race-
based identity politics in the United States. By displaying the interconnectivity between seemingly disparate people, drawing on his
own family history and then using the examples of others, Obama
demonstrates the limitations of fixed identities based on race that
have driven black politics relative to the Democratic Party since the
early 1970s. He points instead to the shared experiences among
Americans in the process of forming "a more perfect union."

Just weeks before the 2008 general election, Obama, a black
Democrat, was called a "transformational figure" by former secretary of state Colin Powell, a black Republican. The movement surrounding Obama's candidacy was characterized as a search for "a

new paradigm, new partnerships and a new way of doing politics" by Dr. Lenora Fulani, a developmental psychologist who in 1988 became the first woman and the first African American to get on the ballot in all fifty states running as an independent for president. The Reverend Jesse Jackson, who ran historic presidential campaigns in 1984 and 1988 as an insurgent Democratic candidate, offered his endorsement one year before Obama's now-famous speech—long before high-ranking elected black Democrats were willing to lend their support. In some ways, Powell, Fulani, and Jackson represent three key elements of the black electorate—liberal Republicans, progressive independents, and reform-oriented Democrats—joined in 2008 to back Obama's candidacy.

Obama first gained national attention when he delivered a stirring keynote address at the 2004 Democratic National Convention in which he tied his personal story—as the son of an African and an American—to the nation's history. He was noted as a new kind of black politician from both within and outside of his party. Four years later, Obama challenged partisan convention by reaching out to independents and Republicans, in addition to rank-and-file Democrats, in the two dozen statewide open-primary contests and caucuses. Doing so won him significant early victories in the primaries, pushing his candidacy through the final stretch and, ultimately, to a stunning victory in the general election. Throughout much of his campaign, but most poignantly in his March 18 speech, Obama also challenged the nation to examine its understanding of race and politics.

Several questions come to mind regarding his speech. If we begin with the premise that race is to be understood as a matter of political power (not just as a social or cultural construct, and certainly not as based in genetics or biology), what does his speech tell us about the state of American democracy? Is he attempting to transcend race in his speech, or simply explain away racism in America? What does the speech mean in terms of the black community in particular? Is he suggesting that the Black Agenda, dating to the

1972 National Black Political Convention in Gary, Indiana, has been subsumed into mainstream politics, so as to render a separate agenda for African Americans no longer necessary? And, in light of Obama's decisive victory in the general election, making him the first African American to win the office of the president of the United States, are we now talking about the end of black politics?

A number of commentators on Obama, and black politics generally, have either declared or implied that traditional black politics is coming to an end: Errol Louis's "Meet the New Guard Black Politicians" (*New York Daily News*, February 17, 2008) and Matt Bai's "Is Obama the End of Black Politics?" (*New York Times Magazine*, August 10, 2008) stand out among the articles published. But as historian Eric Foner underscored on the eve of the 2008 general election in "Rooted in Reconstruction" (*Nation*, November 3, 2008), there have been various and competing strands of black politics since the days of the abolitionist movement—not a single approach. The various strands have included black nationalist, populist, socialist, communist, liberal, and conservative affiliations. Indeed, some African Americans have adopted a variety of political views and approaches simultaneously, or changed their affiliations over time. The scholar and political activist W. E. B. Du Bois, for instance, supported the Progressive Party, the Socialist Party, and the American Labor Party, before joining the Communist Party.

Historically, African Americans have worked with both major parties, but they have also worked with third parties and have run as independent candidates. African Americans, including Frederick Douglass, joined the Liberty Party in the 1840s in calling for the abolition of slavery. Black voters later threw their support behind the Republican Party, whose radical faction successfully drove democracy beyond emancipation by securing voting rights for black men with the Fifteenth Amendment.

During the late nineteenth century, some African Americans—Black Populists—supported the People's Party in the South to challenge Democratic rule, even as most black people remained loyal to "Lincoln's party." However, black loyalty began shifting from the Republican Party to the Democratic Party starting in 1936, with African Americans in the North casting their ballots in support of President Franklin D. Roosevelt and his New Deal policies. Black voters in the South remained disenfranchised under Jim Crow until the mid-1960s. Since that time, at least two out of three African Americans in the nation have identified themselves with the Democratic Party. For the older generation of black voters, this has been a function of Democrats' having enacted key legislation, most notably the Voting Rights Act of 1965, demanded by civil rights leaders—from Dr. Martin Luther King Jr., pushing from outside of government, to Congressman Adam Clayton Powell Jr., pushing from within government.

Today, over 30 percent of African Americans identify as independent (neither Democrat nor Republican); among the younger demographic, black voters eighteen to thirty-five years old, the percentage of those who identify as independent increases by five points. Studies by the Joint Center for Political and Economic Studies, the Pew Research Center, the Suffolk University Political Research Center, and Columbia University's Center for African American Politics and Society all point to a combination of *increasing* independence and *decreasing* partisanship in the overall black electorate. Still, most black voters continue to identify themselves as Democrats.

Obama gave his speech in the midst of a heated Democratic presidential primary battle between himself and the party establishment's choice, Senator Hillary Clinton. He was responding to the uproar surrounding comments made by his former pastor, the Reverend Jeremiah Wright. The reverend's impassioned words "God damn America!," exclaimed during a sermon—words directed at the wrongs inflicted on black people by the white power structure—were perceived by many, including Obama, as inflammatory and divisive. As Obama puts it in "A More Perfect Union," Wright "express[ed] views that have the potential not only to widen the racial divide, but views that denigrate both the greatness and the goodness of our nation, that rightly offend white and black alike." In practical political terms, Obama *had* to respond to the firestorm resulting from his pastor's comments, as his level of support in opinion polls began to dip, it seemed, with each passing replay of clips of Wright on cable news or YouTube. For Obama, the question was not whether to respond, but how.

There are, of course, a number of ways to interpret Obama's speech on race. A superficial reading would suggest nothing more than that it is a defense against attacks on his character due to his long-standing association with Wright—a kind of guilt by association. In this reading, the junior senator from Illinois is simply seeking to justify the "incendiary language" of his black preacher on the grounds of cultural misunderstanding among white people of one thread in the black religious experience: the social gospel (a form of black liberation theology) of Wright and his Trinity United Church of Christ, on Chicago's South Side.

Read another way, the speech is an invocation of "e pluribus unum," wherein Americans of every color and background—patriots one and all—are viewed in their shared humanity as advancing democracy through generational struggles. And read yet another way, the speech is a rebuke of politics based on race; it even takes a stab, albeit circuitously, at the role of both Democratic and Republican politicians in regards to fomenting race-based identity politics for partisan advancement. As Obama is known to convey in his speeches, most things in life (and politics) are complicated, or even contradictory, and require nuanced expression. Perhaps elements of all three readings were at play.

Paradoxically, Obama would need to employ the language of

race in order to advance a more historical, process-oriented approach to the nation's political state of affairs that goes beyond static notions of identity—be they racial or partisan. In this author's reading of the speech (one among many readings, as this collection attests), race is fundamentally a question of power with social and political implications. The fact is that there are at least as many ways to interpret the words contained within this or any other speech as there are people listening to or reading such words. No single interpretation can capture the entirety of what a particular speaker intends, or all the ways in which their speech is received. Words take on different meanings based on the context in which they are used. The larger context of Obama's speech—beyond the electoral politicking of the Democratic presidential primary—is not only the post–civil rights era but a postmodern era, in which identity (racial and otherwise) as well as political affiliation (Democratic, in particular, relative to African Americans) are increasingly being called into question.

Obama is of a generation that came of age after the modern civil rights era, after second-wave feminism, the demonstrations against the war in Vietnam, the Stonewall riots (marking the beginning of the gay rights movement), and the Black Power movement. He came of age with the rise of identity politics in the 1970s, which had grown out of the political struggles of the prior decade. He came of age with the promise that reforming the Democratic Party—by getting more black men and women elected to office via the party (the de facto strategy that came out of the Gary convention)—was the way for poor and working black people to ultimately gain a greater say in policy making. And he also came of age to see the limits of race-based politics and, by extension, the politics of the Democratic Party.

Obama, indeed many Americans, had begun to seek out new alliances that pushed beyond the New Deal coalition of African

Americans, organized labor, and white liberals. African Americans had partnered with white liberals and labor via the Democratic Party only to see that strategy keep them locked into a new system of authority and political control. A branching out and diversification of strategies was required. During the 2008 presidential primaries and caucuses, white liberals broke in slightly larger numbers in favor of Clinton; however, it was African Americans, white independents, and, to a smaller extent, young voters who provided Obama's margins of victory. Had African Americans and white independents formed a new "black and independent alliance," as it has been called by political analyst Jacqueline Salit? And what were the prospects of such an alliance?

Difficult to define, Obama may be progressive, but he is neither a radical nor a moderate. Liberal in his voting record, he is more of a political unifier, and he does not espouse—culturally or in the electoral arena—the kind of black nationalism that has kept African Americans politically isolated. He has been willing to reach out to those whose dominant views he may not necessarily share, but with whom he could work in order to advance specific policies. He has done so by focusing on shared interests and experiences. After all, his personal and political lives have largely been about building bridges and finding common ground.

Obama's history has been well documented: Born in 1961, "the son of a black man from Kenya and a white woman from Kansas," raised by his maternal grandparents, he lived in Hawaii and Indonesia. He graduated from Columbia University and then Harvard Law School, where he served as the first African American president of the *Harvard Law Review*. He became a community organizer in Chicago and then taught constitutional law at the University of Chicago. He did all this before being elected to the U.S. Senate in 2004. By the time Obama entered the electoral arena, winning a state senate seat in Illinois in 1996, identity politics and black Democratic partisanship had long been embedded in the American political landscape.

Obama begins his speech with his affirmation of the power of the U.S. Constitution as an instrument for democratic change—an instrument used by the American people to expand democracy within the nation (from the abolitionists who sought the emancipation of slaves to independents in the modern movement for political reform). The first ten amendments to the Constitution (the Bill of Rights) provided key measures for both the protection and the empowerment of the people: freedom of speech, freedom of the press, freedom of assembly, freedom of religion, and the right to petition, among others. Such liberties and rights from the earliest days of the republic were essential for popular political mobilization, but their usefulness depended upon bipartisan alliances and the ongoing struggle of ordinary people.

As Obama states in symbolic terms, the Constitution was "signed but ultimately unfinished." He notes that it "promised its people liberty, and justice, and a union that could be and should be perfected over time." However, "words on a parchment would not be enough to deliver slaves from bondage, or provide men and women of every color and creed their full rights and obligations as citizens of the United States." Obama then observes, "What would be needed were Americans in successive generations who were willing to do their part—through protest and struggle, on the streets and in the courts, through a civil war and civil disobedience and always at great risk—to narrow that gap between the promise of our ideals and the reality of our time."

In 2006, Obama wrote and published what would become a national bestseller, *The Audacity of Hope: Thoughts on Reclaiming the American Dream*. In chapter three of the book, he discusses the Constitution, giving his own historical and legal interpretation of the founding document. There he states, "Implicit in its structure, in the very idea of ordered liberty, was a rejection of absolute truth—the infallibility of any idea or ideology, or theology, or 'ism,' any tyrannical consistency that might lock future generations into a single unalterable course." He views the Constitution as dynamic. It is a perspective that gets expressed over and over again in his political discourse. And while Obama may not consider himself a postmodernist, it would certainly not be a stretch to say that he represents a new way of doing politics that is not overly determined by identities and that is, in this sense, postmodern. In other words, Obama is this generation's challenge to the partisan gridlock and ideological rigidity that epitomizes modern politics. It may simply be Obama's American pragmatism (in a postmodern age), but his actions seem akin to doing what postmodernists call "relational politics." In the words of philosopher Fred Newman and psychologist Lois Holzman, relational politics—the search for a new politics at the dawn of the twenty-first century—is "a shared, collective, democratic human (citizen) activity." It is less about fixating on programmatic positions and more about creatively connecting with one another, building new kinds of relationships, and opening up new possibilities.

The intimate nature of Obama's speech on race, in which he offers his story and those of the people closest to him as part of the sweep of the narrative of the American experience, surely draws his listeners into what he has to say: "I am married to a black American who carries within her the blood of slaves and slave owners—an inheritance we pass on to our two precious daughters." He continues, "I have brothers, sisters, nieces, nephews, uncles, cousins, of every race and every hue." By bringing himself and his family into the narrative, he demonstrates the interconnectivity of Americans. But he is also aware of the difficulties in deconstructing race and politics in this nation, or, in his words, "the complexities of race in this country that we've never really worked through." As if placing his long, outstretched arms around feuding siblings, he notes, "[If] we walk away now, if we simply retreat into our respective corners, we will never be able to come together and solve challenges like health care, or education, or the need to find good jobs for every American."

It is with empathy that Obama is able to connect with people from diverse social backgrounds, holding a range of ideological positions. He uses the controversy of Wright's comments to do so: "I confess that if all I knew of Reverend Wright were the snippets of those sermons that have run in an endless loop . . . there is no doubt that I would react in much the same way." However, he goes on to show that he is nonetheless tied to his former pastor and uses yet another personal example, that of his own grandmother. He says, "I can no more disown [Wright] than I can my white grandmother—a woman who helped raise me, a woman who sacrificed again and again for me, a woman who loves me as much as she loves anything in this world, but a woman who once confessed her fear of black men who passed by her on the street, and who on more than one occasion has uttered racial or ethnic stereotypes that made me cringe." Obama's connections clearly run in many directions, tying the nation together to make a seamless whole: "These people are a part of me. And they are part of America."

He also shows how the attacks on him for his relationship to Wright are not unlike those attacks launched against his opponents *in support of* him. He uses the case of Geraldine Ferraro, the 1984 Democratic Party candidate for vice president (and 2008 Clinton supporter), who questioned Obama's success based on his merits, stating that his being African American was what had gotten him as far as he had gotten in the race for the White House. Obama: "We can dismiss Reverend Wright as a crank or a demagogue, just as some have dismissed Geraldine Ferraro, in the aftermath of her recent statements, as harboring some deep-seated racial bias." He notes the divisiveness of such politics and later points to the unifying story of "Ashley" and the "elderly black man" and the "single moment of recognition between [them]." Obama, it seems, is constantly looking for that which connects people on both personal and political levels.

He posits that the American people have decisions to make about which way, and *how*, we want to move forward as a people: "[We] have a choice in this country. We can accept a politics that breeds division, and conflict, and cynicism . . . Or, at this moment, in this election, we can come together and say, 'Not this time.'" He hedges, however, in his criticism of "the special interests in Washington," saying, "This time we want to talk about how the lines in the emergency room are filled with whites and blacks and Hispanics who do not have health care; who don't have the power on their own to overcome the special interests in Washington, but who can take them on if we do it together." Deliberately or not, here Obama fails to recognize that the two major parties are *themselves* special interests.

There is, in fact, nothing written in the Constitution about political parties, yet the two major parties have taken over the government, functioning, if you will, as if they are government. And while Obama, in targeting "special interests," deflects blame away from the Democratic and Republican parties, it is doubtful that he is unaware of the extent to which two-party-oriented election laws and regulations make political independents second-class citizens (for instance, through barriers regarding ballot access, closed primaries, and the exclusion of third-party candidates from publicly held debates); it appears that he is choosing to criticize politics- and politicians-as-usual but not take his argument to its logical conclusion so as not to expose his own partisan role in permitting the political and legal marginalization of independents.

Demanding political equality before the law has its precedent in the modern civil rights movement. But laws, in and of themselves, do not substitute for developmental growth; they are only a potential part of the process. Therefore, while mass political action in the 1950s and 1960s helped to produce powerful legislation dismantling Jim Crow and ushering in federal protection and over-sight for the civil and political rights of African Americans (namely, the Civil Rights Act of 1964, followed by the Voting Rights Act of 1965), the cultural and emotional aspects—the "complexities of race"—have yet to be "worked through," as Obama puts it. Working through these challenges appears to be partially under way. However, the issue of political power, upon which race depends, is still an open question.

With whom will African Americans partner in continuing to democratize the United States so that all Americans are included in the political process on equal terms? Will the black and independent alliance seen in the primaries and caucuses gain further traction, or be squashed under the divisive and heavy hand of partisanship and political convention? The divisions that are created in the electoral arena, and the political culture at large, are in good measure driven by race-based politicking. As Obama notes, "anger is exploited by politicians, to gin up votes along racial lines, or to make up for a poli-tician's own failings." It is precisely this kind of politics that Obama seeks to change. He continues, "Anger [be it black or white] . . . keeps us from squarely facing our own complicity in our conditions, and prevents the African American community from forging the alliances it needs to bring about real change."

While Obama was born during the time of the generation that suc-cessfully challenged racially based segregation and dismantled Jim Crow, the segregation of today's partisanship remains. Equality be-fore the law may have been legislated to a great extent. For all intents and purposes, there is no longer legal discrimination based on race in terms of voting, public seating, or other matters. But as a nation, we have yet to come to terms with what Obama describes as "the brutal legacy of slavery and Jim Crow." It is a political legacy enmeshed in the very fabric of American society—one that will require, I believe, generations to deal with. Electing, in Obama, the nation's first black president has created new possibilities. The question is, will Americans embrace the opportunity with which we are presented to (paraphrasing Obama) forge the alliances necessary to bring about meaningful political change?

"This union may never be perfect," says Obama in his speech, "but generation after generation has shown that it can always be perfected. And today, whenever I find myself feeling doubtful or cynical about this possibility, what gives me the most hope is the next generation—the young people whose attitudes and beliefs and openness to change have already made history in this election." The beliefs and openness to change among today's younger generation are not only derived from the political naïveté normally associated with youth by older members of society, but are part of an overall transformation of American political culture that has produced the view that race-based politics and partisanship are unhelpful and unhealthy—a transformation that young people are helping to effect. Obama alludes to the narrowness of race-based politics and partisanship when he states, "[We] need to come together to solve a set of monumental problems—two wars, a terrorist threat, a failing economy, a chronic health care crisis, and potentially devastating climate change, problems that are neither black or white or Latino or Asian, but rather, problems that confront us all."

Today, young people are moving away from partisanship and toward greater political independence. They may have voted for Obama, but they did not necessarily do so because he is a Democrat; they likely did so in spite of his being affiliated with *any* party. Approximately 24 million voters under the age of thirty cast their ballots in 2008, an increase of 2.2 million from the 2004 general election. Of these, 66 percent voted for Obama, meaning that this demographic, composed of all different races and backgrounds, broke two to one for him over Republican nominee Senator John McCain. Many young people were mobilized through popular social networking sites such as Facebook and MySpace, as well as through concerted outreach efforts on college campuses and in the community. But just as Obama and his campaign were organizing young people, these same young people—the next generation—found in his candidacy an opportunity to exert their numbers and express their voices for a new kind of politics. In this way, Obama and his campaign served as *their* vehicle.

As rich in detail and examples as Obama's speech is, it may also serve as a tabula rasa, a blank slate upon which each of us places our own histories, experiences, and ways of working through our thoughts and feelings.* I am the son of an East Indian father and a Peruvian mother; like Obama, I carry a Muslim name and grew up as a Christian; my own two children are of cultures and traditions that include their mother's, which are Colombian, and my own; but they are Americans, to be sure. I have spent much of my adult life as an independent political organizer and a scholar of black political history in the United States and other areas of the African diaspora. These are some of the factors that inform my reading and analysis. For me, it is the invitational character of Obama's speech that makes it so compelling to listen to and read, and I suspect it is the same for others.

Beyond his eloquence, Obama's tall physical presence and calm but firm demeanor, his dark features, his beaming smile, his gender, and his name all figure into how he is perceived and how his speech is "read." As Colin Powell noted on *Meet the Press* when he gave his endorsement to Obama, attacks leveled at "Barack Hussein Obama" for allegedly being Muslim (attacks seen first in the primaries and

---

* My thanks to T. Denean Sharpley-Whiting for inviting me to write this essay and a special thanks to my Abu (Meer Hamid Ali), Leah Worthington, Carrie Sackett, and Cecilia Salvatierra for offering their thoughts and suggestions on aspects of what I have written. Students from my Independent Black Politics seminar at Vanderbilt University also provided helpful feedback, and Maria Worthington-McKenna pointed out the distinction between formal and pragmatic legal theory in constitutional studies.

then in the general election) sent deeply negative messages to Americans, implying that there is something wrong with being Muslim. The fact that Obama is now president of the United States changes things for people of color as they speak to their children about the potential and possibilities they have to embrace. Indeed, all Americans can now speak to their children in new ways about what the nation has achieved and can.

In my particular reading of Obama's speech, both he and the younger generation he has come to embody challenge notions of race and identity politics. With race and politics being inextricably linked in the history of the United States, it is not possible to separate the two. But whether we see the politicization of race or the racialization of politics in action, it is safe to say that discussion of race, politics, and their interconnection will continue to be part of the national conversation for an indefinite period of time.

LIVING THE DREAM

Keli Goff

When I first heard that Barack Obama was going to deliver a
major speech about race, and do so as the Reverend Jeremiah
Wright controversy threatened to envelop his campaign, I did not
have particularly high hopes. I knew that his audience would likely
be filled with plenty of Americans who were unaware of some of our
nation's complicated racial politics and history. And that they were
happy to remain that way.

Clearly Obama knew this as well. He had spent much of the
seemingly endless presidential campaign becoming a master of edu-
cating Americans on his atypical racial and ethnic heritage—and
helping them grow comfortable with it. But helping Americans come
to grips with a foreign-sounding name and an exotic upbringing is
an easier task than publicly shattering the myths of our racial innocence. How could anyone, I mused, address race in a single speech,
one that would seek to tackle the issue in a way that was accessible
for Americans of all ages and all colors? His goals would have to be
multifaceted. He would have to be somber yet transcendent. Painfully honest yet awesomely inspiring. He could take the opportunity
to inform and educate—but most of all he would have to find some
way to unify and uplift and connect, not alienate.

I considered this virtually impossible, until I heard it.

What struck me most about the speech was how effortlessly

Obama balanced looking forward toward the hope and promise of America's future with a few measured glances back at America's sometimes painful past. Yes, it was part history lesson, but in film terms it was much more *Back to the Future*—crashing through history not in an effort to dwell or place blame, but to try to make the present and future a little bit better. Or as Chuck D, hip-hop icon turned political activist, proclaimed, "While not exactly saying the past is just the past," the speech "was still ultimately a message of healing."

When historians look back on the defining moment that ultimately shook up the presidential election and transformed Barack Obama from just another candidate for the presidency into an actual potential president—the moment when the political pundits and voters nationwide morphed from skeptics into believers—it will be the day that Obama won the Iowa caucus. For a black man with a foreign-sounding name to win a caucus in one of the whitest states in our country confirmed that anything truly is possible in America. But Obama could not have won the Iowa caucus without younger voters. An analysis by *Newsweek* published after his victory there noted, "Youth turnout was up 135 percent from 2004, and the under-25 set alone gave Obama 17,000 votes . . . Obama's margin of victory [in Iowa]? Twenty thousand."

To be clear, Obama would not have been elected president of the United States without the overwhelming support of younger voters—of all colors. Throughout the primary season I found myself being asked the same question in interviews: "Every election cycle we hear about the potential for younger voters to be a real force, then they don't show up. Will they this time?" This time, not only did younger voters show up but they showed up big. In addition to playing a crucial role in Obama's caucus and primary wins in states like Iowa, they gave him an advantage on election night, exit polls showed, in states won by the GOP in 2004, such as New Mexico.

Some speculated that Obama's appeal among younger voters was due simply to his age. The rationale went something like "Well, he is the youngest candidate running for president, so of course younger voters are more likely to support him." Some presumed that younger black voters simply wanted to support, to put it bluntly, the black guy. And that their white counterparts—moved by some alleged sense of "white guilt"—felt compelled to do so as well. But as I explained to the various commentators in my rounds on CNN, Fox, and MSNBC who seemed obsessed with the "white guilt" theory, the young white college students in Iowa so passionately waving Obama signs were not around when the stuff that they were allegedly supposed to feel guilty about happened, and at this point their parents, some of them Obama's age, were very young when it happened as well. On the contrary, these were individuals driven not by a sense of guilt about race but by a sense of racial camaraderie that did not exist and, frankly, was not possible within previous generations in this country. So if ever there has been a speech that perfectly encapsulates just why younger voters gravitated toward Barack Obama in the 2008 election, it is "A More Perfect Union."

The speech deftly characterized the American experience of so many younger voters—an experience that is multiethnic, multiracial, and focused on the future, not the past. But more important, it summarized an American experience so much more truly American than that of any previous generation. For all the talk of our country being the ultimate melting pot, we are only now beginning to really melt—and meld—together, and younger voters are at the forefront of this historic change. (It is worth noting that the term "young voters" was thrown around pretty loosely throughout the 2008 presidential election. Officially it applies to voters under the age of thirty, although college-age voters under the age of twenty-five are often discussed as a unique subset. It should also be noted that "the hip-hop generation," a term often used to describe younger black voters, actually applies to voters born between 1964 and 1984, which means that while some younger voters are indeed members of the hip-hop generation, in some cases their parents are too. All of these voters, however, are members of the post–civil rights generation.)

It must be acknowledged that one reason Obama was able to speak so effectively about America's greatest cultural land mine without detonating it—and to do so while demonstrating an extraordinary measure of sensitivity to the feelings of Americans both black and white—was that he is both black and white. As the offspring of a black African father and a white American mother, he was able to translate some of the hopes and fears of Americans on both sides of the color line with a measure of sincerity and credibility. It should come as no surprise that the role of cultural translator would come so effortlessly to him. Indeed, from Indonesia to Hawaii and Harvard, he had been playing the role his entire life.

For many members of the post–civil rights generation, Obama's mere existence is a powerful symbol of just how different their American experience is from their parents' and grandparents'. His multiracial makeup makes him in many ways the perfect political face for a generation that has become so defined by diversity that the growing popularity of racially ambiguous models in advertisements and actors in film was the subject of a 2004 *New York Times* article. Retailers were bending over backward to reach a generation of consumers whose worldview was increasingly defined as a rainbow. Hence the ubiquitous United Colors of Benetton ads that ran for years featuring fair-skinned, freckle-faced models sporting Afros next to almond-colored models with blond curls or Asian models with dreadlocks. While such ads might have caused some to ponder aloud, "Hmmm. I wonder what they are," for this generation the answer was obvious. They are American. That's what America looks like. And there's no reason the president shouldn't look like that.

As a testament to the increasingly fluid notions of race emerging among younger people, that same *New York Times* article described the U.S. Census Bureau as "stumped" by the number of Americans, nearly seven million, who checked more than one racial category in the 2000 census, the first time respondents were able to do so. The trend was particularly popular among younger Americans. Those under the age of eighteen were twice as likely as adults to identify themselves as multiracial, making members of Generation Y under the age of twenty-five the most racially diverse people in American history.

There are plenty of younger Americans who may not have grown up with Obama's braided heritage, yet have grown up poly-lingual and -cultural—that is, speaking and negotiating the multitude of language and cultural registers that those who float between worlds often do. For my young, black female friends and I, speaking the language of *Sex and the City*, with its Manolos, cosmos, and "He's just not that into you's," was just as essential as speaking the language of *Girlfriends—Sex and the City's* browner and sometimes funnier counterpart. For some of my white friends, knowing the lyrics of Dr. Dre's "Ain't Nuthin' but a 'G' Thang" was just as essential as knowing the lyrics of Nirvana's "Smells Like Teen Spirit." And for my friends of all races, growing up knowing and loving the Huxtable family of *The Cosby Show* was just as essential as knowing and loving your own.

When Obama segued seamlessly between discussing black anger and addressing white resentments in his speech (and did so without getting booed off the stage by both groups), it was a testament to his strength as a cultural linguist. He articulated the fears and resentments of Americans black and white, the ones that are often only discussed in the privacy of homes, and never on the political stage. In my mind, there is no question that the most significant part of the speech was when he legitimized the right of Americans of all colors to be a part of the conversation about race in this country and how we move forward. The idea in itself is somewhat revolutionary and indicative of why he was embraced so early by Americans of a certain age, namely younger.

For years the conversation about race followed a familiar arc: White Americans had wronged black Americans, and we would therefore tell white Americans what they needed to do to fix it. Forever. But in validating some of the grievances of white Americans who did not exist during the dark days of segregation—Obama said, when they "hear that an African American is getting an advantage in landing a good job or a spot in a good college because of an injustice that they themselves never committed; when they're told that their fears about crime in urban neighborhoods are somehow prejudiced, resentment builds over time"—he made clear that everyone has a right to have a seat at the table in this conversation. He added that "just as black anger often proved counterproductive, so have these white resentments distracted attention from the real culprits of the middle-class squeeze—a corporate culture rife with inside dealing, questionable accounting practices." While Obama had his critics—those who felt that in an effort to appease white Americans, he unnecessarily criticized black Americans—fundamentally the idea that race, or culture, or anything for that matter, is not a one-sided or one-color conversation only brought him closer in step to the worldview of Americans of the post–civil rights generation.

When I first began interviewing other younger black voters for my book *Party Crashing: How the Hip-hop Generation Declared Political Independence* two years ago, one thing became crystal clear. We are different from our parents and grandparents; in many ways, we are more different from the generations that immediately preceded us than any other American generation before and quite possibly any American generation to come. The reason comes down to one word: race.

Race has been America's greatest obsession since the nation's inception. And yet, in the last two decades, something extraordinary has happened. After more than two centuries of de jure segregation, America has emerged as both a mosaic of cultures held together by its national identity and a melting pot, witnessed by the

45

uptick in transracial/transcultural unions. The hip-hop generation, Generation Y, the O—as in, Obama—generation, millennials—whatever you want to call us, as the generations who have come of age after the civil rights movement in this country, we have emerged as the most racially integrated demographic in our nation's history. But more than that, we are the most socially and culturally integrated.

In many ways, the cultural integration of this country has been more important than the legal one. A common sentiment once expressed by segregationists was that you could not legislate people's feelings. This is fundamentally true. The legal battles for equality were only part of winning the larger war (a very important part but a part nonetheless). Equality as we now know it was ultimately won not in the courtroom or even in the court of public opinion but in the court of cultural opinion, namely the defining cultural moments that have brought us together.

A *Vanity Fair* salute to the legendary music label Motown noted that when the Temptations began performing in the South in the mid-sixties, a rope was placed within the audience to divide blacks from whites. Singer Smokey Robinson recounted receiving letters from young white fans who would say that they loved his music but kept it hidden from their parents, who would not approve. He then noted that only a few short years later he began receiving fan mail from whites that would say, "Our kids turned us on to your music." Around the same time, the rope once used to divide blacks from whites at Temptations concerts was removed.

If music broke down barriers within the baby boomer generation, then it blew them up altogether for the boomers' children and grandchildren. While Motown brought blacks and whites together on the same dance floors and in the same concert halls, hip-hop brought them together period. Even hip-hop's fiercest critics cannot deny that some of our nation's most defining moments of cultural integration have stemmed from hip-hop. When Run-DMC joined

Aerosmith for a rock-meets-rap version of the Aerosmith classic "Walk This Way," the song, and, perhaps more important, the 1986 video, which ended up in nonstop rotation on MTV, sent a powerful message to both blacks and whites that they could not only enjoy the same music but also make beautiful music together—literally. In a nod to the cultural significance of the moment—which was not lost on the artists involved—the video features a wall between the two acts literally being knocked down. A few years later, hip-hop would produce one of its and America's brightest stars. Will Smith introduced America to a different face of hip-hop, one that not only white and black kids but their parents could appreciate (even if those same parents just didn't "understand"). But eventually Smith would go on to become culturally significant beyond the confines of hip-hop. He has emerged as the most bankable film star in Hollywood. This means that a rapper turned actor is now the celebrity with whom a majority of Americans—black, brown, Asian, Native American, and white, young and old—would most like to spend their evening at the movies.

We have come a long way since Motown.

Much as their parents convinced their own parents to give the Supremes and the Temptations a chance, the generation who grew up with "Walk This Way" and *The Fresh Prince of Bel-Air* have in many ways nudged their own parents a step further, introducing them not only to their favorite black artists but to their own black friends. The post–civil rights generation has served as a powerful bridge for racial reconciliation in this country, and by extension as a powerful bridge for Barack Obama's candidacy.

As the *New York Times* article "Young Obama Backers Twist Parents' Arms" noted, "Young supporters of Mr. Obama, who has captured a majority of under-30 primary voters, seem to be leading in the pestering sweepstakes. They send their parents the latest Obama YouTube videos, blog exhortations and 'Tell Your Mama/ Vote for Obama!' bumper stickers." The article revealed that Senator

Bob Casey of Pennsylvania had decided to endorse Obama largely on the strength of the enthusiasm displayed by his teen daughters for Obama's candidacy. Casey's endorsement was particularly noteworthy because he had initially planned to stay neutral in the race. Additionally, Casey, who is white and Catholic, represented constituencies that Obama had struggled with: Catholics and working-class white voters in Pennsylvania.

Though its place as a defining moment in America's complicated racial history is now secure, upon its debut "A More Perfect Union" was intended to serve, first and foremost, as a defining moment in a presidential campaign. More specifically, it was intended to help save one.

Barack Obama's presidential ambitions were nearly derailed when controversial statements by his former pastor, the Reverend Jeremiah Wright, were discovered and began airing on national television. Obama had spent his campaign trying to avoid being pigeonholed as "the black candidate," or worse, being viewed as the typical black candidate—one whose candidacy is predicated primarily on running as a black person there to advance black issues or to air black grievances. Then his black pastor is foisted into the national spotlight and becomes the media embodiment of some white Americans' black bogeyman. But more than any other moment on the campaign trail, the speech and the conflict that inspired it epitomize why so many young Americans felt a connection to Obama and his candidacy.

As he stood in Philadelphia that day, clearly pained, he did something that it seemed no politician in his right mind would have done (at least not publicly). Instead of throwing Wright "under the bus"—as 2008's popular political expression went—and hitting the accelerator as most politicians would have done, he sought to defend the good in the man while denouncing the bad in some of his ideas and sermons, noting that Wright "contains within him the contradictions—the good and the bad—of the community that he has served diligently for so many years."

To illustrate his point, he told a particularly poignant story about his beloved white grandmother, Madelyn Dunham, who helped raise him. In defense of his relationship with Wright, Obama said, "I can no more disown him than I can my white grand-mother . . . , a woman who sacrificed again and again for me, . . . but a woman who once confessed her fear of black men . . . who on more than one occasion has uttered racial or ethnic stereotypes that made me cringe." This statement was referenced endlessly on television and in cyberspace in the hours, days, and weeks after the speech; months later, the anecdote would be remembered with even greater poi-gnancy when Obama took leave from his presidential campaign to be with an ailing Dunham, who passed away only two days before his historic election as president.

Obama's anecdote about his grandmother and his nuanced yet impassioned defense of Wright provide a window on the qualities that many younger Americans found most compelling about him. At its core "A More Perfect Union" is really the culmination of Obama's lifelong struggle to make peace between the America he sees and be-lieves in and the America that some—even those closest to him— see. As Obama said, "the profound mistake of Reverend Wright's sermons is not that he spoke about racism in our society. It's that he spoke as if our society was static; as if no progress has been made; as if this country—a country that has made it possible for one of his own members to run for the highest office in the land and build a coalition of white and black, Latino and Asian, rich and poor, young and old—is still irrevocably bound to a tragic past."

Many of the younger people listening to his speech had had their very own "A More Perfect Union" moments, whether it was the time a parent said, "I'm not prejudiced or anything, but . . ." or the time that a grandparent used a racial slur. But unlike Obama, most of us have been fortunate enough not to have ours played out on a national stage.

Comedian Chris Rock once irreverently declared that the most prejudiced person in America is an older black man. Though he was joking, he had in fact tapped into some universal truth. Many of us who have come of age after the civil rights movement, who have reaped its rewards without the burden of the injustices that precipitated it, have often grappled quietly with the Reverend Wrights in our own lives. Hip-hop artist Pierce Freelon, who is the founding editor of the popular blog Blackademics, echoed this sentiment, noting, of the likely reaction among his readership to the catalyst for the speech, that "most probably have a 'Reverend Wright' in their family, whether it be a grandparent, uncle or pastor."

In my own case, I was reminded of a member of my family whom as a child I viewed as a sort of embarrassing but humorous and ultimately harmless George Jefferson–like figure. Only instead of calling white folks "honky" à la Mr. Jefferson's slur-cum-endearment for his neighbor turned friend Tom Willis, this family member was notorious for bouts of political incorrectness that included incessantly referring to biracial children as "half-breeds," along with the occasional "cracker" reference to whites who had sparked a particular ire. It was only upon reaching adulthood that I gained an appreciation for the level of bitterness that had consumed him since his years growing up as a young black boy in America's segregated South. The wounds from those years had never fully healed, and in fact had never really been treated. My mother revealed that this family member had confided to her that around the age of six he had been warned by a white adult that if he was ever caught playing with a childhood neighbor—a white girl—he would be found "swinging from a tree." When my mother asked if he had reported the incident to his parents, he replied, "Of course not. I didn't want them to get into trouble."

When we watch other countries plagued by wars and genocide,

we Americans usually find ourselves able to sit back with a comfortable, disconnected empathy peppered with smugness, knowing that even on our worst day no American will be forced to flee this country as a dislocated refugee. And yet we have millions of black Americans who have spent the last forty years feeling like emotional refugees in their own homes. The level of dysfunctional denial some parts of our country must have relied upon to coexist in the immediate aftermath of the end of Jim Crow is extraordinary, and the silence surrounding it—even among black Americans, including my relative—is audible. I am reminded of a critical scene from *The Prince of Tides*.

After a group of men attack a mother and her children while the father is away, the mother decides that the best course of action is for them all to pretend that nothing happened when the father returns. This silence leads to a lifetime of tragedy and despair for all of them.

While I would never defend some of Wright's more unsettling rhetoric, I also don't think that any of us are in a position to judge the source or even the extent of his anger. This is a sentiment that Obama clearly struggled with as he sought to reconcile his optimism about our great country with the skepticism, the cynicism, that plagued those who lived through some of the nation's less than laudable eras. As Obama would note in his speech, "for the men and women of Reverend Wright's generation, the memories of humiliation and doubt and fear have not gone away; nor has the anger and the bitterness of those years." It was as though Obama was running a campaign that was predicated on a theme—"Yes We Can"—that ran counter to everything that so many Americans of Wright's generation had been raised to believe: "No we can't and never will."

The conflict between the ideals of America and a past abounding with racial upheaval has been a recurring theme throughout Barack Obama's political career. His first, and only, major political defeat came at the hands of Bobby Rush, the former Black Panther turned congressman. His political peer group of younger black elected officials, including current Newark mayor Cory Booker and Congressman Artur Davis of Alabama, Obama's law school classmate, faced similar defeats during early runs against civil rights–era black leaders in campaigns marked by accusations that the younger generation lacked the life experience to be "black enough." (Sharpe James, Booker's predecessor as mayor, went so far as to declare, "You have to learn to be an African-American . . . and we don't have time to train you.")

This notion was unfortunately given new life early in the presidential primary, largely on the strength of a few inflammatory quotes and commentaries from some older African American gadflies. Even among those who eventually supported Obama, such as the Reverend Jesse Jackson, there were signs of resentment. In addition to allegedly accusing Obama of "acting white" during the Jena 6 controversy, there was his infamous pronouncement that he wanted to "cut [Obama's] nuts off," which drew a strong rebuke from Jackson's own son, himself a younger elected official. There was undeniably a sense that Obama would enjoy the fruits of the political promised land without having had to endure the long, hot, perilous walk through the desert that Jackson and others had to get there. It simply wasn't fair.

But aside from concerns about his sufficient blackness (which were, quite frankly, overblown by the media), the greatest concern among some older black Americans was that Obama's quest for the presidency was merely an impossible dream. And yet, their children and grandchildren knew from the beginning that it wasn't impossible at all. Not in the America that we knew. And soon enough, after Iowa proved that America had become a place in which the "Yes We Can" mantra no longer came with a "whites only" sign attached, these older black Americans too became true "hope mongers."

It is only natural that historians, pundits, and others would strive to compare "A More Perfect Union" to that other landmark speech on race, Dr. Martin Luther King Jr.'s "I Have a Dream." Subject matter aside, however, the speeches are markedly different, shaped by the different experiences of the men who gave them and the vastly different circumstances under which they were compelled to give them. While Dr. King was trying to convince Americans of different colors not to fear one another, Obama was ultimately trying to convince Americans to trust one another and, in their capacity, to perfect the union. Though they may sound similar, these are in fact two very different goals. The greatest difference between the two men's speeches lies in the audiences to which they delivered them. King found himself speaking to an audience primarily populated by generations bracketed by 1896's *Plessy v. Ferguson* and 1954's *Brown v. Board of Education*. For many of these Americans, little had really changed in their day-to-day lives.

Obama spoke to a very different audience, one populated by some Americans who could still recall the America that King had dreamed of bringing *change* to all those years before, but increasingly by more Americans who were living the dream—as was Obama himself. While King's speech represented a lofty dream for many, Obama's "A More Perfect Union" represented reality for many more—particularly younger Americans.

Obama issued a disclaimer regarding just what he believed "A More Perfect Union" could ultimately accomplish: "Contrary to the claims of some of my critics, black and white, I have never been so naive as to believe that we can get beyond our racial divisions in a single election cycle, or with a single candidacy—particularly a candidacy as imperfect as my own." Clearly he sold himself and the speech short. The speech's greatest legacy is that by talking frankly and openly about race, it finally allowed our nation to begin to move forward in a way we had been unable to before. Journalist and cultural critic Michaela Angela Davis noted in the aftermath of "A More Perfect Union," "By not ignoring the issue of race, I felt many folks like me could actually start to let it go. You can only forgive if you promise never to forget. His speech was a promise that we didn't need to fully identify ourselves and our work by race and racism, nor did we have to turn our backs on it and live in denial." She continued, "Though I identify myself as a post–civil rights, hip-hop generation, 'Barack generation' woman, I am not [of the] post-race generation. This speech helped lighten the burden of full identity by race and started giving us permission to begin being, just simply being."

When I asked my incredibly optimistic and full-of-life eighty-seven-year-old grandmother if she had ever thought that she would see a black president elected in her lifetime, she responded that she hadn't given the matter much thought over the years, but fundamentally, "no." She didn't have it down on her list of things she would get to see in her long, extraordinary life. And yet, she—a woman who had endured a life that had included segregation, the Great Depression, and hard, backbreaking work in the cotton fields—lived long enough to see America become a country in which her granddaughter *could* grow up believing that the election of a black president was not only a possible dream but a viable reality. And in some ways this says more about the evolution of our nation than Obama's actual election to the presidency does. However, it is Barack Obama's ability to successfully bridge the gap between vastly different American experiences with his message of hope, forgiveness, and, most of all, letting go and looking forward that makes "A More Perfect Union" such an important contribution to the American conversation.

And it gives me hope that one day my young niece will also grow up and live in a continuously evolving and *changed* America, one where she will read this essay that ponders the issue of race and politics and find herself asking, "What was all the fuss about?"

BLACK LIKE BARACK

Joan Morgan

I chose to run for the presidency at this moment in history because I
believe deeply that we cannot solve the challenges of our time unless
we solve them together, unless we perfect our union by understanding
that we may have different stories, but we hold common hopes; that
we may not look the same and we may not have come from the same
place, but we all want to move in the same direction—towards a
better future for our children and our grandchildren.

It's a story that hasn't made me the most conventional candidate.
But it is a story that has seared into my genetic makeup the idea that
this nation is more than the sum of its parts—that out of many,
we are truly one.
—SENATOR BARACK OBAMA, "A More Perfect Union," 2008

If there was ever a time when I doubted that Barack Obama could
become the forty-fourth president of the United States, it was in
the weeks before he addressed an uneasy nation about his controversial relationship with the Reverend Jeremiah Wright. Today that
speech, "A More Perfect Union," stands poised to take its rightful
place in the prestigious canon of seminal American speeches—right

on up there with "I Have a Dream" and the Gettysburg Address. But back in March 2008 its outcome was uncertain. At best.

Locked in an epic battle with then–Democratic heir apparent Senator Hillary Clinton, Obama was down in the polls, struggling to overcome consistent attacks that ranged from the unfounded (closet Muslim, elitist, out-of-touch intellectual) to the absurd (unqualified male who'd, according to irate pro-Hill white feminists, only gotten this far because America's sexism is so intractable that the country would rather see any man, even a—gasp!—black one, occupy the highest office than a woman). No one could doubt the man's abilities as a skilled orator and a gifted writer. His address at 2004's Democratic National Convention and two best-selling books, *Dreams from My Father* and *The Audacity of Hope*, were partially responsible for the veritable rock star status accorded his candidacy even in its infancy. But the emergent maelstrom unleashed by Wright's comments shook the delicate tightrope Obama walked when it came to race, specifically the tactical and prudent decision to let his skin color be everyone else's obsession and not his own.

Still, when Obama began his address that day, he must have known that this no-holds-barred "Come to Jesus" moment regarding American race relations had been inevitable. Love him or hate him, Wright had driven home the inescapable reality that the man vying to be the de facto leader of the free world was, at the end of the day, a black man in America—a country whose racial history was deeply and ineradicably embedded in both its social and its political DNA. It was highly unlikely that its citizens—black, white, or other—were going to hand over the keys to the White House without knowing exactly how Obama felt about Wright specifically and race in general. The question was never *if* race would morph from the pink elephant in the room into the raging tiger that needed to be sedated and tamed. It was always when and who, if anyone, would emerge intact once the beast was unleashed.

For Obama, who must also have been aware that political careers had imploded over far less than the fire-and-brimstone race rhetoric excerpted from the good reverend's Sunday sermons, the situation was as difficult to defuse as it was likely to detonate. For the most fearful of white folks, Wright's heated three-minute critique of white racism and American foreign policy tapped into deep-seated anxieties regarding the mythic cauldron of collective black anger that has allegedly been boiling since slavery. He was a frightening confirmation that blacks would be unable to resist the seductive call of "Get Whitey!" retribution if, God forbid, a black man actually sat in the Oval Office. Or, as a white customer in my local coffee shop dared to wonder aloud, "So, what? If he wins, we have to sit in the back of the bus now?"

Obama's standing with African Americans was equally precarious. In the aftermath of his presidential victory and the warm fuzziness it invokes, the tendency is to be revisionist, but if truth be told, African American support before the primaries was far from unilateral. Not that there weren't core black supporters from the onset. There were. There were also members of the generations old enough to remember the King, Kennedy, and Malcolm X assassinations who repeatedly voiced fears about Obama's living long enough to finish the election. Some questioned his inexperience, while others doubted America's readiness for a black president. Both groups thought their vote would be more wisely cast for a candidate who actually had a shot in hell at winning. Among Clinton's loyalists were black feminists who thought the country could be better served by a substantial infusion of estrogen, as well as political allies who were slow to turn their support away from the wife of the man unofficially dubbed "the first black president of the United States"— even after Bubba's infamous display of sour grapes during the South Carolina primary.

Still, African Americans were not likely to dismiss the obvious: The rage and the racism that had fed Wright's tirade were hardly unfamiliar, or even unjustified. In very real ways, Wright was being scapegoated for sentiments many African Americans shared—just usually not when white folks were watching. Any subsequent decisions he made to stand "wrong and strong" by justifying his stance in the media might have been seen as everything from politically imprudent to embarrassingly crab-in-a-barrelish; still, there was little question that as far as the black vote was concerned, Wright would sooner be forgiven for potentially torpedoing the chances of the first black man to have a serious shot at the presidency than Obama would be for appearing to save his political ass by throwing another black man under the bus.

By all counts, the Wright debacle was a live grenade that threatened to damage an essential tenet of the Obama campaign: the sexy new multiracial, youth-driven, socioeconomically diverse, bipartisan "CHANGE" he was promising America. Any failure to neutralize the race drama caused by Wright's sound bites would pose a direct challenge to the veracity of what my colleague T. Denean Sharpley-Whiting, in following Du Bois, calls Obama's "averred gift of 'second sight.'" Throughout the campaign, Obama carefully positioned Clinton as a polarizing force, all the while subtly maintaining that his biracial identity and multiethnic upbringing had made him both insider and outsider, capable of viewing America and her problems from multiple vantage points, both within and outside the frame. This "second sight" made him the candidate in the running uniquely suited to acting as a unifying force between racially, economically, and politically disparate groups. "A More Perfect Union" was the senator's critical shot to show and prove, or be forever branded way too *kumbaya* for the country's own good.

And yet, as a Jamaican-born, black American woman, I listened to "A More Perfect Union" with a distinctly different ear, acutely aware that the senator's relationship with Wright was incidental to the real issue at hand. At the end of the day, the issue being raised wasn't Obama's potential for covert racism, or even his race loyalty. It was the legitimacy of his particular brand of blackness itself: "At various stages in the campaign, some commentators have deemed me either 'too black' or 'not black enough' . . . The press has scoured every exit poll for the latest evidence of racial polarization, not just in terms of white and black, but black and brown as well."

For months I'd watched America fumble around its own racial history and neurosis, struggling to define a man who is black and undeniably American, who identifies himself as African American but is not a direct descendant of American slaves, or what is otherwise broadly referred to as African American. As a first-generation immigrant, I am well aware of the proprietary tendency of native-born Americans to use "black" and "African American" interchangeably—as if to be black in America is necessarily to be descended from this ancestry. In 2009, however, this is an increasingly dated reality. Today the number of black immigrants (hailing predominantly from the Caribbean, Latin America, and Africa) living in the United States is in the millions. According to Mary Mederios Kent in "Immigration and America's Black Population," "immigration contributed to at least one-fifth of the growth in the U.S. black population between 2001 and 2006 with the number of foreign-born blacks rising from 125,000 in 1980 to 2,815,000 in 2005. More than one-fourth of the black population in New York, Boston, and Miami is foreign-born."* Moreover, a 2005 article by Sam Roberts that appeared in the *New York Times* suggests that more people of African descent arrived in the United States voluntarily from 1990 to 2000 than the total who came as slaves prior to 1807, when the country outlawed the slave trade.

Obama's presidential run forced all Americans to grapple with the fact that "black" in America is a diverse, multiethnic, sometimes biracial, and often bicultural experience that can no longer be confined to the rich but limited prism of U.S. slavery and its historical aftermath. As a first-generation black immigrant, I also know that

---

* In *Population Bulletin* 62, no. 4 (2007).

Obama's precarious footing was caused less by Jeremiah Wright than by the confusion and distrust this identity tends to provoke among whites and African Americans alike—precisely because it complicates, quite beautifully, not only existing constructs of race but all the traditional expectations, stereotypes, and explanations we have come to expect from discussions around what it means to be black in America.

Ironically, the same racial exoticism and "second sight" that seemingly had the potential to help unify a polarized America left Obama simultaneously fighting to transcend limited notions of black possibility and reassuring African Americans that he was indeed deserving of his black card. The former reaction was easy to dismiss as an expected by-product of racism. The latter, however, I found more disturbing.

In a January 22, 2007, piece titled "Colorblind" on Salon.com, author and cultural critic Debra Dickerson wrote,

> I didn't have the heart (or the stomach) to point out the obvious: Obama isn't black.
>
> "Black," in our political and social reality, means those descended from West African slaves. Voluntary immigrants of African descent (even those descended from West Indian slaves) are just that, voluntary immigrants of African descent with markedly different outlooks on the role of race in their lives and in politics. At a minimum, it can't be assumed that a Nigerian cabdriver and a third-generation Harlemite have more in common than the fact a cop won't bother to make the distinction. They're both "black" as a matter of skin color and DNA, but only the Harlemite, for better or worse, is politically and culturally black, as we use the term.

Dickerson was not the only one. A *New York Times* article, "So Far Obama Can't Take the Black Vote for Granted," broke the apparently startling news that African Americans would not automatically cast their vote for president solely on the basis of a mutual melanin count. I expected an article centered on the assertion that African Americans, like their white counterparts, were politically astute enough to base their votes on the ability of the candidate to effect change in the areas most pertinent to them—educational reform, health care, the economy, to name a few. What I got instead was a roundup of voices arguing that the distinction of being the first black president of the United States was one that should be reserved for an African American, a sentiment summarized by a brother the reporter interviewed in a D.C. barbershop.

> Mr. Lanier pointed to Mr. Obama's heritage—he is the American-born son of a black father from Kenya and a white mother from Kansas—and the fact that he did not embody the experiences of most African Americans whose ancestors endured slavery, segregation and the bitter struggle for civil rights.
>
> "When you think of a president, you think of an American," continued Mr. Lanier, a 58-year-old barber who was still considering whether to support Mr. Obama. "We've been taught that a president should come from right here, born, raised, bred, fed in America. To go outside and bring somebody in from another nationality, now that doesn't feel right to some people."

To see some black folk so closely mimic the very prejudices that white America reserved for European immigrants saddened me, especially since white folks finally figured this out: when Europeans immigrated to America, became citizens, paid taxes, and contributed their substantial labor force to the economic, cultural, and political growth of the country, they stopped being European immigrants and became just regular white folk and easily united in the common interest of holding on to every bit of entitlement that whiteness grants in a country like America whose emergence as a superpower is partially based on the maintenance of very specific forms of racial oppression. The fact that we voluntary immigrants of African, Caribbean, and South American descent often do the same—become citizens, pay taxes, and contribute substantially to the economic, cultural, and political growth of the country—and will be subjected inevitably to the very same racism as African Americans is not enough to convince folks like Dickerson to grant us the elusive black card. This stems, in part, from a failure to acknowledge our common histories, to understand that, despite the atrocities of America's "original sin," African Americans do not hold the monopoly on the painful legacy of colonialism, slavery, and imperialism, which descendants of West African slaves have experienced around the globe. The difference between rice and peas and black-eyed peas is hardly as great as one might think. Same shit, different boat: the mere distance between stops on a slave ship.

Refusing to see us as black Americans is also a matter of willful ignorance. As Dickerson accurately points out, "we know a great deal about black people. We know next to nothing about immigrants of African descent (woe be unto blacks when the latter groups find their voice and start saying all kinds of things we don't want said)." Perhaps not. But there is a necessary discourse that's long overdue if we are remotely serious about channeling the potential power we hold when we expand our notion of black American culture to include the diverse, multiethnic power base that was savvy enough to elect one of the most dynamic and capable leaders the free world has ever seen, at least in this millennium. If current black leadership, which has remained stubbornly committed to defining black struggle through a solely African American lens, hopes to apply that same political force to the issues that affect us all as black people—health care, education, poverty, police brutality, and racism among them—it's time to stop ignoring the millions of other voices that comprise the American black experience.

There is a bit of stubborn American ethnocentricity at play. I suspect, though, another reason for the reluctance. Delving into the differences between native-born and immigrant blacks is potentially messy and painful stuff, in part because of mutually held prejudices and stereotypes, in part because the hyphenated identity of black immigrant Americans is by no means a clear-cut one. As Obama lingers between two distinct worlds, so do we, navigating what is often a culturally schizophrenic identity, one whose influences are often as innate as they are discordant.

African American ancestry and its many cultural influences are simply not ours to claim. Whether they are fostered by memory or parental influence, most of us retain a profound love of and a fierce loyalty to our countries of origin. We are more likely to see ourselves as Jamaican/Haitian/Ghanaian/Nigerian/Guyanese before we see ourselves as black by this country's definition. We are not all exempt from the experience of being African American—and not only because we will inevitably be subjected to American racism. As a matter of both acclimation and survival, we learn the history. We absorb the culture. Some of us even acquire the accent. But for many of us, the connection to and longing for our mother countries never go away, irrespective of how many years we've lived here.

To the untrained, unlearned American ear, my Jamaicanness is not easily detected. I am at my core also a black girl who came of age in the Boogie Down. I have no resistance to a righteous plate of soul food or the communal funk of a soul clap. I can easily pass for African American if and when I want to. Most people will never hear the easy patois I naturally slip into in the company of my family or see that my hips find their most natural sway to the drive of a wicked reggae riddim. But after more than four decades of living in America, majoring in African American studies in college, and having countless African American lovers and friends, I never feel completely American. I still feel a visceral need to return to the home I left before I was two, to walk barefoot on Jamaican soil. The profound irony in this is that once I arrive, my Americanness sticks out like a sore thumb. Jamaicans embrace me as their daughter, yes, but are quick to notice the unmarred skin that marks an absence of hard physical labor, the patois spoken with stilted tongue that screams "she just come from foreign." My connection to Jamaica is encouraged, but Jamaicans will never consider me completely Jamaican.

Unlike Italian Americans, whose whiteness is never questioned when they embrace their cultural identity, then meld it into their distinctly American one, black immigrants who reject an African American identity to acknowledge an ongoing cultural influence from and spiritual connection to our native countries are sometimes looked at as separatist or divisive. This is due to a critical lapse in communication. Unlike the ongoing discourse on biracial identity that continues with President Obama's victory, there has yet to be a meaningful exchange about what it means to be black and bicultural in America. But black and bicultural we are. We grow up in homes with different political histories, foods, cultures, languages, patois, customs, and music. As first- and second-generation immigrants, we are often more conservative in our political ideology, are less likely to publicly embrace social programs like welfare, and tend to be very stalwart in our opinions about black complicity in our own conditions. Racism for us is an undeniable reality, but it is also not the ultimate determinant. At our very core, we view America as a land of infinite possibilities because we know firsthand that it is possible to arrive in this country with nothing and build a life infinitely richer than the one that was left behind. We are, in short, very up-from-the-bootstraps kind of people, a bit more Republican (although we tend not to vote that way), if not moderately Democratic, in nature than black political leaders care to recognize.

And if we are to be unabashedly honest about it, some of us share the same prejudices about African Americans as working- and middle-class whites. The ones who, as Obama eloquently pointed out in his speech, "don't feel that they have been particularly privileged by their race. Their experience is the immigrant experience—

as far as they're concerned, no one's handed them anything; they've built it from scratch." In the comfortable presence of countrymen, we are prone to superior, spirited rants—ones deriding the "laziness" of African Americans and their seeming willingness to use racism as an excuse not to succeed in a land of obvious opportunity, when we are sure African Americans are not listening.

Those of us who know better, and many of us do, connect the dots between the oppression and poverty we left our mother countries to escape and the imperialist, racist drive that fostered American slavery. We also recognize that our insights as bicultural outsiders imbue us with our own "second sight," and with it a keen advantage and a responsibility to bridge the communication gaps that exist between us.

The fact is that the comments that have been made and the issues that have surfaced over the last few weeks reflect the complexities of race in this country that we've never really worked through—a part of our union that we have yet to perfect. And if we walk away now, if we simply retreat into our respective corners, we will never be able to come together and solve challenges like health care, or education, or the need to find good jobs for every American.
—SENATOR BARACK OBAMA, "A More Perfect Union," 2008

While Obama's speech may have centered specifically on the differences between blacks and whites, his calm, eloquent call for all Americans to push themselves out of the safety of their respective comfort zones to address long-lingering tensions around race also felt particularly prescriptive for addressing the undeniable tensions between first- and second-generation immigrant blacks and African Americans. His gentle reminder to white America "that so many of the disparities that exist in the African American community today can be directly traced to inequalities passed on from an earlier generation that suffered under the brutal legacy of slavery and Jim Crow" also functioned as a much-needed reminder to immigrant blacks that African Americans live the aftermath of this country's original sin daily; its generational impact is imprinted on their DNA.

Obama poignantly attempted to evaluate and temper Reverend Wright's anger: "They came of age in the late fifties and early sixties, a time when segregation was still the law of the land and opportunity was systematically constricted. What's remarkable is not how many failed in the face of discrimination, but rather, how many men and women overcame the odds, how many were able to make a way out of no way for those like me who would come after them." And in doing so, he reminded America "how we arrived at this point." This moment in the speech was also a pointed reminder to every immigrant black who too readily adopts the very same prejudices and stereotypes about African Americans as part and parcel of a seemingly intractable racist American tendency to dismiss the continuing impact of over four hundred years of slavery and the sanctioned inequities of Jim Crow. It was a none too subtle reminder that we arrived here without that baggage, and that as a result we appear able to move a little lighter and a little faster on what is still a vastly unequal playing field.

When we criticize African American blacks for their laziness, but willingly participate in social programs that were created to address the disparities of America's racism—I don't know many blacks who refuse to check the African American box on a job or school application—we participate in a profoundly unhealthy and hurtful hypocrisy. So is it any wonder that when we arrive on those campuses and refuse to "get involved," scorning opportunities to form necessary political alliances with African Americans, we inevitably bear the brunt of righteous anger and frustration? We can't have it both ways.

Reminding ourselves how we arrived here might also free us

from the convenient amnesia we seem to have about the painful legacy that slavery, imperialism, and colonialism left on our own countries. We might recall that even in these predominantly black, and in many cases black-governed, countries, there is a notable discrepancy between white and black privilege and wealth, and as a result a deeply entrenched class- and complexion-based caste system that makes social/economic advancement difficult, if not impossible. And that our desire to avoid this fate was the reason many of us, if not our parents, willingly took the figurative "banana boat" in the first place.

It might also leave us less inclined to let white folks off the hook as they enlist us in their project of painting a picture of a "post-racism" society, lauding our progress as examples of the American dream and a direct indictment of the hopelessness of African Americans. "Look at how well you've done. It's clearly their fault that they are where they are." It would help us recognize that there are tremendous psychological and emotional advantages when you can sit in your American history class and not have your entry begin with the "stigma" of slavery. And then there is not having to reach back as far as the vagueness of Africa, denying the vastness of the continent and its own complicity in the transatlantic slave trade, to retrieve a meaningful connection to a land that fortifies your identity. Racism has so coded and corroded African American experiences in America that the possibility of an African American president seemed remote. And yet our experiences as immigrants in many ways make us natural by-products of the American dream. So much so that an Obama victory was not especially unfathomable to a group of people taught to believe that if you work hard enough in America, almost anything can happen.

So I listened to "A More Perfect Union" with high hopes that he would become the forty-fourth president of the United States, and that his own "exotic" origins and his struggle with those origins would bring to light the schisms that exist in black American identity and bring us closer to healing them. And I hoped that in years to come, this speech and his subsequent victory would encourage all of us, as black folks, to embrace the diversity of our collective American experience. Once we draw on the similarities within that collective experience, we can start building bridges. Of course, this means acknowledging the stereotypes and prejudices between us, but that's where the healing begins. And it is work that's long overdue.

THE AUDACITY OF POST-RACISM

Adam Mansbach

Other essayists in this volume, more politically astute than I, will surely situate Barack Obama's "A More Perfect Union" historically. I trust that someone else will detail the surge of amazement, the sense of possibility, that gripped so many Americans upon sitting down to hear a black man with a good chance of becoming president speak about race and racism on national television for half an hour. Doubtless, one of my colleagues will note that such an eloquent and thoughtful discourse on *any* topic far exceeds what we have come to accept of American politics, and that to hold forth on an issue so pernicious and so seldom approached honestly is remarkable. The fact that this soaring oration was delivered largely out of necessity, the candidate's back against the wall after weeks of mounting controversy about his former pastor, will also, I'm confident, be discussed elsewhere, as will the fact that Obama has scarcely revisited the subject in the months since.

For my part, I watched the speech in my living room, on a laptop computer with tinny speakers, and I was with Obama until he let white people off the hook. Though I grasped the political necessity of the move, my expectations of this man were sufficiently high that it was disheartening to hear him fudge the difference between institutional racism and white bitterness. Three weeks earlier, I'd felt a similar sense of letdown when, challenged at a debate in

Ohio to further denounce Minister Louis Farrakhan, Obama responded by articulating the need to mend black-Jewish relations, then proceeded to reinscribe the very paradigm that has served to rend them.

I say this as a white person, a Jew, and an enthusiastic Obama supporter. My reactions, it also bears mentioning, are colored by the fact that when the Ohio debate aired, I had just published a novel titled *The End of the Jews*, which chronicles three generations of a Jewish American family and also takes as its subject the evolving relations between black and Jewish artists throughout the twentieth century. "A More Perfect Union" marked the first time I'd sat on my couch in weeks; I had just returned from a book tour speckled with dates at Jewish Community Centers and synagogues, in addition to the standard bookstores and universities.

This level of interaction with Jewish communities was utterly new to me. No one had ever considered me a Jewish writer before, except the white supremacists who'd protested the speaking gigs for my previous novel, *Angry Black White Boy*, and accused me of "masquerading as white." I was raised by secular parents raised by secular parents, and at the age of twelve I was expelled from the Sunday School and Half-Price Car Wash for the Children of Agnostic Cultural Jews after getting into a fight with my teacher about whether Satch Sanders of the 1940s Boston Celtics was the only black person in history not to abandon his community after achieving success. It was the culmination of a lesson devoted to the great Jewish Exodus—from Roxbury, Massachusetts, in the 1950s, when the blacks moved in.

I won't blame the encounter for my souring on Judaism; more accurate would be to say that as a kid growing up in a largely Jewish suburb, I simply conflated Jewish with white, and thus my frustration with the complacency and hypocrisy of white liberals (I didn't know any conservatives) extended automatically to Jews.

The pervasiveness of injustice was something I had always intuited; obsessing over fairness on a personal level is a childhood instinct that can remain personal and fade or broaden into an analysis of the world and grow stronger. But my absorption in the still-underground culture of hip-hop was what allowed me to confirm that things were not well, very close by and yet in another world altogether.

I believe that the music to which one is exposed at twelve is the most important one will ever hear; I was that age in 1988, when Public Enemy, Boogie Down Productions, Stetsasonic, the Jungle Brothers, and N.W.A. were articulating the insidious realities of police brutality, a Eurocentric school system, American collusion in South African apartheid, and ghettos ravaged by crack and guns—all over unbelievably dope beats. Thanks to METCO, a busing program that constituted Boston's unidirectional form of school integration, tapes of these groups made their way to the suburbs and to me.

Hip-hop, at the time, was one of the only sites in American life to dislocate whiteness from its presumed position of centrality. By listening, I was listening in. And only by physically seeking out the parties, the shows, and the record stores that sold 12-inch singles—all located in the aforementioned Roxbury and other equally unwhite neighborhoods—could I hope to participate. Doing so meant venturing outside of comfort zones, rendering myself visible as different.

Soon, it also meant a chance to step away—semantically, momentarily—from the nimbus of skin privilege and the complicity in injustice it afforded me. This is to say that hip-hop became a different kind of comfort zone: contested, and all the more beloved for it. Hip-hop demanded that I cast off romantic notions of color blindness and investigate oppression. Not just as a relic of the past, as it was presented in school. Nor as something held at bay by regular donations to the NAACP or the Southern Poverty Law Center. But as something monstrously alive, a fact of life even a fool could see—so long as that fool knew where to look.

By taking casual and institutional racism for granted, hip-hop created space for follow-up questions—quintessentially hip-hop questions like *how do we flip this?* Well, by exploiting exploitation: By using the black kid as a decoy in the art supply store, while the white kid steals the spray paint. By having the black kid buy the beer in the white neighborhood, since the old white store owner can't tell fifteen from twenty-one so long as fifteen is darker than blue.

Of course, nobody ever got carded at Giant Liquors in the 'Bury; you could ride in on a tricycle and leave with a case of Olde English 800. The realization was sobering, and it was not the only one.

Though it opened my eyes, hip-hop also let me bullshit myself. It permitted me to believe that the opposite of white privilege was not working to dismantle that privilege but embracing and being embraced by blackness. Thus, as long as my friends were black people who didn't like white people, I figured I was doing my part. The experience of being a token white boy was one of being identified, tested, and ultimately accepted; it was about feeling exceptional, in the word's truest sense. Had I pondered my status a bit harder, I might have concluded that it was to be attributed not to an uncanny understanding of the plight of black people and the true nature of racism, but rather to the fact that I was a little less oblivious and smug than the average white kid, a little more willing to put myself on the line. Also, I could rap.

It would take me years to realize the flawed nature of some of the racial equations by which I lived, but one thing I did grasp immediately, given the company I kept, was the unspoken difference between the political and the personal. Between whiteness, as a concept that engendered fury and pointed jokes, and an individual white person, who would be judged on his merits—if he stuck around long enough to realize that a rant about The White Man didn't mean he ought to leave before he got his ass kicked, but rather the opposite.

I delve into the race politics that marked my adolescence (and hip-hop's) because the manner in which their sharpness has blurred is the backdrop for "A More Perfect Union." Hip-hop is now America's dominant youth culture. It still dislocates whiteness, but in a way far less conducive to personal growth or rigorous assessment of injustice. White hip-hoppers of my era constructed elaborate rhetorical structures intended to accommodate paradox, to acknowledge the devilishness of white supremacy without condemning ourselves. Today, white youth are confounded by a different paradox: the divergence of cultural capital and hard capital in American life.

Largely because of hip-hop, American coolness is coded and commodified more than ever as American blackness. White kids all over the country believe, based on the signifiers flashing on their TV screens, that blackness equals flashy wealth, supreme masculinity, and ultra-sexualized femininity—interrupted occasionally by bursts of glamorous violence, and situated in a thrilling ghetto that is both dangerous and host to a constant party. They feel locked out of the possibility of attaining that lifestyle, because of the color of their skin. They don't know where to find a workable identity, unless they embrace the "I'm a fucking redneck" ethos of Levi Johnston, Sarah Palin's once future son-in-law. All this strikes them as oppressive, and their resentment is compounded by the fact that they possess no language with which to discuss it.

Were any of this utterable, one could present them with reams of evidence demonstrating that in all the important ways white people in America are anything but marginal. Traditional markers of prosperity—rates of wealth inheritance and home ownership, comparative levels of education and income and incarceration—reveal just how privileged whites remain relative to blacks. A recent study conducted at Princeton University revealed that a white felon stands an equal chance of being granted a job interview as a black applicant with no criminal record, and there are dozens of other studies that each speak volumes.

Nonetheless, confusion persists even among the kind of

coast-dwelling, liberally raised, relatively well-educated white kid I once was about the basic facts of racism today—to say nothing of everyone to their ideological right. They want to know if the playing field is level; they can't tell, and they've got their fingers crossed that it is, because if it's not, they've got to confront things no one has prepared them to face. Many of them would rather believe, and in fact suspect, that it is slanted in black people's favor.

At the very least, they're eager for a kind of moral compromise, one with an air of the fairness so appealing to young minds: *Racism cuts in both directions. Anyone can be its victim, just as anyone can refuse to perpetrate it.*

This is what Barack Obama provided on March 18, 2008, in Philadelphia. After a succinct but powerful summary of institutional racism's history and its practical and psychic effects on black people, he added,

A similar anger exists within segments of the white community. Most working- and middle-class white Americans don't feel that they have been particularly privileged by their race . . . As far as they're concerned, no one's handed them anything . . . So when they are told to bus their children to a school across town; when they hear that an African American is getting an advantage in landing a good job or a spot in a good college because of an injustice that they themselves never committed; when they're told that their fears about crime in urban neighborhoods are somehow prejudiced, resentment builds over time . . .

. . . To wish away the resentments of white Americans, to label them as misguided or even racist, without recognizing they are grounded in legitimate concerns—this too widens the racial divide, and blocks the path to understanding.

Obama's insights about white anger were salient, but to characterize ire at affirmative action and at *the thought that others might think them prejudiced* as "similar" to the frustration felt by the victims of entrenched structural racism was disingenuous, and even irresponsible. I don't dispute that white resentments should be addressed, if only because white people will refuse to grapple with race unless they are allowed to centralize themselves. But to begin such a discussion—the mythic National Dialogue on Race—without acknowledging that structural racism is a cancer metastasizing through every aspect of American life is impossible. Call it, to borrow a catchphrase from the foreign policy side of the election, a precondition.

Implicit in the resentment Obama identified is whites' belief that they *should* be significantly advantaged because of their race. They are not angry because people *think* they're advantaged when they aren't; they're angry because they don't feel advantaged *enough*. The essence of white privilege is not knowing you have it; white people in America are bicyclists riding with the wind at their backs, never realizing that they owe part of their speed—whatever speed that is—to forces beyond their control. By no means does this guarantee success. But few whites are conditioned to contemplate how much worse off they might be if they had to grapple with factors like police profiling and housing discrimination, in addition to the other travails of being an American in the twenty-first century.

To place the experiences of white and black Americans on an equal footing, Obama had to abandon the empirical and speak the language of the emotional. Hence, the focus on how people "feel"—privileged or not, racist or not—rather than on the objective realities of what they have and do and say.

The soft-focus abstraction of racial realities goes beyond Obama's speech. It was a hallmark of the entire presidential campaign, with its musings on whether Obama was too black, black enough, or "post-race." Naturally, one must be black to be post-race, for the same reason that no one thought to ask whether Hillary Clinton or Mitt Romney was too white or not white enough. The purpose of abstracting race is to obscure racism, to elide the fact that a black person is never so lacking in blackness—culturally, person-ally, politically, or by any other standard—as to find himself exempt from discrimination.

The desire for personal post-race status is an impulse I encounter frequently. Without fail, it comes from well-intentioned white people looking to be absolved of whiteness—not through their poli-tics, but through their biographies. They listen studiously to my take on race privilege, then raise their hands to identify themselves as white but gay, or white but Irish and thus part of an ethnicity that was once considered nonwhite, or white but from an all-Dominican neighborhood.

My response to such statements is always the same. I have no desire to belittle any aspect of your identity, I say, but either you walk through this world with white-skin privilege or you don't. There's no such thing as being pulled over for Driving While Want-ing to Be Black. Sometimes how you "self-identify" is irrelevant. You could be a gay Irish dude from the heart of Washington Heights, with a Senegalese lover and a degree from Morehouse to boot. The cop and the judge and the loan officer and the potential employer are only going to check one mental box. And when they do, you're going to benefit from the way they see you, like it or not.

"Post-race" suggests, not without an air of self-congratulation, that we are moving toward an acceptance of the multifaceted nature of identity—learning to assimilate, for instance, the idea that a hu-man being can be both Kenyan and Kansan. This may be true. The problem is that "post-race" inevitably implies post-*racism*. To con-flate the two ignores the very nature of oppression.

I witnessed this perspective recently at a talk I gave in Minne-apolis. A woman in the audience stood up to explain that racism would soon be vanquished without any concerted effort on our part, and cited the infant on her hip as proof. She was Korean, she said, and her husband black and Italian. Their son was all three. Any ma-chine that attempted to categorize him would explode.

The sad truth that this child will someday be forced to color in a single bubble on a Scantron form like everyone else speaks to the particular insidiousness of race. It is a construct, not a question of biology or self-image. It will not vanish in the face of multiethnicity, because it exists for a purpose, and that purpose is hierarchy.

Had Obama not lent so much currency to the notion of a kind of equality of racial bitterness, enacted on a field that everyone thinks favors the other team, the case of Geraldine Ferraro might not have played out as it did: as a spectacular example of racist action forgiven because racist "feeling" is not found, and as an abject, to-the-political-death refusal to acknowledge the difference between structural racism and white resentment.

The former congresswoman and vice presidential nominee forfeited her place in the Clinton campaign when, a week before Obama delivered the speech, she told reporters that "if Obama was a white man, he would not be in this position," just as she would not have been tapped for the vice presidency by Walter Mondale had she not been a woman. The difference between being appointed to a ticket and winning a record number of primary votes across the entire nation seemingly escaped Ferraro, who elaborated on her remarks a few weeks later in a stunning *Boston Globe* op-ed:

> Since March, when I was accused of being racist for a statement I made about the influence of blacks on Obama's historic campaign, people have been stopping me to express a common sentiment: If you're white you can't open your mouth without being accused of being racist. They see Obama's playing the race card throughout the campaign and no one calling him for it as frightening. They're not upset with Obama because he's black; they're upset because they don't expect to be treated fairly because they're white.

Contrary to Ferraro's recollection, the most striking aspect of the media's response to her initial comments was the consistency with which pundits and commentators across the ideological spectrum fell all over themselves to *avoid* accusing her of racism. Seldom, in political life, has the sinner been granted such immediate distance from her sin.

But this has become the blueprint for public figures who make inflammatory remarks about race—as long as they're white. First comes the claim that their words do not reflect their hearts. This puts the ball in the commentariat's court. The commentariat duly concurs that the figure is not racist, despite all evidence to the contrary. Then, after a probationary period of a few months, the figure quietly resumes his or her role in public life.

"I am not a racist." So said Bill Clinton on ABC News shortly after the conclusion of his wife's presidential bid, defending himself against accusations of race-baiting.

"I'm not a racist, that's what's so insane about this." So said *Seinfeld*'s Michael Richards in 2006, explaining himself on *The David Letterman Show* after a video surfaced of him dropping multiple n-bombs on a black heckler at a comedy club. Mel Gibson, who disgraced himself with an anti-Semitic rant the same year, put forth the same argument: *I'm not a racist, merely a guy who said something racist. It came out of nowhere, for no reason, and it doesn't reflect who I am.* Ditto Don Imus, after his 2007 "nappy-headed hos" remark. And Senator Trent Lott, whose pro-segregation comments cost him his role as majority leader in 2002, though not his job.

It is a dramatic reversal of the standard criterion for judgment. Usually, we seek to be judged by our actions, not our thoughts, and we accept that the former are a manifestation of the latter. The success of the Richards-Imus-Lott strategy, it would seem, hinges on the fact that it has become more acceptable to spout racism in the public arena than to accuse someone else of spouting racism.

On to the thesis Ferraro put forth: that whites in America have been rendered voiceless, that to be black is to be "lucky" (to paraphrase another of her comments about Obama), that whites are the new racial underclass, that "they're attacking me because I'm white." They were notions that rhymed neatly with the identity frustrations of white youth. And Obama's speech would seem to have granted them legitimacy, if we accept the argument that whatever people feel about race must be treated with the same respect as the facts.

I have no problem believing that people were stopping Ferraro—although I suspect "sidling up to" would be more accurate—to voice this "common sentiment." One might well ask, though, how she was so unaffected by the racial gag order against which she railed. One might wonder why her silent majority of whites can so readily muster outrage at their own unfair treatment, yet remain so blissfully un-ruffled by anyone else's. If one were feeling particularly optimistic, one might contemplate how to turn such complaints into what's known as a "teaching moment." Could white America's cresting indignation at its own marginalization be the Rosetta stone that allows it to under-stand how other people in the country feel?

Eh. Probably not.

On the other hand, the pressure on Obama to denounce Minis-ter Farrakhan—which directly preceded the pressure to denounce the Reverend Jeremiah Wright—offered the candidate a chance to speak a difficult truth to a valuable constituency and play a role in genuine healing. Certainly, Obama's rhetoric spoke to a desire to do so:

> What I want to do is rebuild what I consider to be a historic rela-tionship between the African-American community and the Jew-ish community. I would not be sitting here were it not for a whole host of Jewish Americans who supported the civil rights movement and helped to ensure that justice was served in the South. And that coalition has frayed over time around a whole host of issues, and part of my task . . . is making sure that those lines of communica-tion and understanding are reopened.

But rather than turning to that task, Obama proceeded to do precisely what the current, sorry state of black-Jewish relations demands. He iterated his rejection of Farrakhan's endorsement, citing the Nation of Islam leader's anti-Semitism, and left it at that.

For twenty-five years now, the specter of black anti-Semitism has been used as the rationale for tremendous Jewish disinvestment—practically, emotionally, financially—from the black community and the legacy of progressive work that blacks and Jews share. A handful of comments from civil rights–era black leaders provide most of the evidence. For many in the Jewish community, the Reverend Jesse Jackson will always be the man who called New York City "Hymietown" in 1984. The Reverend Al Sharpton will always be the man who inflamed a tense situation in Crown Heights in 1991, and Farrakhan will always be the man who, in 1983, called Judaism a "gutter religion."

The fact that all three have apologized, moved on, and made amends does not seem to matter—that Jackson was instrumental in restoring peace to Crown Heights, that Sharpton's 2004 presidential run was an exemplar of inclusiveness, that Farrakhan has been meeting regularly with a group of rabbis for more than ten years now, in an effort to mend fences.

Nor does it seem to matter that none of these men speaks for the black community at large, or that Obama's candidacy and the emergence of hip-hop generation leaders and grassroots political organizations prove that the civil rights generation is no longer in the driver's seat. They remain central in the Jewish memory of my parents' and grandparents' generations. Their comments are frozen in amber, never to be forgotten or forgiven. Thus, denunciations of Farrakhan—despite the declining influence of his organization and his own outreach to the Jewish community—remain red meat for many Jewish voters.

How can this be, when the Ferraros, Imuses, and Lotts of the world tiptoe back into the mainstream after a brief time-out, their best intentions unimpugned? Even Gibson, whose anti-Semitic rant was truly epic, had his incoherent, responsibility-dodging apology promptly accepted by the Anti-Defamation League, a Jewish watchdog group that has never stopped vilifying Farrakhan.

The story behind the story is complex, one of changing identity in a changing country. Perhaps no two groups in America share such an intimate history as Jews and blacks; by turns it has been beautiful and tense, unified and vituperative. Both groups have been shattered and scattered, displaced and enslaved, and both have made outsized contributions to the cultural life of America. Both communities, perhaps by the nature of diaspora, have wide margins, in addition to existing on the margins of American life. By this I mean that the number of people who feel ambivalent, ambiguous, full of unresolved questions about their blackness or their Jewishness, is large in relation to the number of people nestled snugly in the bosoms of those communities. The pain and perspective engendered by this double marginality are important ingredients in making art, and in the desire for social justice.

Jews and blacks have been united by this shared otherness and also pitted against one another because of it. At the root of the Jewish retreat from the coalition of which Obama speaks is the way in which Jews, in assimilating, have relied on the immutability of black otherness as a foil. It has been an other more other than their own, and sometimes one to measure progress by their distance from.

As the Jews have been accorded more and more of the privileges of whiteness, many have decided, consciously or otherwise, that it behooves them to change their bedfellows. Fifty years ago, it was far more difficult for Jews to be complacent or hypocritical about race: They didn't have the option of paying mere lip service to the cause because they understood that they were implicated in it, both as potential victims and as potential oppressors. The benefits of whiteness were fewer for Jews and more readily contested. Thus, the morality of allowing them to accrue was easier to address honestly, and find lacking.

There is, of course, much more to the story—more than I have the space to go into and also more than I know. I realize, too, that I have addressed the reasons for Jewish pullback from Obama's "historic relationship" and said nothing of black actions or motivations. This is not because I wish to cast all the blame on one side, but simply out of a desire to stick to what I know, as someone who has discussed race with Jewish audiences quite a bit lately.

One question I was asked regularly at JCCs, as I proposed that more disturbing than the pickled comments of Farrakhan, Jackson, and Sharpton were the reasons Jews held them so dear, was "What about Jeremiah Wright?"

The query was always met by nods and murmurs of agreement from the audience—which, I should add for the sake of context, tended to be made up largely of people born well before the Truman administration.

"What about him?"

"Well, he's said some things . . . some anti-Semitic things . . ."

"Like what?"

Silence. Had my interlocutors responded that Wright's church had honored Farrakhan as "exemplifying greatness," that would have been something. But it never happened. Rather, the logic at work seemed to be that a black religious leader was in the news for inflammatory statements, and therefore he must be an anti-Semite. Even if no evidence to that effect came to mind.

What will it take, then, to reverse the fraying? What more could Obama have said in Ohio about blacks and Jews, or in Pennsylvania about the larger conundrum of race?

Any answer begins with radical honesty of the sort most politicians can ill afford to muster. In Ohio, Obama could have risked declaring himself committed to moving beyond the old politics of suspicion and condemnation, detailed the reasons for the splintering of the black-Jewish alliance, and laid out a plan for reestablishing trust and a commonality of purpose. In Pennsylvania, he could have framed the road to racial reconciliation in the same terms he has been brave enough to apply to climate control: as a journey that will require real sacrifice and profound reevaluation of our lifestyles and the unsustainable practices on which they're built. He could have looked into the living rooms of white America and declared that institutional racism is alive and well—that it benefits all those considered white and also exacts from them a high moral toll.

But the political costs of such statements would have overwhelmed Obama's campaign. And while the senator's commitment to presiding over a sea change in America's racial climate appears to be perfectly sincere, it is the level of commitment for which he is willing to call that matters. Soft-pedaling the reality of white privilege might help bring people to the table, but if they come under false pretenses, they won't stay.

All of this points to the fallacy of a national conversation on race led by a president, no matter how thoughtful or inspiring. Not just because political constraints prevent him from addressing the issue with the candor we need, but because a chief executive's role in moving the country toward a state of post-racism should be addressing structural discrimination on the level of policy. Dismantling the system of racist policing and biased judiciary that has led to the epidemic incarceration of black men will do more to heal the nation's racial wounds than even the most compassionate and sustained dialogue. So will revamping a dysfunctional educational system that reinforces racial and economic disparities.

If President Obama wants to attack the issue on all fronts—as he must—then he should use his healing hands to sign over funding for a national program of community forums, to take place in town halls and high school gyms, JCCs and YMCAs, mosques and movie theaters. The structuring and facilitation of these events could be delegated to people like Vijay Prashad, Tim Wise, Tricia Rose, Robin

Kelley, bell hooks, Van Jones, Rosa Clemente, and hundreds of others who have made drawing people into compassionate dialogue on race their life's work.

There could be incentives for attendance: whatever it took to get people in the door, from parking-ticket forgiveness to free-cable vouchers. The conversations need not tackle race head-on; the issue's pervasiveness is such that almost any topic of universal concern raised in a multiethnic setting will intersect with it, from law enforcement to primary school education to jobs. The appetite for dialogue is there, as surely as the bitterness; what we lack is the language and the context to engage. And nothing can tap the veins of goodwill running through the body politic quite like genuine interaction, particularly in this age of technological mediation and shrinking public space.

What's fascinating is how quickly the imagination falters in anticipating the direction these conversations might take. What happens, for instance, after a young black man in need of employment testifies about the difficulty of overcoming the perception that he's a thug, and a white soccer mom raises her hand to ask, "Well, then, why do you dress like that, with your pants so low and your T-shirt so big?" Who speaks next? Does the black man's grandfather concur with the soccer mom? Does the woman's fourteen-year-old son—attired just like the job seeker—realize, at this moment, that black people don't have it as easy as he thought? What do the local business owner, the high school guidance counselor, and the policewoman have to say?

Our access to one another is so limited, so constrained, that the journey into uncharted territory is a swift one. It is a journey on which Obama's "A More Perfect Union" is an important stop, but the road stretches well beyond it—toward racial critiques more daring, policies more radical, and healing more profound.

BETWEEN EXPEDIENCY AND CONVICTION: WHAT WE MEAN WHEN WE SAY "POST-RACIAL"

Bakari Kitwana

If I could save the Union without freeing any slave, I would do it; and if I could save it by freeing all the slaves, I would do it; and if I could save it by freeing some and leaving others alone, I would also do that.
—PRESIDENT ABRAHAM LINCOLN,
letter to Horace Greeley, 1862

I like to believe that for Lincoln it was never a matter of abandoning conviction for the sake of expediency. Rather, . . . that we must talk and reach for common understandings, precisely because all of us are imperfect and can never act with the certainty that God is on our side.
—SENATOR BARACK OBAMA, *Dreams from My Father*, 2004

On a twenty-degree wintry afternoon in Ohio, a swing state, weeks after the election, I jump in my car after working out and take a short ride from the gym to a favorite coffee shop a stone's throw away. As I'm entering the doorway, a middle-aged postal worker is exiting. We exchange the usual niceties that are standard fare between black men as he courteously holds the door for me. We pass, nearly brushing shoulders, and in that moment he mutters, almost to himself but loud enough for me to hear: "Can't be a real brother?"

As I glance back and look into his eyes, it's clear he's talking about the way I'm dressed (no coat; shorts and a hoodie), given the day's temperature in this once upon a time all-white Cleveland suburb. This is routine American racial stereotype, the kind of assumption that makes conservative-leaning blacks like Manhattan Institute scholar John McWhorter (who often laments the way race gets attached to behavior) cringe: Whites don't mind the cold; blacks do. But the election of Barack Obama as the forty-fourth president of the United States issued such formulaic assumptions about race a resounding checkmate. Given the sheer public visibility of the Obama family over the last two years, no one on either side of the racial divide can any longer feign being unaware that blackness, and whiteness for that matter, comes in a variety of packages. If the phenomenon of the post-racial candidate means anything at all, it's that racial assumptions like these, once and for all, are checked at the door, or at least should be.

Unfortunately, or fortunately, depending on your political orientation, when it comes to the idea of "post-racial," the conversation doesn't end there. Probably no other word that hung in the air during and after the 2008 presidential election was more jarring. The term, like its variations "post-racism" and "post-race," is a loaded expression that on the surface speaks to genetic makeup, culture, politics, and history—all at the same time. But what message gets communicated, and how do we weed through each of these complex terrains, if at all?

Part of what makes the word "post-racial" so volatile, and the very idea of it extremely relevant, is that those on the far left almost instantly find it offensive and those on the right are almost too eager to embrace it. The unspoken implication is that America, a country dogged by a legacy of its own brand of racial apartheid, has miraculously eliminated its race problem. The reaction to this suggestion recalls the feeling folks would get, wherever they stood on the racial-politics divide in the nineties, when commentators described the mass cross-racial appeal of, say, Michael Jordan, Tiger Woods, or even Oprah Winfrey as "transcending race." The term "post-black," advanced by museum curator Thelma Golden in association with her 2001 Studio Museum in Harlem exhibit "Freestyle," evoked a similar feeling, as did the title of journalist Debra Dickerson's 2004 *The End of Blackness* and the more recent *New York Times Magazine* cover story "Is Obama the End of Black Politics?," which came shortly after then-senator Barack Obama sealed up the primary.

But, if we can look past all of the connotations that the term itself evokes, what we will discover is that a new concept has emerged whose very existence was actualized for many with this election. It is a sentiment that offers us insight into an unfolding chapter in American history, which goes far beyond the various historic "firsts" regarding American electoral politics that experts will speak about for years ahead: There is something that Americans in this moment, in this time, are collectively feeling that we've never felt before.

I have spent much of the last decade as a lecturer, journalist, and community organizer traveling to forty-eight of the fifty United States and meeting with Americans across generations in various communities—black, brown, white, urban, suburban, and rural—mostly in public forums and town hall meetings. What quickly becomes apparent in these encounters is that the racial politics articulated daily by the American elite via mainstream media and the political establishment is out of sync with the experiences of everyday people across the nation. This old racial politics, outside of the reinforcement it gains within too many of America's institutions, is also inconsistent with the time. Likewise, internationally the world is far ahead of this elite, a point that Fareed Zakaria makes in his 2008 *New York Times* bestseller *The Post-American World*.

So what we arrive at in the word "post-racial" is a sentiment that speaks to the cognitive dissonance between the reality and the illusion of race. This feeling certainly demands a word. The one that we've settled on for now evolved out of previous eras and still carries their baggage. All of those using it accept that something has changed, even if they can't agree on what it is. "Post-racial," for lack of a better word, is attempting to speak to this new idea.

Although in fact, the idea in and of itself isn't altogether new. Various individuals throughout our history have voiced the senti-ment even if it didn't permeate our national culture. And it persisted in some intellectual circles and in pockets around the country. Take the political preoccupations of the former U.S. congresswoman from Georgia who in 2008 landed on the ballot as the presidential candi-date of the Green Party. Walking into the voting booth and having Cynthia McKinney as a choice for president was arguably the most post-racial moment of this election season.

The former congresswoman's political positions deemed most controversial are in sync with a new racial politics that accepts that the old racial politics, built on a might-makes-right philosophy, shouldn't have the last word. She's been outspoken about the imbalance of U.S. foreign policy in the Middle East, particularly in regard to Is-raeli human rights violations of the Palestinian people. She sug-gested that President George W. Bush had prior knowledge of the 9/11 attacks, and she introduced articles of impeachment against Bush, Dick Cheney, and Condoleezza Rice. She also sponsored the Martin Luther King, Jr. Records Act, calling for the unsealing of the federal records surrounding the assassination of Dr. King. By mainstream congressional standards, unpopular positions all three.

The problem with change candidates like McKinney is that they are on the wrong side of the political winds, even if they are on the right side of social justice. She's been post-racial on race issues but not a post-racial politician—this dichotomy is where public in-tellectual Michael Eric Dyson's race-specific assessment of the con-cept of post-race, "We should not attempt to be post-racial, but post-racist—we should not have to give up who we are or the identi-ties we have accrued over space and time struggling for self-definition in a culture that refused to acknowledge our fundamental humanity," parts with strategist Bill Fletcher Jr.'s scientifically political one: that what we are experiencing is not a post-race shift but a "post civil rights politics." There is a difference, which leads us to a second post-racial moment of Election 2008, Barack Obama's March 18 speech, "A More Perfect Union."

Obama's speech acknowledges the extremes, as well as the range of perspectives in between, and attempts to bring them all together. More important, the speech highlights significant revelations for us all in our collective quest to define what we mean as a nation when we say "post-racial." Although Obama, even before declaring his candidacy, was deemed the quintessential post-racial candidate, I imagine he shares Dyson's sentiment in that regard. But if we can take what he says about race and about the nation in his speeches and in his writings at face value, then I think it's safe to assume that he believes it is possible for Americans to move past the ugly racial history and unify as one nation in the tradition of the dream evoked in Dr. King's legendary "I've Been to the Mountaintop" speech. In "A More Perfect Union," Obama presents his own vision for getting past racial disunity.

We are not a post-racial society, he suggests. There is still a racial caste system in the United States in which race is a barrier for some and an asset for others. But the speech offers several bare-minimum prerequisites for beginning the process of thinking through ways to move us in the right direction. The speech offers two main tenets: (1) that we must understand the complexities of race and the rationalization for perspectives on both sides of the divide and (2) that we must understand the U.S. Constitution as a working document and grapple with the Founding Fathers' vision of unity, accepting that race is part of America's destiny, not separate from it.

Part of the brilliance of the speech is that within the span of nearly forty minutes—it was one of the longest speeches of Obama's campaign—very public national questions are meshed with personal reflections on the candidate's identity. First, there is his identity as a mixed-race American, black and white, African American and African, trapped between America's present and historical racial conflict. Second, there is Obama the American patriot who desires to move the country forward with a fierce commitment to the ideals of the Founding Fathers. And finally, there is Obama the post-racial candidate and his struggle to define what that means, even as commentators all around him attempt to define him in alternate ways. In the aftermath of the speech, the United Church of Christ, the parent denomination of Obama's former church Trinity, called for national discussions on race. The above precepts give us a great place to start.

When it comes to America's unreconciled racial dilemmas today, we have essentially arrived at what Obama calls in the speech "a stalemate." The social transformations of the fifties and sixties marked significant gains, so many that those who enjoy race privilege believe that no more can be conceded, even as those seeking additional change seem to have run out of an effective methodology for achieving further success. More than anything else, for much of recent history what has transpired has been lots of talking past one another across the racial divide. Prerequisite number one is that each of us needs to understand the history of racial struggle on both sides, rather than let those who gain from the stalemate continue to do so. Obama suggests that it is in the interest of both sides to move the country forward. For that we need a place of common understanding.

White Americans who resist conceding to black grievances, Obama makes clear, are not all descendants of slaveholders who benefited from centuries of black free labor. "Most working- and middle-class white Americans don't feel that they have been particularly privileged by their race," he says in the speech. "Their experience is the immigrant experience—as far as they're concerned, no one's handed them anything; they've built it from scratch." Likewise, black Americans pushing for change are not all beneficiaries of affirmative action, and black America is not doing as well economically as the professional athletes and entertainers and other black celebrities who are often deemed the public face of black America. By contrast, regarding the legacy of slavery and de jure and de facto segregation still evident in black communities when we look at the statistics, he comments, "Segregated schools were, and are, inferior schools; we still haven't fixed them, fifty years after *Brown v. Board of Education*, and the inferior education they provided, then and now, helps explain the pervasive achievement gap between today's black and white students." Of other forms of legalized racial discrimination that still affect black life, he says, "Blacks were prevented, often through violence, from owning property, or loans were not granted to African American business owners, or black home owners could not access FHA mortgages, or blacks were excluded from unions, or the police force, or fire departments . . . That history helps explain the wealth and income gap between black and white, and the concentrated pockets of poverty that persist in so many of today's urban and rural communities."

He also delves into another way in which the legacy of race poses an obstacle, as exemplified by how race became a variable on the campaign trail—from the right to the left. In his words, "On one end of the spectrum, we've heard the implication that my candidacy is somehow an exercise in affirmative action, that it's based solely on the desire of wide-eyed liberals to purchase racial reconciliation on the cheap. On the other end, we've heard my former pastor, Reverend Jeremiah Wright, use incendiary language to express views that have the potential . . . to widen the racial divide." Here Obama is reflecting on ways in which both his Democratic opponents and his Republican ones tried to back him into a corner that had become race business as usual in American politics.

By the time the Iowa caucus arrived, Republicans had basically rallied around two main talking points when it came to Obama: first, that because he was black, the media was letting him off easy for fear of being called racist, and second, that whites would over-whelmingly not trust a black candidate to represent their interests (positions that Clinton Democrats would subsequently adopt as their own). Former House of Representatives Speaker Newt Gingrich real-ized early on the threat Obama posed to the Republican Party. He noted in an interview with *Good Morning America* days after Super Tuesday that an Obama rally that had drawn sixteen thousand in Boise, Idaho, had previously been inconceivable for a Democratic candidate in a solidly red state. Similarly, acknowledging a shifting racial-politics landscape, weeks later he and Karl Rove were repeat-edly cautioning Republicans to avoid backing themselves into a cor-ner where they'd be called racist. Playing bad cop, other rank-and-file Republicans like talk show host Bill Cunningham did the opposite. In appearances on Fox News' *Hannity and Colmes* and in his intro-ductory comments at a Senator John McCain town hall meeting, Cunningham went to great pains to emphasize Obama's middle name, Hussein, the surname of the former Iraqi president. From there, conservatives as much as possible left it up to Democrats to duke it out among themselves during the primaries.

At first, the general consensus among civil rights establishment black Democrats was that Obama's candidacy was a cute sideshow, no different than the Reverend Jesse Jackson's in the eighties. For them, by contrast, a Hillary Clinton presidency would be an exten-sion of Bill Clinton's: meaning, the unprecedented political support and access that Bill had afforded them as the black political elite would be extended by Hillary as well. And why not? An obscure black christened by neither themselves nor the Clintons didn't stand a snowball's chance in hell of winning the presidency as a Democrat. As Congressman James Clyburn put it in an interview with the *New*

York Times Magazine, speaking for himself and other Democratic Party insiders, "We expected this to be over by March." The (late) Congresswoman Stephanie Tubbs Jones said she'd support Clinton no matter what her constituency did, a position civil rights icon Congressman John Lewis shared for months. Andrew Young, the former Atlanta mayor and Martin Luther King associate went so far as to say that Bill Clinton was blacker than Obama by virtue of his sexual peccadilloes with numerous black women.

But as the primary season heated up after Iowa and Super Tuesday, the same black civil rights establishment was thrown into a tailspin as blacks and whites turned out for Obama in record numbers, including in several of their own districts—despite their pronouncements. Subsequently, some leading white Clinton Democrats inevitably turned to Republican talking points in hopes of neutralizing him. Hillary Clinton pressed Obama to denounce Minister Louis Farrakhan. Bill Clinton suggested that Obama's South Carolina win leveled him to *just* a black candidate. And Geraldine Ferraro charged that Obama's blackness was giving him an unfair advantage.

Obama struck back: "At various stages in the campaign, some commentators have deemed me either 'too black' or 'not black enough.' We saw racial tensions bubble to the surface during the week before the South Carolina primary. The press has scoured every exit poll for the latest evidence of racial polarization, not just in terms of white and black, but black and brown as well." These political maneuverings against Obama from both the right and the left were divide-and-conquer strategies perfected in the era of privatization, shrinking government, and deregulation that followed the rise of the conservative right in American politics. Thomas Frank's 2006 *Harper's* essay "Taking Names: Anti-liberalism in Theory and Practice," like Allan J. Lichtman's 2008 book *White Protestant Nation*, documents the ways in which this ruling elite gained dominance in media and politics, reframed the race discussion, and pushed critical voices to the margins. Add to that the way in which the very idea of racial justice has been framed in the post–civil rights era, and the emergence of the terminology of "post-race" among liberals may be more a euphoric sigh of relief than anything else.

The various factions launching barbs at Obama in the months leading up to the speech on race all operated within this context, arising from an old racial-politics framework. His speech, then, is in part a reaction to these limited attempts to define his candidacy. He shakes off the faulty definitions and proceeds to define himself, offering himself up as an example of someone who understands both sides, both personally and politically. "I am the son of a black man from Kenya and a white woman from Kansas," he says, repeating the two most significant facts most Americans have remembered about him since his speech in 2004 at the Democratic National Convention. "I was raised with the help of a white grandfather who survived a depression to serve in Patton's army during World War II and a white grandmother who worked on a bomber assembly line at Fort Leavenworth while he was overseas. I've gone to some of the best schools in America and lived in one of the world's poorest nations. I am married to a black American who carries within her the blood of slaves and slave owners—an inheritance we pass on to our two precious daughters."

Obama points to himself as an example of a person who in his personal life has had to straddle both sides and implies that voters should trust that he has a vested interest all around. He is an example, not only because he's "biracial," but because of his generation. He says that he can offer a new approach. He suggests that for the generation to which his grandmother ("a woman who . . . on more than one occasion has uttered racial or ethnic stereotypes that made me cringe") and Jeremiah Wright ("as imperfect as he may be, he has been like family to me") belong, such change was not deemed possible. By contrast, the Obama generation and his legion of young, multiracial supporters aren't psychologically bound by the racial caste system of the past.

But even if Obama is a convincing example of someone with a stake on both sides of the racial divide, the ways in which the speech informs us about post-racism don't end there. The speech focuses on the theme that good citizenship requires each of us to rethink the Founding Fathers' vision for the country, particularly their preoccupation with unity. The understanding of unity that Obama presents here is useful in our effort to define what we mean when we say post-race. The speech suggests that as much as Barack Obama recounts racial reconciliation and American destiny as historically separate projects, he sees them as one.

He begins the speech by pointing out the fact that "America's improbable experiment in democracy" and its constitution remain unfinished:

> The document . . . was stained by this nation's original sin of slavery, a question that divided the colonies and brought the convention to a stalemate until the founders chose to allow the slave trade to continue for at least twenty more years, and to leave any final resolution to future generations.
>
> Of course, the answer to the slavery question was already embedded within our Constitution—a Constitution that had at its very core the ideal of equal citizenship under the law; a Constitution that promised its people liberty, and justice, and a union that could be and should be perfected over time.

The question he refers to is of course in part about slavery and race in America, but it is also a larger philosophical question about unity and the difficulty of bringing together diverse perspectives under one banner, what Benjamin Franklin, Thomas Jefferson, and

John Adams called, when drafting the motto for the seal of the United States, e pluribus unum, out of many one. These Founding Fathers, as well as George Washington, all saw unity as a central component of the "improbable experiment." It was an idea that re-emerged with Abraham Lincoln, the great conciliator, and again with John F. Kennedy and Lyndon Johnson during the King years. As a former constitutional law professor, Obama, by no small coincidence, made "unity" the centerpiece of his campaign. In his January 26, 2008, speech after he won the Democratic presidential primary in South Carolina, he described it this way: "The choice in this election is not between regions or religions or genders. It's not about rich vs. poor, young vs. old. And it is not about black vs. white. This election is about the past vs. the future. It's about whether we settle for the same divisions and distractions and drama that passes for politics today or whether we reach for a politics of common sense and innovation, a politics of shared sacrifice and shared prosperity."

Weeks earlier, in his January 8 speech in Nashua, New Hampshire, after he lost the Democratic primary in that state, he alluded to the significance of unity like this:

> Tomorrow, as we take this campaign South and West; as we learn that the struggles of the textile worker in Spartanburg are not so different than the plight of the dishwasher in Las Vegas; that the hopes of the little girl who goes to a crumbling school in Dillon are the same as the dreams of the boy who learns on the streets of LA; we will remember that there is something happening in America; that we are not as divided as our politics suggests; that we are one people; we are one nation; and together, we will begin the next great chapter in America's story.

In the race speech, reflecting on a moment on the campaign trail that he suggests transcends race, he makes this more vivid:

By itself, that single moment of recognition between that young white girl and that old black man is not enough. It is not enough to give health care to the sick, or jobs to the jobless, or education to our children.

But it is where we start. It is where our union grows stronger. And as so many generations have come to realize over the course of the two hundred and twenty-one years since a band of patriots signed that document in Philadelphia, that is where the perfection begins.

A large part of what he means in his call for unity is racial unity, something the Founding Fathers left to future generations to resolve. But he also makes references to unity across various spectrums, including party, culture, class, and age. As a potential president, he was thinking of ways to rise to the challenges facing the country. So the emergence of Jeremiah Wright as a controversial and central figure during the primary, although a major obstacle, offered him an opportunity to reflect again on the black political tradition that influenced Wright's brand of liberation theology. For Obama, it seemed that the black social justice tradition, out of which Wright had emerged, might offer possibilities—not only within the racial context, but in other arenas in which we are divided as well.

Harvard philosophy professor Tommie Shelby, in his *We Who Are Dark: The Philosophical Roots of Black Solidarity*, writes of the distinctiveness of this philosophical political tradition that African Americans built over centuries in their struggle for inclusion. From Frederick Douglass, Martin Delany, and Sojourner Truth to Ida B. Wells, W. E. B. Du Bois, and Ella Baker, to name a few, African Americans drawing on the tradition have been the conscience of the nation, reminding America at key points in its history to, as Dr. King intoned, "live out the true meaning of its creed." It is a political philosophy rooted in social justice that held lessons for Obama as he struggled with not only the race issue, but larger questions of unity in continuing to build the nation the Founding Fathers envisioned; not only for the campaign, but for the country; not only for the personal, but for the public.

According to black studies scholars as diverse as Cornel West and Maulana Karenga, it is because of Obama's exposure to this tradition in Wright's church that he can't completely abandon all things Jeremiah Wright. It would be like throwing out the proverbial baby with the bathwater. In the speech, Obama says of Wright,

> If all that I knew of Reverend Wright were the snippets of those sermons that have run in an endless loop on the television and YouTube . . . there is no doubt that I would react in much the same way.
>
> But the truth is, that isn't all that I know of the man. The man I met more than twenty years ago is a man who helped introduce me to my Christian faith, a man who spoke to me about our obligations to love one another, to care for the sick and lift up the poor.

He continues, recalling his description in his book *Dreams from My Father* of what he learned from Wright at Trinity:

> Those stories—of survival, and freedom, and hope—became our story, my story; the blood that had spilled was our blood, the tears our tears; until this black church, on this bright day, seemed once more a vessel carrying the story of a people into future generations and into a larger world. Our trials and triumphs became at once unique and universal, black and more than black; in chronicling our journey, the stories and songs gave us a means to reclaim memories that we didn't need to feel shame about . . . memories that all people might study and cherish—and with which we could start to rebuild.

So it is not difficult to imagine that Obama has in mind both this tradition and the Founding Fathers' vision of unity when, in a speech primarily focused on the Jeremiah Wright controversy, his range is much more broad. And he poses a contrast between the usual divide-and-conquer approach that American politics has become and an alternate vision. "I would not be running for president if I didn't believe with all my heart that this is what the vast majority of Americans want for this country," he says. "This union may never be perfect, but generation after generation has shown that it can always be perfected."

What Obama is saying here takes us deeper into our engagement with the most post-racial discussion facing us all. How does a diverse citizenry build a unified society? In his message of unity, he's looking to the great questions that should preoccupy every president. So his sights here are not only on the architects of the Constitution but on past presidents he admires. On the campaign trail, his style and demeanor and the circumstances of our time drew comparisons to Lincoln, Kennedy, Bill Clinton, Ronald Reagan, and Franklin D. Roosevelt. He's even made some of these suggestions himself. More than any others, Obama has gone to great lengths to make the strongest connection to Lincoln. They are both state legislators turned U.S. senators. They are both presidents from Illinois. After winning the election, Obama even chose to be sworn in on the same Bible. But for Obama there is an even bigger picture, which is less obvious. Where Dr. King's vision was of a promised land of racial equality, Obama is more concerned with the great conciliator's struggle for national unity in the face of the Civil War and its aftermath. It is no small distinction.

Lincoln wrote in a letter to *New York Tribune* editor Horace Greeley on August 22, 1862, in the midst of the Civil War, prior to signing the Emancipation Proclamation, and in response to Greeley's editorial on Lincoln three days earlier that challenged his indecision,

"If I could save the Union without freeing *any* slave, I would do it; and if I could save it by freeing *all* the slaves, I would do it; and if I could save it by freeing some and leaving others alone, I would also do that . . . I have here stated my purpose according to my views of *official* duty and I intend no modification of my oft-expressed *personal* wish that all men everywhere could be free" [italics by author]. Most students of African American history read these lines and see ambivalence toward the black freedom struggle and the project of social justice. Obama, by contrast, sees a greater value in Lincoln's lofty philosophical conflict, something Larissa MacFarquhar picked up on in her May 7, 2007, *New Yorker* essay "The Conciliator" early on in Obama's campaign.

In *Dreams from My Father*, reflecting on Lincoln's dilemma, Obama writes, "I like to believe that for Lincoln it was never a matter of abandoning conviction for the sake of expediency. Rather, . . . that we must talk and reach for common understandings, precisely because all of us are imperfect and can never act with the certainty that God is on our side." With this crucial point in mind, part of what Obama presents in the speech is a vision of what he can do as a candidate and as a president, not as an activist. One of his closest advisers, Valerie Jarrett, the *New York Times* reported on November 24, 2008, echoed this sentiment in her comments to a handful of black leaders who were disappointed that Obama wasn't responding more vigorously to racial stereotypes in the months after he sealed the nomination: "There are those who are going to fight the race gap, but that's not our role." That said, Bill Fletcher points us in the right direction. What we have entered is the arena of "post civil rights politics." In Obama, what we are too often *visualizing* (mostly via our knowledge of his genetic makeup, which he routinely reminds us of, and the national preoccupation with race) is a post-racial moment, but what we are *witnessing* is a post-racial candidate.

The speech "A More Perfect Union," whether consciously or not, defines what it means to be a post-racial politician. Rather than duplicating the ways in which D.C. mayor Adrian Fenty, Newark mayor Cory Booker, Massachusetts governor Deval Patrick, and even former Virginia governor Douglas Wilder maneuver, Obama builds upon them. The speech is a blueprint for how politicians in the post–civil rights era should be thinking and talking about race even as they escape the civil rights–era stalemate. Rather than suggesting that America is post-race, he answers the question, how do you run as a black man in a majority-white country and not be deemed a black candidate, even when forces all around you are trying to define you as such?

In the days ahead, it will no longer be guesswork to determine if Obama's success as a post-racial candidate will extend into governing, or if it was simply a "get elected" strategy. Again, the international community is waiting for us to catch up. So where Obama weighs in on Iran, Cuba, environmental treaties, global trade, Africa, the Middle East, and more will be the final test of whether or not America can answer the call that every great empire before her has failed to answer: Can the wealthiest and most technologically advanced civilization on earth do more to resolve the great questions of human existence concerning world hunger, disease, and war, or will we continue down a path of self-destruction, self-absorption, and fear?

No one should expect Barack Obama alone to answer all of the above. But can he help create a climate that moves us away from the old racial politics to a new one? This is what is ultimately asked when we utter the word "post-racial," even if we don't have the precise word or phrase or language for it yet. This is why Cynthia McKinney's politics and the very idea of a third party move us closer to the territory. It is why Colin Powell's endorsement of Obama and postelection criticism of the Republican Party's old racial politics struck a chord throughout the nation. Visions like those of McKinney, Powell, and others are ahead of the curve. Obama's speech is a vehicle in the moment. Time will tell if he's swimming against the current, or if the political winds are blowing effortlessly at his back.

HIS GRANDMOTHER, MY FATHER, YOUR UNCLE . . .

Connie Schultz

In the summer of 1968, my father grounded me for having a crush on a black boy. "Not in my house," he yelled. "Not my daughter."

I was confounded by my father's rage. I was a skinny white kid, yes, but I'd just completed my grade school years learning and playing side by side with black children. They were the majority in my little corner of the world, and none of us kids ever seemed to notice. I was the only white girl on the sixth-grade cheerleading squad, for example, but I can't recall a single time when any of the other girls even mentioned it, let alone objected. We were classmates, and we were friends. So, it seemed only natural that my adolescent gaze would fix upon one of the boys I'd known since kindergarten.

Natural to me, maybe, but my father was a whole other story. He was a proud union member who was willing to pray to God but counted on the Democrats to make life better.

Like so many white Americans in the late 1960s, he was afraid of the shifting sands in his universe. He was afraid of a race of people he'd never known until he'd married, left the family farm, and started working in maintenance for the local utility company. He was afraid of Malcolm X and the Black Panthers. And he was afraid of his seventh-grade daughter, who was so taken with Motown and the notion of civil rights that she permed her hair into a white girl's

Afro and grinned herself silly whenever a boy named Adrian walked past the house.

My father couldn't control the tethers of Malcolm or Marvin Gaye, but sure as he was a red-haired German, he could pull hard on his daughter's reins. Despite his iron will, though, or maybe because of it, the seeds of my own activism took root in the fertile ground of that long and hostile summer. In some ways, I guess, I've been trying to make up for that part of my family history for fifty years and counting.

I share this story because I am like millions of other white Americans who grow up loving relatives like my father but hating their prejudices. I know these people because I come from them. They are the same white people who generated so much hand-wringing among Barack Obama supporters in 2008, particularly after the videos of the raging Reverend Jeremiah Wright exploded onto their television screens.

They also seemed to be the target audience for Obama's historic speech on race. Obama knew he would never win over the racists and far-right conservatives. They were lost to him. What he did know was that he needed at least some of those white Americans who called themselves Democrats but never imagined they could vote for an African American for president. Democrats like many of my relatives. Democrats like my father, had he lived to see the day.

In the wake of Barack Obama's election, in which some of his most commanding victories were in states with some of the whitest populations in the country, the question looms: How much impact did his eloquent speech on race have on that section of white America he was trying to reach? The answer? Not so much. If the goal was to budge the needle at that precise point in time, he failed. His words, however moving, sparked few mind-bending epiphanies among the whites who most needed to reconsider their own lines in the sand.

If his speech is viewed as the beginning of a movement, however, he succeeded beyond what white people like me dared to hope for. Some white people's views of Obama evolved over time, as more of them came to believe they knew him. He was a lot for many whites to get used to, after all, but only in Appalachia did his efforts fail to convert more than a fraction of the population.

In the immediate aftermath of his speech, though, much of Obama's attempt to bridge racial divides, both real and imaginary, was lost in the punditry that followed. Conservatives, in particular, acted as if they'd just been handed the gift of a brand-new victim, and an especially sympathetic one at that. Much of the ensuing coverage focused not on Obama's sparse but compelling attempt to illustrate why equality should be every American's burning desire, but rather on a single paragraph that included a reference to his beloved grandmother:

> I can no more disown [Reverend Wright] than I can disown the black community. I can no more disown him than I can my white grandmother—a woman who helped raise me, a woman who sacrificed again and again for me, a woman who loves me as much as she loves anything in this world, but a woman who once confessed her fear of black men who passed by her on the street, and who on more than one occasion has uttered racial or ethnic stereotypes that made me cringe.

Joe Scarborough, the former Republican congressman and host of the MSNBC talk show *Morning Joe*, was quick to pounce. "I really wonder why anybody, why any man, would throw his grandmother under the bus during a political speech, regardless of the point he was trying to make," he said on his show the next day.

From accusation to mantra. Even as I write, in January 2009, a Google search of "Obama" and "grandmother under the bus" generates more than two hundred thousand hits. Back in 2008, Bush strategist Karl Rove kept the chant going in an April 4 speech to the Harvard University Republicans. Rove "denounced Obama's response to the comments made by his pastor," the *Harvard Crimson* reported, "saying that Obama 'threw his grandmother under the bus' in his speech when he equated her 'fear of black men' with the comments of the reverend."

Two full months after the speech, *Atlanta Journal-Constitution* columnist Jim Wooten resurrected the charge after recounting how Obama had told a group of senior citizens in Gresham, Oregon, that John McCain would threaten their social security checks. "He throws his own grandmother under the bus because that's what he needed to do to win," Wooten wrote, "and then frightens ours into jumping under it for the same reason. For shame." For a time, it seemed that white Americans, particularly working-class men, were immovable. Certainly, that was the tone and tenor of much of the reader mail I received as a columnist for the Cleveland *Plain Dealer*, the largest newspaper in Ohio. But then again, that was nothing new.

Early in the 2008 presidential campaign, most newspaper columnists knew that anything—anything—we wrote about Barack Obama would elicit a flurry of responses from white readers. Mention Obama's necktie, and the onslaught of e-mails and calls was sure to follow. This was certainly the case for me at the *Plain Dealer*, where my in-box routinely filled with mail about Obama, regardless of whether I'd written about him in any particular week. Weeks after he delivered his speech on race, he remained the embodiment of everything some whites feared about people who didn't look like them. Their responses ranged from dismissive to toxic, fueled by a seemingly endless stream of chain e-mails that questioned everything from his place of birth (he's not American!) to his choice of pastor (he's un-American!).

At one point, I called fellow journalist Bill Adair, editor of the *St. Petersburg Times'* PolitiFact.com in Washington, D.C., which monitored presidential campaign claims and political ads, to ask what kind of response his staff's fact-checking evoked from Obama detractors. "It doesn't matter how much documentation we provide, some of them will not be persuaded," he told me. He offered as an example the question of Obama's citizenship. "Even after we posted a copy of his birth certificate online, there were all these people who refused to believe it," he said. "There it was, on the screen, his birth certificate proving that he was born in Hawaii, and they just accused us of making it up. It gets really frustrating at times." For these people, no matter what the argument, no matter how much proof, their response was always the same: He is not one of us. And that was that.

But, over time, it became increasingly apparent that there was a growing group of white voters who found Obama's differences to be the source of his appeal: liberals, of course, but also young people from virtually every demographic, including the working class. They saw the first viable African American candidate with the unusual name as change personified in a country all but worn out by the status quo. And, just as apparently, they were trying to work up the courage to say so to the people they loved most but feared would never listen. Their relatives didn't know, or they chose to ignore, that Obama had acknowledged the very grievances they held dear. At the center of his speech, he made it clear that he understood why they were so angry:

In fact, a similar anger exists within segments of the white community. Most working- and middle-class white Americans don't feel that they have been particularly privileged by their race. Their experience is the immigrant experience—as far as they're concerned, no one's handed them anything; they've built it from scratch. They've worked hard all their lives, many times only to see their jobs shipped overseas or their pension dumped after a lifetime of labor. They are anxious about their futures, and feel their dreams slipping away; in an era of stagnant wages and global competition, opportunity comes to be seen as a zero sum game, in which your dreams come at my expense. So when they are told to bus their children to a school across town; when they hear that an African American is getting an advantage in landing a good job or a spot in a good college because of an injustice that they themselves never committed; when they're told that their fears about crime in urban neighborhoods are somehow prejudiced, resentment builds over time.

In less than two hundred words, Obama offered what, to me and to so many fellow white Americans, was a devastating but dead-on description of some of the people most dear to our hearts. He made it clear that he understood our relatives' rage, however misdirected, and he insisted that his own minister's controversial remarks "expressed a profoundly distorted view of this country—a view that sees white racism as endemic, and that elevates what is wrong with America above all that we know is right with America." His willingness to include his own grandmother's struggle with race conveyed an understanding that, at some level, he shared our shame.

"If we walk away now," he warned, "if we simply retreat into our respective corners, we will never be able to come together and solve challenges like health care, or education, or the need to find good jobs for every American." His unspoken request was clear: Would we, as white people, initiate the most painful of conversations with people we loved? We needed this dialogue to heal our oldest wounds as a nation; he needed us to have it now for him to win.

In July, I decided to piggyback on Obama's speech and beseeched white readers to have the tough talk back home. Looking back, I think I was driven as much by a personal need as by a political one. For one thing, I wanted the heartland to live up to its name. But I also had family wounds to heal. My father had died two years earlier at sixty-nine, and I still longed to have the conversation we were never very good at while he was alive. It was one of the hardest columns I had ever written, because a part of me felt I was betraying my father, even though both of my sisters assured me I was not. "Obama would have been a hard sell with Dad," my sister Leslie said. "But we would have worked him hard; we would have won him over." I wanted to believe she was right. Maybe saying it out loud would make it so.

In the column, I wrote about how my father taught me how to tie my shoes when I was four, how his big, gnarly hands gently guided my tiny fingers over and over. I described him running alongside me the first time I rode my bike without training wheels, and how when I was in eighth grade, he took one look at my tearful face and offered to break the legs of the boy who had just stood me up at the spring dance.

That was the dad I loved. Then I described the part that wasn't so lovable:

Most of his life, my father struggled mightily with bigotry. And I do mean it when I say he struggled, because the older I got, the more he saw what his views were doing to my view of him. That hurt him, and me, and for years the only thing we knew to do was yell about it.

It's hard for me to talk about this, harder still to write about it, because I want everyone to know only what I loved about my dad. It feels disloyal to acknowledge this part of him and shameful to admit that this is part of my legacy.

In the past few months, though, I've heard from so many whites whose hearts are breaking over what Barack Obama's candidacy has brought out in some of the people they love. Time and again, from strangers and some of my oldest friends, I hear about an awful remark that is usually followed by guilty silence.

"I hate that my uncle said it, hate even more that I didn't say anything," one of my friends said. "But I didn't want to throw a grenade in the middle of the family picnic."

A whole lot of us know that feeling, and in the past most of us tried to avoid bringing up the issue of race when we knew it was bound to flare tempers and wound hearts.

Those days came to an abrupt end during this presidential race. Suddenly, even those who seldom uttered a peep are now sharing views on race that make our skin crawl. They are not idiots or knuckle-draggers. They are people we love, and that's what makes this so difficult. We can't defend their views, but we can't stop loving them, either.

What we can do is have the conversation we fear most.

I finished the column and hit "send." Then I waited for the onslaught that never came. That's when I knew Barack Obama would win in battleground states like Ohio, which some journalists were still declaring was steeped in mourning over Hillary Clinton's defeat.

Sure, some readers were outraged at me. Among the hundreds of e-mails that poured in, one subject line stood out: "You never understood your father. Never." Those are the kind of notes that require a deep breath or two before being opened, because there's always a little part of you that worries they are right. The writer, who identified himself only as "XManFas," sounded as conflicted as he was angry:

> I am nearing my 70th birthday. I moved into Cleveland Heights 43 years ago. I am a very liberal Democrat and have always been one. I will most certainly cast my vote for Obama, no question. Ms. Schultz, your father was not a racist, not a bigot. He was a realist. Accept the fact. Why is it so impossible for rational people, like you, to accept the fact that the emperor is not wearing any clothes?

Duh? So, he was voting for Obama, but he didn't really want to? A reader from a southwestern suburb of Cleveland didn't mince words: "You have hit a new low. Criticizing your Father for racial remarks that are not his fault is beyond belief, even for a Democrat." He went on to say that he had once been a die-hard liberal, actively engaged in the civil rights movement, but he had changed. "I now suffer from racism, but not the racism of ignorance that my parents suffered from. I suffer from the racism of reality."

There were more than a few like his. Some, of course, accused me of throwing my dad under the bus, "just like Obama did to his grandmother." Overwhelmingly, though, the readers who called and wrote letters, from the Midwest and then from around the country, wanted to share their own stories about friends and relatives whose long-held beliefs or recent comments were driving these readers to despair. One after another, they described the awkward family gathering, the shocking argument with a friend at lunch, the hurt feelings over a forwarded chain e-mail.

"If Mom were alive today," wrote a woman from Kent, Ohio, "she and I would not be able to talk about the current presidential election. My father lives nearby, but because he has many of the same racial biases as did Mom, he and I rarely talk about anything of substance, such as race, religion, politics. Our conversations are bland, sticking to sports, as he and I, by choice, even watch different news coverage on TV and subscribe to different newspapers." The calls and letters continued through Election Day, but over time a majority of the messages seemed to evolve from "How do we have this conversation?" to "Here's how it went."

I remember, in particular, a woman with a nervous voice who called me in the newsroom in September just to say that she had finally told her father, "Stop." "He said he wouldn't vote for a black man," she told me. "And I held up my hand and said, 'Daddy, stop.'" It was the first time in her forty-six years that she had stood up to her father, and her knees were trembling after she did it. When I asked her what happened next, she laughed. "Well, after he got over the shock, we talked. And we're still talking. I don't know if he's going to vote for Obama, but at least he understands now why I will."

It was hard to hear from so many readers like her and not think that Obama's entreaty had hit its mark. On the final Saturday before the election, it was easy to see that, consciously or not so consciously, an awful lot of so-called unlikely white voters were ever so likely to prove the pundits wrong. I was sitting in a packed labor hall in Cleveland where only three months earlier a longtime union activist in his seventies had vented his fears about some of his fellow laborers. "I'm hearing things come out of brothers' mouths that are breaking my heart," he told me then. His blue eyes pooled as he added, "We did an internal poll of our union, and the results were so bad we didn't release them."

On that Saturday, though, that same union member sat two chairs away from me with a grin wider than the Cuyahoga River as the president of the Laborers' International Union, Terry O'Sullivan, took the stage and rattled off the ways in which Barack Obama was just like all the white guys in the room. "He looks like us, he thinks like us, and he works like us," O'Sullivan shouted. "And he's going to fight for us. That's why we're going to elect Barack Obama."*

The crowd cheered, many of them laughing as they clapped. It was an audacious, maybe even outrageous, declaration of support— and it was exactly what many of them needed to hear. O'Sullivan was a middle-aged working stiff with a face redder than a beet as he assured his fellow laborers that not only could they vote for an African American, but they could pick up their campaign packets and canvass their own neighborhoods too. "You didn't join a labor union for social issues," he said. "You joined a labor union because you care about workers, and so does Barack Obama."

Months after the election, the evidence of Obama's inroads with white America keeps mounting in my in-box. These days, the

---

* The anecdotes about the woman caller who finally stood up to her dad and the labor union speaker appeared in slightly different forms in a short postelection piece I wrote for the *Nation*.

e-mails tend to echo the one I received on January 11, 2009, from a woman who lives in Mayfield Heights, on Cleveland's east side:

> I hope you would be willing to listen to something I feel is injustice and needs correcting. The new President is not African-American. The President is biracial. I realize he looks more like his African father then [*sic*] his very white mother, but. This really bothers me and I am sure others also. He was raised by his mother and her parents after his father left him and his mother. His grandmother tried so hard to stay alive until after the election and she died the day before. I really appreciate you taking the time to read this. Thank You.

At the beginning of Barack Obama's campaign, I could count on one hand the number of white readers who wanted to claim him as one of their own. Now, this is one of the most persistent themes in calls and letters from white readers who continue to weigh in about Obama. As evidence, it's purely anecdotal. But we are in a time when one man's personal narrative has changed the trajectory of an entire nation.

His story is now our story. It continues, one anecdote at a time.

NUANCED GENIUS

PART II

Derrick Z. Jackson

On their editorial pages, America's major newspapers barely contained their awe of "A More Perfect Union."

The *Dallas Morning News* called it "true genius" and asked, "Has any major US politician in modern times ever given a speech about race in America as unflinching, human and ultimately hopeful?" The *Arizona Republic* said that Barack Obama "took on the nation's most radioactive issue. And instead of running away, he confronted it [and] made an eloquent, nuanced analysis."

The *Los Angeles Times* said, "No single speech will recalibrate America's consideration of race and politics, but we are closer today, thanks to this remarkable address, to facing our history and perfecting our nation." The *Washington Post* called the speech "an extraordinary moment of truth-telling." The *San Jose Mercury News* said, "If Obama is, as we hope, the leader who can draw people across political divides to create real change and a renewed optimism in America, then confronting race head-on was inevitable. Perhaps Pastor Wright did us all a favor."

The *New York Times*, which had endorsed Hillary Clinton in the primaries, called it a "Profile in Courage," comparing it to inaugural addresses by Abraham Lincoln and Franklin D. Roosevelt. "It is hard to imagine how he could have handled it better," the *Times* wrote, adding that the "eloquent speech should end the debate over his ties to Mr. Wright." The *Boston Globe* said, "Obama took the opportunity to engage the question of race in America, starting a bold, uncomfortably honest conversation. He asked Americans to talk openly about the deep wells of anger and resentment over racism, discrimination and affirmative action. It's a call to break out of the country's racial stalemate."

In Obama's home city, the *Chicago Sun-Times* echoed the *New York Times*, saying, "It called to mind other piercing addresses by the likes of FDR, Kennedy and King. Obama's speech won't sway everybody—within two hours Rush Limbaugh was sneering that Rodney King said it just as well with 'Why can't we all just get along.' But among those Americans who sincerely yearn for relief from the divisive and diversionary politics of the last couple of decades, this was a speech to move the head and heart."

Indeed, the speech did not sway everybody, though few of the cynics were known for racial sensitivity. On Fox, former House of Representatives Speaker Newt Gingrich, who marshaled the 1990s "values" attack on welfare and affirmative action—only to admit last year that he was having an affair at the same time that he led the call for the impeachment of President Bill Clinton for his affair with Monica Lewinsky—offered, "He's a great speechmaker." Gingrich continued, "I also think it was, intellectually, fundamentally dishonest." Sean Hannity said, "I don't think it's believable." The alleged dishonesty and disbelief was related to how much Obama must have known about the Reverend Jeremiah Wright's words, even though no clip of Obama being present for Wright's most fiery attacks had been unearthed.

Fred Barnes, editor of the archconservative, Rupert Murdoch–owned *Weekly Standard*, said that the famous passage in which Obama noted that he could no more disown Wright than his white grandmother, "who once confessed her fear of black men," was tantamount to throwing his grandmother "under the bus." On MSNBC, Tucker Carlson ranted about how Obama had defended a pastor who sowed "hatred, to make people fear their government, to hate other people based on their skin color." Former presidential candidate Pat Buchanan, who owns a long past of controversial racial statements, said on MSNBC that Obama's speech was smart, but also "like a defense of Louis Farrakhan."

The difficulty for conservatives trying to poke serious holes in Obama's speech was summed up by the *National Review*, the magazine founded by the late William F. Buckley Jr. An online commentary called it "eloquently written and at times moving." And at one point, a Buchanan tirade on Obama's hanging around with Wright was checkmated by radio talk show host Joe Madison, who told Buchanan, "This is such a double standard. What was Trent Lott doing hanging around with Strom Thurmond?"

Conservatives, however, had reason to believe in their power as members of the chattering classes, since it had worked for the better part of a quarter century to repress any sane analysis of race, wipe out affirmative action programs to right historic disadvantage, and brainwash a lazy mainstream media to scapegoat African Americans for welfare and crime. Several studies in the 1990s, by professors at Yale University, North Carolina State University, and the Berkeley Media Studies Group, had demonstrated how negative news was grossly overcolorized, even though the majority of women on welfare were white and the percentages of Americans consuming illegal drugs in each racial demographic were roughly equivalent, relative to the demographics' actual shares of the nation's population.

That made it a huge gamble for Obama to explain that Wright's over-the-top anger was borne of real grievances, particularly as a military veteran. As many editorials noted, it would have been easy for Obama to stop at saying that Wright's words were "a profoundly distorted view of this country—a view that sees white racism as endemic." That would have played very well in a nation in denial of today's structural disparities.

But Obama kept going, saying,

We do need to remind ourselves that so many of the disparities that exist in the African-American community today can be directly traced to inequalities passed on from an earlier generation that suffered under the brutal legacy of slavery and Jim Crow.

Segregated schools were, and are, inferior schools; we still haven't fixed them, fifty years after *Brown v. Board of Education*, and the inferior education they provided, then and now, helps explain the pervasive achievement gap between today's black and white student.

A lack of economic opportunity among black men, and the shame and frustration that came from not being able to provide for one's family, contributed to the erosion of black families . . .

This is the reality in which Reverend Wright and other African-Americans of his generation grew up.

Obama also took the gamble of asking African Americans to understand white resentment over black protests for equality, saying, "In an era of stagnant wages and global competition, opportunity comes to be seen as a zero-sum game." It was a double gamble that worked. In the two weeks before the speech, Obama saw a six-point lead in the Gallup tracking polls become a seven-point deficit. A week after the speech, he regained a three-point lead. Former presidential candidate Bill Richardson, the governor of New Mexico, endorsed Obama three days after the speech, saying, "I've been troubled by the demonization of immigrants, specifically Hispanics, by too many in this country." He said Obama's words were those of "a courageous, thoughtful leader who understands that a house divided against itself cannot stand."

Richardson's words had a double meaning. He had served in the Clinton administration, but had grown concerned about the increasingly bitter race between Hillary Clinton and Obama. By this point in the race, Clinton, outmaneuvered by Obama's fifty-state strategy, needed to run the table of big states like Pennsylvania and Ohio and hope that Obama would simply choke. Despite her name power and the aura of a happier 1990s under her husband, she ran a surprisingly sloppy campaign. She threw away any chance at the black vote when Bill ham-handedly patronized Obama in South Carolina. Her war-authorization vote lost her younger female voters. Her ratings suffered further when she made an exaggerated reference to dodging sniper fire on a trip to Bosnia as first lady.

The extent to which Clinton was reduced in the homestretch to a win-at-all-costs pitch to lesser-educated white working-class voters came through in an interview with the *Pittsburgh Tribune-Review*'s editorial board. The newspaper's owner, Richard Mellon Scaife, had funded investigations that had led to Bill Clinton's impeachment. Hillary Clinton had once called Scaife part of a vast right-wing conspiracy. But when asked about Wright, she said, "He would not have been my pastor. You don't choose your family, but you choose what church you want to attend."

This momentary alignment with the right paid only momentary dividends for Clinton. She won Pennsylvania and Ohio, but Obama was winning just about everything else. Superdelegates were falling his way. In a conference call with the Trotter Group of African American newspaper columnists, I asked Clinton why she had been so sparse in her praising of Obama's race speech and why she kept fanning the flames of Jeremiah Wright. Republican presidential candidate Mike Huckabee struck a more sympathetic tone when he said, "I grew up in a very segregated South. And I think that you have to cut some slack—and I'm going to be probably the only conservative in America who's going to say something like this, but I'm just telling you—we've got to cut some slack to people who grew up being called names, being told, 'You have to sit in the balcony when you go to the movie, you have to go to the back door to go into the restaurant.'"

All Clinton would do was repeat her very brief praise from right after the speech that it was "commendable" and that she was "very glad" he had given it. In reality, she probably realized that its glowing reception by the mainstream media was a huge nail in the coffin of her presidential bid. Obama gave his speech precisely at a unique moment in America's history when all Americans were tired of stagnant wages, losing out to global competition, watching Detroit automakers sink under the weight of their incompetency, embarrassed by the U.S. government's response to Hurricane Katrina, increasingly feeling robbed by Wall Street, and mired in two wars, one of them a deadly travesty launched under false pretenses. As rare a moment as it was for an African American to be given a national stage to talk about race, it was just as rare that white Americans were so fed up with the country that—whether they would be willing to admit it or not—they were now feeling at least a tiny bit of what too many black people had felt for decades. The speech hit America, the world even, in the deepest parts of the psyche at a time when it was so vulnerable, it had to listen.

L'EFFET OBAMA: DIVERSITY AND "A MORE PERFECT REPUBLIC"

Dominic Thomas

It was the best of times, it was the worst of times, it was the age of
wisdom, it was the age of foolishness, it was the epoch of belief, it was
the epoch of incredulity, it was the season of Light, it was the season
of Darkness, it was the spring of hope, it was the winter of despair, we
had everything before us, we had nothing before us, we were all going
direct to Heaven, we were all going direct the other way—in short,
the period was so far like the present period, that some of its
noisiest authorities insisted on its being received, for good or for evil,
in the superlative degree of comparison only.
—CHARLES DICKENS, *A Tale of Two Cities*, 1859

Senator Barack Obama's presidential campaign captured the attention and imagination of people around the world in unprecedented ways. But in France, where tensions between the authorities
and immigrant/minority populations have been exacerbated in recent years, Obama's candidacy reverberated with a particular degree
of intensity. Media coverage of every stage of the electoral campaign
was unparalleled. Newspaper columns were devoted to various aspects of the American political process. Obama support groups
brought people together in micro-communities; presidential debates
were televised live and then rebroadcast on the Internet. Books by

and about the candidate were bestsellers. Magazines featured essays on him in every issue, while Internet sites and blogs were alive with debates, and public intellectuals weighed in. Astute observers and critics of American society have never been lacking in France. But such interest has not always translated into introspection. While the French have long endeavored to further enhance their understanding of a society that continues to fascinate and surprise them, on this occasion their interest was accompanied by a concerted look at domestic challenges—more pointedly, race relations.

By the end of the election season, most French people had developed competency in American electoral parlance—the primaries, the Electoral College, the balance of power on Capitol Hill—and familiarity with the rivalries within each political party and the intricacies of political life in America. Whatever their degree of fluency in English, most French citizens could now confidently pronounce, "Yes We Can," three simple words that encapsulated the successful campaign. But key questions were posed: Could this outcome be reproduced in France? Was this even feasible? To what extent had their own three words, "Liberty, Equality, Fraternity," upon which the French Republic is built, proved adequate? France has struggled to define the parameters of cultural and religious diversity, to foster a productive debate on the legacy of slavery and colonialism, to address the various "memory wars" and competing claims that have been made by disparate groups for recognition, to negotiate immigration from former colonial territories, and to interpret the causes of race riots and social unrest.

The consequences in France of economic marginalization and social exclusion are similar to those found across the Atlantic. In many ways, then, the particular reasons for the appeal and importance of Obama's "A More Perfect Union" speech there are manifold. The United States and France may well exhibit their own particularities, but both countries' ultimate objectives of achieving national reconciliation and implementing reform remain incontrovertible. Naturally, these objectives have not occurred without controversy, without contradictory measures that reveal lingering concerns for balancing electoral appeal with social progress. The nature of the debate, though, in France has been permanently reshaped and expectations elevated.

Shortly after the delivery in Philadelphia on March 18, 2008, of "A More Perfect Union," the prestigious Paris-based publishing house Grasset released a bilingual edition of the text along with an introduction. In order to fully appreciate the impact on and reception of the speech within the French political landscape, certain fundamental differences and distinctions between America and France should be highlighted. Slavery has now been acknowledged as a shameful chapter in American history (a history, as Obama argued, "stained by this nation's original sin of slavery"), and the key contributions made by African Americans to building the modern nation have seemingly been recognized. Immigration, however, in American history has been primarily structured around a post-migrant narrative, and informed by the trials and tribulations associated with the resettlement experience that have followed. It is essentially understood as an overwhelmingly positive and foundational component of American national history.

More recently, the term "immigration" has adopted negative connotations as the debate has shifted toward border control and undocumented aliens. Ethnic minorities (Asian, African American, Hispanic, Native American, etc.) continue to experience discrimination, but legal segregation is now a thing of the past. America has for a long time appreciated the intrinsic value of diversity. In France, a country second only to the United States during the 1920s in terms of immigration numbers, the situation has been quite different. Since the end of the Second World War, the main nationality groups as a percentage of France's foreign population have shifted from a primarily European and Judeo-Christian base toward former colonial and often Muslim regions. In this framework, immigration has been understood as a supplement to a preexisting nation rather than as a foundational component of it. To this end, the term has been used to designate both facets of the migratory experience, namely the control of populations entering France *and* the internal dynamics of race relations. Somewhat paradoxically, the histories of France and the United States are closely intertwined; from the 1920s through the 1950s, France was particularly receptive to African American writers and performers (Richard Wright, James Baldwin, Josephine Baker) who sought refuge from racial segregation in America, at a historical juncture when France was itself fully engaged in its own particular form of racial exploitation, namely colonialism.

Inevitably, "A More Perfect Union" allows for an intriguing comparative element. There is tremendous admiration for America's capacity to navigate the post-slavery and post-segregation eras so that a candidate like Barack Obama could emerge. Yet references in the media to a post-racial American society lead French observers to point to lingering examples of discrimination: over-representation of minorities in prison, in disadvantaged urban areas, as victims of violence, and so on, as corroborated by Obama's own speech. Others argue that Obama's almost forty-minute disquisition on race was essential in order to detract from the negative attention generated by the Reverend Jeremiah Wright's sermons, sermons that subsequently contributed to a portrait of an amorphous candidate with whom some potential voters would feel "uncomfortable" and "uneasy," "unclear" as to his suitability for the nation's highest political office. Some even contend that Obama was forced to downplay the role of race in America. In the end, such perspectives only serve to further draw attention to the centrality of these issues in France, where measures enacted by the authorities over the years to address racial and religious intolerance have proved grossly inadequate.

America is far from being homogenous. Like France's, its demographics include populations with histories anchored in extirpation, slavery and the slave trade, colonialism, and contemporary immigrant experiences. To this day, France continues to control overseas departments (French Guiana, Réunion, Martinique, and Guadeloupe) and territories collectively known as the DOM-TOM. Its national population includes people from former colonial territories in Africa (sub-Saharan and North African) and Asia. France's uniqueness comes from the fact that according to Republican ideals, all citizens are considered equal and *indistinguishable*. The French Republic operates a color-blind model in which official government records are not maintained by ethnicity or race. This color blindness has been a significant obstacle to advancing racial integration. Obama underscored the collective responsibility of addressing race:

> But race is an issue that I believe this nation cannot afford to ignore right now . . .
>
> The fact is that the comments that have been made [by Reverend Wright] and the issues that have surfaced over the last few weeks reflect the complexities of race in this country that we've never really worked through—a part of our union that we have yet to perfect. And if we walk away now, if we simply retreat into our respective corners, we will never be able to come together and solve challenges like health care, or education, or the need to find good jobs for every American.

Segregated schools, lack of economic opportunity, and high unemployment in poor areas are problems shared by the socially disadvantaged in France. Unlike American or British "inner cities" or "housing projects," the French have promoted *banlieues* projects located at the periphery of urban centers. Accepting that these inequities have their roots in "racial history" is a prerequisite to redressing them. And yet, finding a way to proceed outside of a rhetoric of culpability and blame is a gesture, offered by Obama's "A More Perfect Union," that has especially appealed to the French authorities, who want to avoid at all costs appearing to privilege individual groups. "We do not need to recite here the history of racial injustice in this country," Obama argued. "But we do need to remind ourselves that so many of the disparities that exist in the African American community today can be directly traced to inequalities passed on from an earlier generation that suffered under the brutal legacy of slavery and Jim Crow."

As far as slavery and the slave trade are concerned, the French have been ahead of many other European nations. On May 21, 2001, the government enacted the Taubira Law (named after Christiane Taubira, a deputy in France's National Assembly from French Guiana), which recognized slavery as a crime against humanity. However, France's colonial history, structured around a carefully articulated "civilizing mission" premised on the cultural superiority of the West and the white man's burden, remains a contested terrain whose "positive role" was still being debated in the National Assembly as late as 2005. These connections with the colonial past inform current representations of immigrants and ethnic minorities (or "visible minorities," as they are referred to in France).

Obama's conciliatory approach to America's racial history was then of tremendous appeal in France:

> That anger is not always productive; indeed, all too often it distracts attention from solving real problems; it keeps us from squarely facing our own complicity in our condition, and prevents the African American community from forging the alliances it needs to bring about real change. But the anger is real; it is powerful; and to simply wish it away, to condemn it without understanding its roots, only serves to widen the chasm of misunderstanding that exists between the races.

The recognition of injustice comes here with a call for agency; it is a constructive road map for advancing the conversation. The first signs of a French-style civil rights consciousness occurred during the

1980s, when young people mobilized and brought attention to race. Ultimately, these demonstrations never gained the kind of momentum needed for substantial change to occur.

Since 2005, a combination of factors have brought race back to the forefront. Several apartment building fires occurred in Paris during the summer of 2005 that resulted in the deaths of low-income sub-Saharan African immigrants. Large-scale riots later that year further emphasized the failure of the republic to fulfill its promise of ensuring equality. The link with America was immediately made through references to the negligence of the French state as a "French Katrina."

Prior to these riots, then–minister of the interior Nicolas Sarkozy had visited various *banlieues* located outside of Paris. The provocative statements he made on those occasions, promising to use "a high-pressure hose" to rid the projects of their "*racaille*" (scum), contributed to heightening tensions between the authorities and residents of these communities. When on October 27, 2005, two teenage boys (both ethnic minorities) were electrocuted in a power plant as they fled police, riots ensued. The authorities were quick to attribute blame, preferring to see in the protests an indication of unsuccessful integration into Frenchness rather than expressions of frustration with the arbitrary raids, racial profiling, and control of movements that characterize life in these neighborhoods. The singular lack of organization on the part of the rioters, however, undermined the demands for increased government assistance that were being made.

Obama outlined how social change occurred in the United States, and the French have taken this lesson to heart: "What would be needed were Americans in successive generations who were willing to do their part—through protests and struggle, on the streets and in the courts, through a civil war and civil disobedience and always at great risk—to narrow that gap between the promise of our ideals and the reality of their time." In fact, during his visit to Europe, the complexity of the situation was underscored at a press conference on July 25, 2008, by CNN's chief international correspondent, Christiane Amanpour. Amanpour asked now-president Sarkozy to reflect on his usage of the word "scum." His response was awkward, somewhat evasive, but nevertheless pointed in the right direction to the extent that he underlined the urgency of addressing these questions. Obama's campaign message and "A More Perfect Union" have proved to be a major catalyst in reinvigorating the discussion of race relations in France and in motivating a shift away from obstacles and toward identifying solutions that will enhance diversity.

This is a daunting challenge for France. It is now widely accepted that ethnicity and "race" constitute categories of discrimination in France, and that while the republic may be color-blind, people are not; judgments are made based on how people are seen and interpreted, and research has corroborated such conclusions. President Sarkozy had been an advocate of a French-style affirmative action policy known as "positive discrimination," a model that has been associated with redressing social inequality by considering social class (economics) rather than ethnicity/race. For example, an experiment conducted at the prestigious Institut d'Études Politiques (Sciences-Po) has allowed disadvantaged students to gain access to this elite school. However, the glaring underrepresentation of visible minorities in the National Assembly (in the June 2007 legislative elections, out of the 555 deputies elected, there was 1 minority from mainland metropolitan France) as well as in universities, industry, and entertainment has of course meant a relative absence of role models (thus explaining the identification with a transnational figure such as Obama). The notion of a French *plafond de verre* (glass ceiling) is increasingly invoked, and people are asking how one can expect the situation to improve when there are no mechanisms in place for identifying discrimination based on ethnicity/race. No matter how controversial measures such as affirmative action in the United States and the Race Relations Act of 1976 (which yielded the Commission for Racial Equality) in Britain may have proved, they nevertheless required employers to adopt monitoring in order to identify racial discrimination *and* offered the legal recognition that discrimination exists.

Though Sarkozy rode into office in 2007 on promises to extreme right-wing constituencies, it is particularly revealing to explore how his position has evolved since then, and the extent to which his decision making has been infused by Obama's vision of race relations in the twenty-first century, as laid out in "A More Perfect Union."

In July 2007, Sarkozy created the Ministry for Immigration, National Identity, Integration, and Co-Development. His electoral campaign had carried a message of unity, epitomized by the slogan "Together, everything is possible." Yet this message had been compromised by harsher statements such as "France, either love her or leave her." For Sarkozy, the cornerstone of the new ministry was selective immigration, the fight over illegals, and the use of integration contracts* in response to concerns over the erosion of French national identity. Obama's repeated allusions to his own "story," "a story that has seared into my genetic makeup the idea that this nation is more than the sum of its parts—that out of many, we are truly one," would stand diametrically opposed to this kind of divisive politics. Furthermore, during an official state visit on July 26, 2007, to Dakar, the capital of Senegal, an African country with whom France shares a long history, Sarkozy delivered a disturbing speech that descended into colonial stereotypes and in turn undermined his other calls for new policies on integration: "The problem with Africans is that they continue to live in symbiosis with nature . . . The problem with Africa is that it continues to hold on to a lost paradise."

By 2008, though, "*L'effet Obama*" (the Obama factor) appeared to have indelibly changed the French political landscape. Sarkozy

---

* Newly arriving immigrants must sign a contract stipulating that they will undergo language training and instruction on French values.

declared that he would be favorable to constitutional reform. He called for a commission chaired by Simone Veil (a lawyer and former government minister) to explore an amendment that would accommodate greater diversity. The commission's report, *Veil Report on the Preamble to the Constitution*, submitted on December 17, 2008, cites a fairly long passage from *De la race en Amérique* ("A More Perfect Union") on white privilege and white resentment, racial grievances, and an inclusive American identity to demonstrate its adaptability in the French context:

> Most working- and middle-class white Americans don't feel that they have been particularly privileged by their race. Their experience is the immigrant experience . . . no one's handed them anything; they've built it from scratch. They've worked hard all their lives, many times only to see their jobs shipped overseas or their pension dumped after a lifetime of labor . . .
>
> For the African American community, that path means embracing the burdens of our past without becoming victims of our past. It means continuing to insist on a full measure of justice in every aspect of American life. But it also means binding our particular grievances—for better health care, and better schools, and better jobs—to the larger aspirations of all Americans.

The Veil Commission and Sarkozy concurred that no modification to Article 1 of the Constitution should be made, agreeing that the existing text provided for "equality before the law of all citizens without distinction of national origin, race or religion." Adhering to the Constitution, which allows for a color-blind procedure to remain in place, and rejecting any specific consideration of ethnicity or religion, the Veil report preferred to address a more generalized social inequality (one that implicitly targets visible minorities, who are disproportionately impacted by economic disadvantages). Accordingly, the report and Sarkozy fastened on to that dimension of Obama's speech while also opting to conceive of the immigrant experience as a constitutive element of the French nation.

The report's publication coincided with a much-publicized speech given by Sarkozy titled "On Equal Opportunities and the Promotion of Diversity" and with his appointment of Yazid Sabeg (an Algerian-born industrialist) to the inaugural post of high commissioner for diversity and equal opportunities. Sarkozy's appropriation of Obama's insights and rhetorical strategies on plurality, inclusion, and difference reveal what a "More Perfect Republic" may look like. The connections between "On Equal Opportunities" and "A More Perfect Union" are striking; Obama too invoked the American Constitution as having "at its very core the ideal of equal citizenship under the law; a Constitution that promised its people liberty, and justice, and a union that could be and should be perfected over time."

Regarding diversity and inclusion, Sarkozy claimed, "France has always been, over the centuries, the product of mixing. A mixing of cultures, ideas, and histories . . . The best antidote for ethnic factionalism, well, it's quite simple, it is for the Republic to be more true to its promises." Such speech making should in no way be seen as somehow indemnifying the French Republic. For in the same way that recognition of discrimination in America has been an important step for "those who scratched and clawed their way to get a piece of the American dream," young artists, filmmakers, musicians, and writers from France's *banlieues* came together in 2007 and formed a collective known as Qui Fait La France? (Who makes up France?). Their claims were not for special rights, but rather for inclusion in the republic:

> *We*, the children of a plural France, want to promote this diversity which is an asset and an opportunity for tomorrow . . . *We*, a composite of mixed identities, *we* are joining forces in the struggle for equal rights and respect for all, above and beyond geographic origins and social conditions; *we*, citizens from here and elsewhere, open to the world and to its richness, intend to fight against the

shameful prejudices that have fossilized our country and undermined our ability to live together . . . *We*, the children of the Republic, want to be participants in spreading the power of its message, its inspirational power, and in translating its values and principles into action.

As Obama would later claim, "It requires all Americans to realize that your dreams do not have to come at the expense of my dreams."

We now know that the forty-fourth U.S. president is African American. His election has created a favorable climate for addressing these difficult questions outside of America, and traces of his speech are to be found in President Sarkozy's public statements. One should remain both suspicious and vigilant, however, regarding these gestures, for it remains questionable whether reform can occur in France without constitutional amendment. As Sarkozy himself has argued, there is a world of difference between words and deeds: "Equal opportunities must not remain a priority at the level of words, but rather a priority in terms of deeds." The terrain ahead is uncharted; the optimism enjoyed by visible minorities in France as a result of Obama's election is one thing, but the work it will take for Sarkozy to gain the trust of the most underprivileged members of French society is another. Clearly, a commitment to equal opportunity will be insufficient unless the racism that is currently endemic to French society is denounced. These are the challenges that lie ahead in order to form "a more perfect union" or "a more perfect Republic," spaces where the principles of equality, fairness, and justice are values embraced by all.

With the speech, Barack Obama embraced the benefits of working toward a shared future: "Working together we can move beyond some of our old racial wounds, and . . . in fact we have no choice if we are to continue on the path of a more perfect union." And in turn President Sarkozy called for a more dynamic republic, "a formidable willingness to live together, to share a language, a history, a way of being and thinking, in which we all recognize an ideal and common destiny . . . For the Republic is about movement, progress, it is a call for justice. A dream forever in the making, it is a project." Needless to say, for any of these goals to be achieved, irrespective of their particular articulations or the demands and exigencies leaders will face on each side of the Atlantic, change will be a prerequisite, and a comprehensive overhaul of French society will be indispensable. "But what we know," Obama maintained, "what we have seen—is that America can change." "We must change our behavior," Sarkozy reaffirmed. "We must change our habits. We have to change so that the Republic can remain alive. We have to change so that no French person ever feels like a foreigner in their country . . . I am convinced that many French people want these changes, that many French people are hoping for them . . . people who love this country and who feel that loving their country consists in making a place for all of its children."

As both America and France face the realities of a global economic downturn, commitment to diversity and racial and religious tolerance in the twenty-first century will be tested, as will our willingness to share with the most underprivileged inhabitants of the planet the possibilities of the twenty-first century. As Obama insisted, "we may have different stories, but we hold common hopes . . . We may not look the same and we may not have come from the same place, but we all want to move in the same direction—towards a better future for our children and our grandchildren." So together we recognize our common and shared existence; yes, we may dream, but, more important, we may *dare*, dare to think of America and France as they are and as they could be, rather than as they were.

WHY OBAMA'S RACE SPEECH IS A MODEL FOR THE POLITICAL FRAMING OF RACE AND POVERTY

William Julius Wilson

Generating political support from Americans, who tend to place far more emphasis on cultural factors and individual behavior than on social structural inequities in explaining social and economic outcomes,* is one of the greatest challenges facing policy makers committed to reform. After all, beliefs that attribute joblessness and poverty to individual shortcomings do not engender strong support for social programs to end inequality. But in addressing the problem of social structural inequities, it would not be wise to leave the impression in public discussions that cultural problems do not matter. Indeed, any proposal to address racial inequality should

---

This article is adapted from my forthcoming book, *More than Just Race: Being Black and Poor in the Inner City* (New York: W. W. Norton, 2009).

* A 2007 survey by the Pew Research Center revealed that "fully two-thirds of all Americans believe personal factors, rather than racial discrimination, explain why many African Americans have difficulty getting ahead in life; just 19% blame discrimination." Nearly three quarters of U.S. whites (71 percent), a majority of Hispanics (59 percent), and even a slight majority of blacks (53 percent) "believe that blacks who have not gotten ahead in life are mainly responsible for their own situation." *Optimism About Black Progress Declines: Blacks See Growing Values Gap Between Poor and Middle Class,* Pew Research Center, Washington, D.C., November 13, 2007, p. 33.

reflect awareness of the inextricable link between aspects of social structure and culture.

The ongoing social science debate over the role of social structure versus culture in shaping the social outcomes of African Americans has apparently done little to educate Americans on the importance of a relationship between structural inequities and culture. Ideological inclinations often predict what position is taken. Whereas liberals tend to focus on structural conditions, especially racialist structural factors such as segregation and discrimination, conservatives tend to emphasize cultural factors, such as individual attitudes and behavior.

Over the years, I have reflected on this debate. However, not until I attended a panel discussion at the University of Chicago in 1995 on Richard J. Herrnstein and Charles Murray's controversial book, *The Bell Curve: Intelligence and Class Structure in American Life*, did I see the most compelling reason for *combining* cultural arguments with structural arguments. Integration of the two could be used to construct a truly comprehensive explanation of the social and economic outcomes of poor people of color and provide more compelling arguments for those policy makers truly committed to eradicating racial inequality in our society.

In *The Bell Curve*, Herrnstein and Murray found differences in the test scores of blacks and whites even after they included social environmental factors such as family education, father's occupation, and household income in their analyses. They used this difference in test scores to support the argument that the social and economic outcomes of blacks and whites differ at least in part because of genetic endowment—a position that suggests that African Americans are innately inferior. To my mind, none of the panelists gathered that day at the University of Chicago provided a satisfactory rebuttal. And I left the discussion thinking that Herrnstein and Murray's argument for the importance of group differences in cognitive ability was based on an incredibly weak measure of the social environment. In other words, simply controlling for differences in family education, father's occupation, and household income hardly captures differences in cumulative environmental experiences. Herrnstein and Murray did not provide measures of the cumulative and durable effects of race, including the effects of prolonged residence in racially segregated neighborhoods.

Two recent groundbreaking longitudinal studies show that these cumulative effects are both structural and cultural.* Unfortunately, these effects had not been adequately captured in the quantitative research on race and poverty that dominated debates at the time *The Bell Curve* was published.† Paradoxically, although liberal social scientists rejected the book's "inferiority thesis," in effect they were playing into the hands of Herrnstein and Murray by not conducting research that would illuminate all the dimensions of the social environment. Because they ignored the impact of culture and how it interacts with structural forces, they were not able to capture all the important features of the social environment.

If culture is the sharing of outlooks and modes of behavior that are sustained through social interaction within a community and often transmitted from generation to generation, then patterns of behavior in racially segregated inner-city neighborhoods often represent particular cultural traits that emanate from or are the prod-

---

* Patrick Sharkey, "The Intergenerational Transmission of Context," *American Journal of Sociology* 113 (2008): 931–69; Robert J. Sampson, Patrick Sharkey, and Stephen W. Raudenbush, "Durable Effects of Concentrated Disadvantage on Verbal Ability Among African-American Children," *Proceedings of the National Academy of Sciences of the United States of America* 105 (2008): 845–52.

† Other social scientists have reached similar conclusions in their critique of *The Bell Curve*. For a discussion of these reactions, see Orlando Patterson, "Taking Culture Seriously: A Framework and an Afro-American Illustration," in *Culture Matters: How Values Shape Human Progress*, ed. Lawrence E. Harrison and Samuel P. Huntington (New York: Basic Books, 2000), 202–18.

ucts of racial exclusion.* Obviously, some of these traits may impede successful maneuvering in the larger society.† Accordingly, to fully explain or understand the divergent social and economic outcomes of racial groups, we must take cultural influences in the environment into account.

For all of these reasons, it is extremely important to discuss how the issues of race and poverty are framed in public policy discussions. How we situate social issues in the larger context of society says a lot about our commitment to change. A useful example of how this works comes to me from Robert Asen, a professor in the Department of Communication Arts at the University of Wisconsin. He has reminded me that the *political framing* of poverty—that is, the way in which political leaders formulate arguments about how we as a nation should talk about and address issues of poverty—in the New Deal era was quite different from the political framing of poverty in our own times.

During the New Deal era, the emphasis was on structure: namely, the devastating impact of the economic crisis. Americans clearly recognized that hundreds of thousands of citizens were poor or unemployed mainly because of a severe and prolonged job shortage. In the public arena today, poverty tends to be discussed in reference to individual initiative. This distinction, Asen points out, reveals how larger shifts in society have influenced our understanding of the nature of poverty. Therefore, we ought to consider the contingency of political frames at particular moments in time. These "deliberative frames" not only orient our debates on public policy, but can also be

---

* Ulf Hannerz, *Soulside: Inquiries into Ghetto Culture and Community* (New York: Columbia University Press, 1969).

† See, for example, Elijah Anderson, *Code of the Street: Decency, Violence, and the Moral Life of the Inner City* (New York: W. W. Norton, 1999); Sudhir Alladi Venkatesh, *Off the Books: The Underground Economy of the Urban Poor* (Cambridge, MA: Harvard University Press, 2006).

shifted through debate. So just because cultural explanations resonate with policy makers and the public today does not mean that
structural explanations cannot resonate with them tomorrow. To
shift political frames, however, and hopefully provide a more balanced discussion, requires parallel efforts among politicians, engaged
citizens, and scholars.*

Sociological research provides some examples of how political
frames might be shifted to address racial inequities, not in a cynical
way to manipulate public opinion, but to make a true case for needed
political and social reform. In 1990, almost seven in ten white Americans opposed quotas for the admission of black students in colleges and universities, and more than eight in ten objected to the
idea of the preferential hiring and promotion of blacks. However,
research suggests that such strong white opposition to quotas and
preferential hiring and promotion should not lead us to overlook
the fact that there are some affirmative action policies that are supported by wide segments of the white population, regardless of racial attitudes.

As the Harvard sociologist Lawrence Bobo points out, the view
that white opposition to affirmative action is monolithic is distorted.
"Affirmative action policies span a range of policy goals and strategies. Some formulations of which (e.g., race-targeted scholarships or
special job outreach and training efforts) can be quite popular."[†]
For example, recent studies reveal that although they oppose the
"preferential" racial policies associated with quotas and job hiring
and promotion strategies designed to achieve equal outcomes, most
white Americans approve of "opportunity-enhancing" affirmative

---

* Robert Asen, private communication, May 7, 2008. Readers interested in Asen's
work should consult his book *Visions of Poverty: Welfare Policy and the Political
Imagination* (Lansing: Michigan State University Press, 2002).

† Lawrence Bobo, "Race, Interests, and Beliefs About Affirmative Action," *American
Behavioral Scientist* 41 (1998): 986.

action policies, such as race-targeted programs for job training, education, and recruitment. In the 1990 General Social Survey, 68 percent of all whites favored spending more money on the schools in black neighborhoods, especially for early-education programs. And 70 percent favored granting special college scholarships to black children who maintained good grades.* In their large survey of households in the Boston metropolitan area, Barry Bluestone and Mary Huff Stevenson found that whereas only 18 percent of the white male and 13 percent of the white female respondents favored or strongly favored job *preferences* for blacks, 59 percent of the white males and 70 percent of the white females favored or strongly favored special job training and education for blacks.†

Accordingly, programs that enable blacks to take advantage of opportunities are less likely to be "perceived as challenging the values of individualism and the work ethic."‡ The implications for political framing are obvious: Opportunity-enhancing affirmative action programs are supported because they reinforce the belief that the allocation of jobs and economic rewards should be based on individual effort, training, and talent.

Ronald Haskins, a policy analyst at the Brookings Institution, suggests a shift in framing to aid the working poor. He argues that a way to frame policy issues today would be to emphasize personal responsibility with government support. He points out that bipartisan support for working families increased in Congress following the

---

* Lawrence Bobo and Ryan A. Smith, "Antipoverty Politics, Affirmative Action, and Racial Attitudes," in *Confronting Poverty: Prescriptions for Change*, ed. Sheldon H. Danziger, Gary D. Sandefur, and Daniel H. Weinberg (Cambridge, MA: Harvard University Press, 1994), 365–95.

† Barry Bluestone and Mary Huff Stevenson, *Greater Boston in Transition: Race and Ethnicity in a Renaissance Region* (New York: Russell Sage Foundation, 1999).

‡ Lawrence Bobo and James R. Kuegel, "Opposition to Race Targeting: Self-Interest, Stratification Ideology, or Racial Attitudes?," *American Sociological Review* 58 (1993): 446.

passage of the 1996 welfare reform legislation. And he notes that the slogan "People who are working should not be poor" resonated with those on Capitol Hill and led to increased support for child care, the State Children's Health Insurance Program (SCHIP), child tax credits, Medicaid, and the Earned Income Tax Credit (EITC) in the years immediately following the passage of the 1996 welfare reform bill.*

Still, much of the welfare reform debate in the Republican-controlled Congress prior to the legislation of 1996, a debate that was framed narrowly in terms of individual factors and cultural explanations (not structural explanations, such as those that highlight the impact of joblessness), influenced the enactment of welfare legislation. For example, one of the most widely discussed policies associated with the welfare reform bill was the marriage promotion legislation, which focuses solely on cultural factors—that is, changing the attitudes and behavior of individuals. The challenge facing those of us who seek to change outcomes for the poor and the marginalized is to frame the issues so that the American public comes to recognize that structural inequities are the most powerful forces shaping individual and family responses, and that cultural programs, although desirable, should be combined with strong efforts to attack structural inequities.

In my previous writings, specifically *The Truly Disadvantaged* and *When Work Disappears*, I called for the framing of issues in a way designed to appeal to broad segments of the population. Key to this framing, I argued, would be an emphasis on policies that would

---

* Comments by Ronald Haskins at the conference "The Moynihan Report Revisited: Lessons and Reflections After Four Decades," Harvard University, Cambridge, MA, September 27, 2007. I use the words "in the years immediately following the passage of the 1996 welfare reform bill" deliberately. With the subsequent drain on the budget caused by the Bush regressive tax policy, the Iraq War, the war in Afghanistan, and the fight against terrorism, all of these programs have suffered deep cuts.

directly benefit all groups, not just people of color. My thinking was that, given American views about poverty and race, a color-blind agenda would be the most realistic way to generate the broad political support that would be necessary to enact the required legislation. I no longer hold to this view.

The question is not whether the policy should be race neutral or universal; the question is whether the policy is framed to facilitate a frank discussion of the problems that ought to be addressed and to generate broad political support to alleviate them. So now my position has changed: In framing public policy, we should not shy away from an explicit discussion of the specific issues of race and poverty; on the contrary, we should highlight them in our attempt to convince the nation that these problems should be seriously confronted and that there is an urgent need to address them. The issues of race and poverty should be framed in such a way that not only is a sense of the fairness and justice of combating inequality generated, but also people are made aware that our country would be better off if these problems were seriously addressed and eradicated.

In considering this change of frame—indeed, a change of mind-set on race and poverty—I am drawn to then-senator Barack Obama's speech on race given March 18, 2008. His oratory provides a model for the type of framing I have in mind. In taking on the tough topic of race in America, Obama spoke to the issue of structure and culture, as well as their interaction. He drew America's attention to the many disparities that exist in the African American community today that "can be directly traced to inequalities passed on from an earlier generation that suffered under the brutal legacy of slavery and Jim Crow." He also discussed the lack of economic opportunity among black men and how "the shame and frustration that came from not being able to provide for one's family . . . contributed to the erosion of black families." Obama called on whites to acknowledge that the path to a more perfect union means acknowledging that what ails the African American community does not just exist in the minds of black people; that the legacy of discrimination and current incidents of discrimination, while less overt than in the past, are real and must be addressed. Not just with words, but with deeds—by investing in our schools and our communities; by enforcing our civil rights laws and ensuring fairness in our criminal justice system; by providing this generation with ladders of opportunity that were unavailable for previous generations. It requires all Americans to realize that your dreams do not have to come at the expense of my dreams; that investing in the health, welfare, and education of black and brown and white children will ultimately help all of America prosper.

However, Obama did not restrict his speech to addressing structural inequities; he also focused on problematic cultural and behavioral responses to these inequities, including a cycle of violence among black men and a "legacy of defeat" that has been passed on to future generations. And he urged those in the African American community to take full responsibility for their lives by demanding more from their fathers and spending more time with their children, "reading to them, and teaching them that while they may face challenges and discrimination in their own lives, they must never succumb to despair or cynicism; they must always believe that they can write their own destiny."

By combining a powerful discussion of structural inequities with an emphasis on personal responsibility, Obama did not isolate the latter from the former, as is so often the case in the remarks of talk show hosts, journalists, and conservative politicians and commentators. He gave an honest appraisal of structural racial inequality as he called for all Americans to support blacks in their struggle to help themselves. As I think back on my discussion of white support for opportunity-enhancing affirmative action programs and the congressional support for programs to help the working poor during the first term of the George W. Bush administration, I feel that the perspective offered in Obama's speech is exactly the type of framing that can result in broad support for addressing the problems of race and poverty. Indeed, I feel that it is a model for the political framing of issues involving race and poverty in the United States.

A BELIEF IN THE UNSEEN: A NATION STILL AT RISK

Gilman W. Whiting

When you control a man's thinking, you don't have to worry about his actions. You do not have to tell him to stand there or go yonder. He will find his "proper place" and will stay in it. You do not need to send him to the back door. He will go without being told. In fact, if there is no back door, he will cut one for his special benefit. His education makes it necessary. History shows that it does not matter who is in power . . . Those who have not learned to do for themselves and have to depend solely on others never obtain any more rights or privileges in the end than they did in the beginning.

—CARTER G. WOODSON, *The Mis-Education of the Negro*, 1933

And I finally said to him that it's a nice thing to say to people that you oughta lift yourself by your own bootstraps, but it is a cruel jest to say to a bootless man that he oughta lift himself by his own bootstraps. And the fact is that millions of Negroes, as a result of centuries of denial and neglect, have been left bootless.

—DR. MARTIN LUTHER KING JR., "The Other America," 1967

Carter G. Woodson, sometimes referred to as the "Father of Black History," was an African American historian, journalist, and prolific author. A professor at the historically black Howard

University, in Washington, D.C., Woodson earned a master's degree from the University of Chicago and was the second African American to earn a Ph.D. from Harvard University, in 1912. He was also deeply committed to "Negro" education in the United States. He authored sixteen books and was the editor of the *Journal of Negro History* and the *Negro History Bulletin*. Woodson created Negro History Week. That week eventually became Black History Month. While he left a number of legacies, among them an academic professional organization, the Association for the Study of African American Life and History (originally the Association for the Study of Negro Life and History), his most referenced work is *The Mis-Education of the Negro* (1933). This farsighted volume, unknown for the most part in mainstream America, is an important historical read for educators working with underrepresented minority children and anyone seeking a political office with educational-policy mandates, and it is certainly required reading for the holder of the privileged position of president of the United States.

Between the pages of this tour de force, Woodson makes plain a history of substandard schooling in America that ultimately created minority students who believe they have little to offer, who accept and expect underachievement. *Mis-Education* was a harbinger of the landmark *Brown v. Board of Education* decision, which would become a hallmark piece of legislation in the civil rights movement of the 1950s. However, in Great Depression–era America, racial segregation was the law of the land, extralegal white terrorism against blacks known as lynching had attenuated somewhat, and academic achievement for blacks was thought to be an express improbability. According to *America 1930–1939: Education*, there were over two hundred counties in the South that did not have a high school for black students in 1932, the year before Woodson's classic tome was published. These same counties had high schools for whites. With respect to advanced degrees, sixteen states had no state-supported black institutions that offered graduate or professional-training programs. This educational vacuum for Americans of African descent was the back-drop for Woodson's *Mis-Education*. It would inform his philosophy of education, one bookended by self-reliance and self-knowledge, with reform sandwiched in between.

Years later, in 1981, U.S. Secretary of Education Terrel Howard Bell lobbied to appoint a commission to take an in-depth look at America's education system after a meeting with the National Council on Black American Affairs in Atlanta, Georgia. Bell had the distinction of being President Ronald Reagan's thirteenth and thus last cabinet appointment in the new administration. His "thirteenth man" status certainly gave some indication of education's place on Reagan's list of domestic priorities. Indeed, Reagan sought to dismantle the U.S. Department of Education, which had only been signed into law under President Jimmy Carter in 1979. And he had selected Bell to carry out the deed. As if in defiance of his "last man, last priority" standing, Bell elevated the issue of educational reform to a national level.

In 1983, the secretary of education was delivered a sixty-five-page report from the National Commission on Excellence in Education. The American people were subsequently presented with the eighteen-month finding titled *A Nation at Risk: The Imperative for Educational Reform*. Though underfunding persisted for the Department of Education and its initiatives throughout the Reagan Revolution, after *A Nation at Risk*'s positive public reception and reviews, education emerged as a new White House priority. Echoing Woodson's condemnation of the American educational system writ large, the report states,

> Our Nation is at risk . . . The educational foundations of our society are presently being eroded by a rising tide of mediocrity that threatens our very future as a Nation and a people . . . If an unfriendly foreign power had attempted to impose on America the mediocre educational performance that exists today, we might

well have viewed it as an act of war. As it stands, we have allowed this to happen to ourselves . . . We have, in effect, been committing an act of unthinking, unilateral educational disarmament.

In this fifty-fifth year of the anniversary of the *Brown v. Board of Education* decision, which sought to abjure educational inequality and uphold the Fourteenth Amendment, and twenty-five years after the release of *A Nation at Risk*, public education in America and its students, particularly black, brown, and lower-income whites, are still at risk.

I listen to the *entire* "I Have a Dream" speech. I am flooded with a range of emotions. It is a speech whose narrative exceeds its commonly distilled dream of racial integration and reconciliation. Most people remember the climactic arcs of "I have a dream," "Let freedom ring," and "Free at last!," rather than the "horrors of police brutality," still with us today, and "America has given the Negro people a bad check, a check which has come back marked 'insufficient funds.'" But in its beginning and middle, Dr. Martin Luther King Jr. explores the messiness of our history. My listening is accompanied by an upsurge of exasperation because of the conditions in which so many lived in a nation of plenty, commingled with pride, hope, and joy because I have been able to experience this historic moment, the words, their intent, through the miracle of technology; and there is a sadness because I am listening to a visionary leader whose future I know will end in violence in Memphis, Tennessee, five years later. All of these emotions I associate with King's speech. But what of Barack Obama's "race speech," this post–civil rights speech? How will time treat Obama's words and ideological leanings? The immediate events leading up to its national offering were not water-hosed bodies, dog-bitten limbs, or billy-clubbed heads on the streets of Selma, Alabama. It all came to a head, almost like an ultimatum, over the rousing homilies of a Chicago South Side preacher, the Reverend Jeremiah Wright. The speech was necessary, an essential part of a presidential campaign. The time was right, the stage had been set, and it was do it or let Senator Barack Obama's road to the White House end.

Many immediately reached for King's August 1963 address as a point of comparison to Obama's "A More Perfect Union." But the measured tone, the racial realism, required of Obama's race speech, the studied urgency, and the smaller political venue—though its reach would be broadened via the technological innovation of YouTube—were more in keeping with King's oft-overlooked "The Other America" address of 1967. The venue for "The Other America" was smaller than the Lincoln Memorial. It was an auditorium at Stanford University. In the same way that "A More Perfect Union" is frequently referred to as the "race speech," the "Other America" address on "race problems" is also called the "white backlash speech." Interestingly, Obama's speech on the "racial stalemate" in America was given because of a looming white backlash, not the phenomenally violent kind of King's era, but the presidential-bid-dooming kind in the polls. However, they are both race speeches.

Four years after "I Have a Dream," King felt an urgency to tackle head-on poverty, the Vietnam War, the resolve of white apathy and resentment, the rising tide of the Black Power movement, and the bubbling up of black frustrations that were erupting in riots across America.* But he also felt an urgency to take apart arguments for strategies such as gradualism that impeded black progress and "genuine equality." His patriotic, soul-bearing address at the Lin-

---

* The title and substance of King's "Other America" address (as well as 2008 Democratic presidential candidate John Edwards's "Two Americas" campaign slogan), particularly as it relates to poverty, were drawn from the work of the late Michael Harrington, an American Democratic Socialist, political writer, and public intellectual. Harrington was the author of *The Other America: Poverty in the United States* (1962). His work on poverty greatly influenced both president John F. Kennedy's and eventually Lyndon Johnson's War on Poverty.

coln Memorial in 1963 had been met with "white backlash" seven-
teen days later in "Bombingham," Alabama, where the lives of four
little black girls were cut short by a bomb planted at the Sixteenth
Street Baptist Church. King was restless. He knew, like Barack
Obama after him, that it was time, as civil rights lawyer and former
Harvard law professor Derrick Bell wrote in *Faces at the Bottom of the
Well: The Permanence of Racism*, "to get real about race" in America.
Two men of their times, King and Obama each felt like never before
the "fierce urgency of now."*

Let us indulge in a lengthy citation from King's "The Other
America":

> Today I would like to talk mainly about the race problems . . .
>
> . . . I'd like to use as a subject from which to speak this af-
> ternoon, the Other America. And I use this subject because there
> are literally two Americas. One America is beautiful for situation.
> And, in a sense, this America is flowing with the milk of prosper-
> ity and the honey of opportunity. This America is the habitat of
> millions of people who have food and material necessities for their
> bodies; and culture and education for their minds . . .
>
> But tragically and unfortunately, there is another America.
> This other America has a daily ugliness about it that constantly
> transforms the ebulliency of hope into the fatigue of despair . . .
>
> . . . The greatest tragedy of this other America is what it does
> to little children. Little children in this other America are forced
> to grow up with clouds of inferiority forming every day in their
> little mental skies . . . Many people of various backgrounds live in
> this other America. Some are Mexican-Americans, some are
> Puerto Ricans, some are Indians, some happen to be from other
> groups. Millions of them are Appalachian whites. But probably

---

* In his August 28, 1963, speech in Washington, D.C., King talked about the "fierce
urgency of now." On February 15, 2008, in Milwaukee, Obama cites King.

the largest group in this other America in proportion to its size in the population is the American Negro.

. . . We are seeking to make America one nation, indivisible, with liberty and justice for all.

. . . The struggle to make these two Americas one America, is much more difficult today than it was five or ten years ago . . .

. . . [We are] in reality standing up for the best in the American dream and seeking to take the whole nation back to those great wells of democracy which were dug deep by the Founding Fathers in the formulation of the Constitution and the Declaration of Independence . . .

I submit that however unpleasant it is we must honestly see and admit that racism is still deeply rooted all over America . . . And this leads me to say something about another discussion that we hear a great deal, and that is the so-called "white backlash." I would like to honestly say to you that the white backlash is merely a new name for an old phenomenon. It's not something that just came into being because of shouts of Black Power, or because Negroes engaged in riots in Watts, for instance . . .

It may well be that shouts of Black Power and riots in Watts . . . are the consequences of the white backlash rather than the cause of them.

What is necessary to see is that there has never been a single solid monistic determined commitment on the part of the vast majority of white Americans on the whole question of Civil Rights and on the whole question of racial equality. This is something that truth impels all men of good will to admit.

It is said on the Statue of Liberty that America is a home of exiles. It doesn't take us long to realize that America has been the home of its white exiles from Europe. But it has not evinced the same kind of maternal care and concern for its black exiles from Africa. It is no wonder that in one of his sorrow songs, the Negro could sing out, "Sometimes I feel like a motherless child." What great estrangement, what great sense of rejection caused a people to emerge with such a metaphor as they looked over their lives.

The similarities between these race speeches are striking. They both go to the "well" of the Founding Fathers. They contrast the experiences of America's black and white exiles. They recognize the diversity that is America, even as they retread the black-white paradigm that continues to dominate American politics of race. And they both confront—one in his time and the other through a backward glance, through the understandably cynical prism of a black liberation theologian's commentary—the politically confrontational and rhetorically uncompromising movement of Black Power.

For King and Obama, "The Other America" and "A More Perfect Union" were also, and more importantly, their *Black Orpheus* moments. Here, they queried their audiences in more nuanced language than French philosopher Jean-Paul Sartre could finesse: "What then did you expect when you unbound the gag that muted those black mouths? That they would chant our praises? Did you think that when those heads that our fathers had forcibly bowed down to the ground were raised again, you would find adoration in their eyes?" There, they struck an openhanded pose with the shock (of whites) at the "Blacklash" manifested in the musings of Black Power and the riots in Watts (King) and the recriminations heaped on America by Wright (Obama).

A law enforcement civil rights model, notably the equal protection of black rights and life, was a fundamental flank in King's agenda. He knew the law could not "change the hearts of men," yet it could restrain their behavior when enforced. But education too moved in lockstep with legal protections, for education could "change the habits of men" and provide American blacks with access to that Other America, with its "milk of prosperity and the honey of opportunity."

So when Barack Obama concluded "A More Perfect Union" on

the eighteenth day of March 2008 in Philadelphia, I felt a renewed amazement. There was no sadness, this time. He spoke of the historical context of the Africans' arrival on the shores of a new, strange, and hostile nation. He spoke with forceful compassion as he unwove, dissected, and described for millions across the globe in real time the status of education in America; he too outlined the veritable reasons for our failed fits and starts in our attempts to reconcile democracy and racial equality. Education became one of the major themes of the speech, if not the major solution for America's missteps and wrong turns. In minute fifteen of this nearly forty-minute speech, the senator uttered the word "education" for the first time. He coupled it with "health care" and "good jobs":

> The fact is that the comments that have been made and the issues that have surfaced over the last few weeks reflect the complexities of race in this country that we've never really worked through—a part of our union that we have yet to perfect. And if we walk away now, if we simply retreat into our respective corners, we will never be able to come together and solve challenges like health care, or education, or the need to find good jobs for every American.

It would be the first time applause would be given. The senator went on to say,

> We do need to remind ourselves that so many of the disparities that exist in the African American community today can be directly traced to inequalities passed on from an earlier generation that suffered under the brutal legacy of slavery and Jim Crow.
>
> Segregated schools were, and are, inferior schools; we still haven't fixed them, fifty years after *Brown v. Board of Education*, and the inferior education they provided, then and now, helps explain the pervasive achievement gap between today's black and white students.

In the span of seconds—two paragraphs—Obama repeated what many before him, among them W. E. B. Du Bois, Woodson, Fannie Lou Hamer, and King, had understood: that despite our greatest efforts at "America's improbable experiment in democracy," there are "two Americas," unequal and rent by race. And in these two Americas, there are markedly different school curricula, resources, educational opportunities, rates of academic success, and expectations.

New York Times bestselling author and educator Jonathan Kozol offers us sobering tales of America's public education system and its disparate effects on black children in *Savage Inequalities: Children in America's Schools* (1992) and *The Shame of the Nation: The Restoration of Apartheid Schooling in America* (2005), where he revisits his findings of nearly fifteen years earlier:

> Thirty-five out of 48 states spend less on students in school districts with the highest numbers of minority children than on students in the districts with the fewest children of minorities . . . In several states, moreover, the funding gap for children of color is a great deal larger than the gap for low income children . . . Inequitable support of public schools . . . has gone on so long . . . that some states have come perilously close to accepting this as the natural order of things.

Not only are America's schools inequitably funded per student by race and income, but teachers and administrators who have the least seniority—in effect, the most inexperienced teachers and administrators—are placed in the most troubled and failing schools. As well, many teachers are woefully underprepared to work with black and brown as well as low-income white students whose backgrounds and cultures are greatly misunderstood and vastly unlike their own.

The unripened fruit of the findings in *A Nation at Risk* is the reform-oriented but controversial Public Law 107–110, the No Child

Left Behind Act of 2001 (NCLB). This national educational-reform policy attempts to redress the issue of the downward trend in achievement in America's schools. America continues to lag behind in literacy, math, and science when compared with other industrialized nations such as China and Japan. NCLB set a national standard based on four pillars: stronger accountability for results, more freedom for states and communities, proven education methods, and more choices for parents. Each school and school district is challenged with reaching federally mandated targets. A theoretically and morally commendable bipartisan educational model that sought to deliver on America's promise, NCLB continues to miss the mark. While benchmarks for schools are standardized, funding levels are still inequitable, master teachers are virtually nonexistent, and student underachievement persists in low-income, predominantly minority school districts. There has been change and progress in the education of black students, but certainly not enough.

A popular mantra in the United States is that earning an education is a significant predictor relative to achieving the American dream. It is an unfortunate reality that while all individuals have legal access to an education (as a result of *Brown v. Board of Education*), the quality of their school experience is not always high and equitable. There is an average of a four-year gap between white and black students in the National Assessment of Educational Progress (NAEP). This achievement gap, highlighted in Obama's "A More Perfect Union," is evidenced not only by NAEP assessments, but also by scores on other tests (the ACT, the SAT, statewide proficiency tests), grades, high school and college graduation rates, underrepresentation in gifted-student and Advanced Placement classes, and overrepresentation in special education, particularly in high-incidence areas such as learning disability (LD), emotional-behavioral disability (EBD), and mild mental retardation (MMR). Seventy percent of all students with special needs are assigned to these areas. However, the diagnostic assessments for LD, EBD, and MMR tend to be the most subjective, and these classrooms have increasingly become the dumping grounds for young black and brown males.

Though NCLB's pillar of stronger accountability for results aims to have "states working to close the achievement gap and make sure all students, including those who are disadvantaged, achieve academic proficiency," the achievement gap exists in the more than sixteen thousand school districts across the nation, and particularly in those schools with the highest concentration of black and brown children. That 1 to 5 percent of America's schools are as segregated as they were at the time of the *Brown v. Board of Education* decision of 1954 is confounding. So many have "march[ed] . . . before us," Obama notes in the race speech, "a march for a more just, more equal, more free, more caring, and more prosperous America," only to have the next generations find that the gateway to the American dream— a quality education—has been barricaded, access denied to those less prosperous and darker hued.

Against these abysmal statistics, the thrust of "A More Perfect Union" tendered hope, hope that as an educational researcher of black male underachievement, perhaps Barack Obama could really be the education president that George W. Bush promised to be in 2001 with the passage of NCLB—one who does more than his predecessors to fix the multitude of problems plaguing our educational system. And after the delivery of the race speech, the possibilities of his candidacy resonated even more, particularly when the media, Hillary Clinton, and the right-wing blogosphere smeared Obama for, as Republican vice presidential candidate Sarah Palin later elegantly put it, "pallin' around with a terrorist," Bill Ayers. That Ayers, while an unabashed radical activist in the sixties, was now a reform-minded, well-respected professor at the University of Illinois at Chicago's College of Education, and that the "pallin' around" with Obama occurred in the context of Chicago-school-reform initiatives, provided Obama with undeniable street credibility with educators on the ground. The speech, with its connect-the-dots-to-education arc, morphed into more than just a brilliant oratorical staging to save a campaign and silence the cacophony of the punditry.

That a speech on race became a bully pulpit for a discourse on education certainly spoke to Obama's deft political skills. Not knowing, not having the opportunity to better oneself, would seem to fall under education's purview; we could all step away from our television sets or computer screens where "A More Perfect Union" streamed live with the conviction, at least Obama would have us believe, that one need only have the opportunity to do better and one would know better and be better: "Yes We Can." We could believe that with access to a quality education all "Americans [would] realize that your dreams do not have to come at the expense of my dreams."

A "nation at risk," a "mis-educated" nation, in the words of Carter G. Woodson, requires bold moves, innovative ideas, and imposing thinkers who must consider the messy past, take stock of the splintered present, and envision a bolder collective future in order to progress audaciously into the new millennium. It also required that after March 18, 2008, more than 50 percent* of that nation's citizens believe in the unseen, the untested but rhetorically committed possibility of the candidate for the Democratic nomination for the presidency, Barack Obama. Yes, we did.

In the end, though, it remains to be seen whether in an Obama administration the provision of a quality education in America will be a categorical imperative rather than an issue of political expediency. We must now turn toward another truism in American politics—hope.

---

* By March 30, Obama had expanded his lead to 52 percent to Clinton's 42 percent, according to Gallup.

A MORE PERFECT (HIGH-TECH) LYNCHING: OBAMA, THE PRESS, AND JEREMIAH WRIGHT

Obery M. Hendricks Jr.

PREFACE

In early April of 1899, in Coweta County, Georgia, Sam Hose, a black laborer, visited the home of his employer, a white farmer named Alfred Cranford, to request wages owed to him. Cranford took umbrage at Hose's request, and the two men argued. The next day, an outraged Cranford confronted Hose as he chopped wood in Cranford's yard, and the argument resumed. Apparently Hose, the sole source of support for his invalid mother and mentally retarded brother, had been too insistent on being treated fairly (read: "uppity") for Cranford's taste; it probably didn't help that Hose was literate at a time when most blacks were not. At any rate, the white man drew his pistol and threatened to kill him. Before Cranford could get off a shot, Hose flung his ax, striking Cranford in the head and killing him instantly. Hose recoiled in terror. He knew he had committed the greatest of sins for a black man in the Deep South: He had killed a white man, even if it had been in self-defense. Terror-struck, Hose fled for his life. He eluded capture by roving white mobs for two weeks. Every day of that span, local newspapers, most prominently the *Atlanta Constitution*, wrote of little else but the crime of Sam Hose and the hunt to bring him to vengeance.

From the first, it was clear that accuracy in reportage was not the goal of the Southern newspapers. Daily, they featured increasingly incendiary—and false—accounts of the events surrounding Cranford's death that seemed more concerned with directing public opinion than with offering substantiated facts. A headline in the *Atlanta Constitution* even suggested a plan of action: "Determined Mob After Hose; He Will Be Lynched if Caught; Assailant of Mrs. Cranford May Be Brought to Palmetto and Burned at the Stake." One account alleged that before leaving Cranford's house (which he had never entered), Hose had said, "Now I am through with my work, let them kill me if they can."

These stories left little doubt that the purpose of the newspapers' journalistic efforts was to fulfill a clear and strategic agenda: maintaining the status quo of white social and political supremacy. This aim was given particularly chilling public voice with the vow of Mississippi governor James Vardaman that white supremacy would reign in Mississippi even if it meant that "every Negro in the state will be lynched." The papers' tactic: stoking the ever-smoldering fires of racial bloodlust high enough to hide any fact that did not serve their ends. Thus, Hose was presented as a murderous fiend who had burst into Cranford's home and planted an ax in his employer's skull as he shared a quiet dinner with his wife, whom, the newspapers screamed, Hose had then raped numerous times "within arm's reach of where the brains were oozing out of her husband's head" while "swimming in her husband's warm blood." It didn't matter that Cranford was found in his yard with a pistol in his hand; if anyone had cared to ask, Mrs. Cranford would have told them what she told an investigator later dispatched by Ida B. Wells: that Hose never set foot in her home, that he neither touched nor even approached her. Hose's life was forfeit the moment he raised his hand to Cranford; surely a noose would have awaited him even had the ax not met its mark.

After the press's demonization of Hose, there was no doubt in most readers' minds that he was guilty of not one but two of the worst crimes a black man could commit: He had spilled a white man's blood and touched a white woman's body. Yet beneath it all, there was an even greater perceived sin for which Hose had to pay, though it was unspoken: By refusing to acquiesce to Cranford's exploitation of him and by defending himself against Cranford's attempt to do him harm, Hose had effectively challenged Southern white people's self-identification as superior to him and to all people of color—any color—which granted them the God-given right to determine how he and his like should think, what they deserved to possess, and how in general they should live. In other words, Sam Hose's monumental sin in the lexicon of white supremacy was failing to acknowledge one and, therefore, all whites, as his superior, merely by lodging a claim to just treatment and claiming the right to defend himself and his interests against harm. These were his only crimes. In other words, Sam Hose was guilty of no sin, and he was guilty of no crime. Sam Hose was an innocent man.

However, so monumental was his perceived transgression beneath the white supremacist gaze that a noose was no longer penalty enough. Hose's punishment had to fit the enormity of the crime in the eyes of whites. And it had to be staged in such a way that it would deter other blacks from stepping out of "their place," an example of the fate that awaited any black person who dared to question the right of white privilege to assert itself in whatever ways it saw fit without challenge or repercussion.

Yet lest the extreme brutality of his end elicit sympathy or defenders, he had to be portrayed as possessed of no emotions save anger against whites and lust for the rights, possessions, and power they cherished as theirs alone. There must be no intimation that Hose was a human being with testimony worthy of being heard to stand in the way of his destruction; there must be no room for consideration that his account of the events could possibly be true. So Sam Hose the human being was transformed into a cipher with no distinguishing motivation save homicidal rage against whites, thus deserving of naught but destruction without compunction or compassion. He was turned by the press into "a monster in human form" and a "beast." A measure of the success of the press's strategy is seen in the outrage their reports raised in one reader, who wrote, "The dog is more worthy of sympathy."

The strategy also succeeded in increasing the violence directed at Hose and, therefore, the deterrence value of his lynching: In the end, it was carried out in the most brutal and terrifying ways imaginable. His face was skinned. His genitals were sliced off. His ears were hacked away. His fingers were chopped off, one by one. Yet for his tormentors, even this was not punishment enough. After torturing him for hours, the mob slowly burned Sam Hose to death. His charred bones were broken into bits and sold for twenty-five cents each; slivers of his cooked liver were sold for a dime. However, the process was still not complete; the public demonization and torture of Hose, as terrible as it was, was not enough. The final step was to also demonize those who not only refused to anoint the lynching of Hose as justice, but also those who refused to accept the myriad systemic injustices heaped upon black Americans as a matter of course.

When Georgia governor Allen Candler was told of Hose's lynching (the April 25, 1899, edition of the *New York Times* reported that a member of the lynch mob brought him the news along with a gift, a piece of Hose's burned liver), his response was two-pronged: He praised the lynch mob for its work, and he denounced blacks for not assisting in Hose's capture. But Candler saved his real ire for "the leaders of [the black] race" for not sharing the lynch mob's bloodthirsty sentiments. After numerous prominent blacks, including Booker T. Washington, T. Thomas Fortune, Ida B. Wells, and W. E. B. Du Bois, publicly decried Hose's lynching, Candler accused them of racism: "They are blinded by race prejudice," he howled, "and can see but one side of the question."

Although uttered under particularly brutal circumstances, the inverted logic of Candler and his ilk, which allowed purveyors of the politics of white racism to demonize their victims for daring to recite the victimizers' transgressions against them—and the abiding and debilitating legacies of those transgressions—was by no means an isolated instance. Indeed, it remains an integral feature of America's political discourse, yet in different and, most often, more subtle discursive forms.

On March 18, 2008, presidential candidate Barack Obama delivered what many pundits and observers consider one of the greatest speeches in American history, joining the august company of the Emancipation Proclamation and Dr. Martin Luther King Jr.'s "I Have a Dream" address. The praise was unstinting. Andrew Sullivan wrote in his blog for the *Atlantic*, "This . . . deeply, deeply Christian speech is the most honest speech on race in America in my adult lifetime. [Obama] does not merely speak as a Christian. He acts like a Christian." The *Wall Street Journal*'s Christopher Cooper declared it "extraordinary." MSNBC commentator Joe Scarborough called the speech "sweeping, some would suggest stunning." Sally Quinn, writing in the *Washington Post*, declared it "probably the most important speech on race since Martin Luther King gave his 'I have a dream' speech."

Despite the accolades, however, it was a speech that Obama had tried mightily not to deliver. Knowing the history of racism in this nation, he had assiduously attempted to avoid any mention of race and racial turmoil.

When initially confronted with statements decrying racism in America by the Reverend Dr. Jeremiah Wright, Obama's longtime pastor at Trinity United Church of Christ in Chicago, rather than respond to the statements, Obama tried to distance himself from Wright's statements by offering an explanation that was probably difficult for him: He likened the brilliant and erudite Wright to a "crazy uncle" with whose views he did not always agree. But many critics found Obama's response inadequate and would not let the controversy die. Their collective skepticism was encapsulated in

Mark Steyn's charge in the *National Review* that Obama's explanation sounded "like the same-old same-old."

Then on March 13, 2008, *ABC World News* played four short video clips of sermons delivered by Wright that cataloged what Wright passionately characterized as sins committed by the United States government against people of color at home and abroad. Without comment upon their accuracy, anchor Charles Gibson called the sound bites "controversial statements," then asked, "Could this reverend become a liability" to Obama's presidential aspirations?

Gibson's colleagues in the media, particularly those on the right wing, answered in the affirmative and set out to make it so. By the next day, the excerpts of Wright delivering those "controversial statements" had begun a continuous twenty-four-hour-a-day loop that was to go on for weeks, each time accompanied by mean-spirited, uninformed, and almost uniformly false portrayals of Wright's patriotism, his ministerial fitness, even his sanity. In the ensuing weeks, Wright was attacked in every major medium—broadcast and cable television, print, blogs, various forms of Internet hosting media—as a delusional and hate-filled demagogue. The onslaught was extraordinary, even by the standards of today's journalistic culture of political sensationalism. Wright was called "a racist," "anti-American," "ranting," "crazy," "divisive," "a self-centered jerk," "militant," "a hate-filled prophet," "angry and threatening," "fiery," "turbulent," "a full blown hater," and "a foaming . . . conceited old fanatic." Fox News's Bill O'Reilly said of Wright, "In my opinion, Reverend Jeremiah Wright is not an honest man. He preaches anti-white and anti-American rhetoric, all the while making money off it." The offending statements were pronounced "racially charged," "anti-American," "eyebrow-raising," "inflammatory," "controversial," "provocative," "offensive," "outrageous," "notorious," "incendiary," "vitriolic," "scandal[ous]," "harsh," and "hate speech." Unsurprisingly, Hillary Clinton, Obama's major opponent for the Democratic nomination, termed Wright's comments "offensive and outrageous."

Even black journalists joined in the frenzy, both before the speech and in the weeks following. The *New York Times'* usually circumspect Bob Herbert called Wright "a loony preacher." The *Nation's* Patricia J. Williams called him a "crazy ex-minister" who spoke "jibber-jabber." Cynthia Tucker of the *Atlanta Journal-Constitution* described Wright's statements as "race-baiting diatribe."

It is clear that the attacks on Wright were initiated as a political ploy whose purpose was to discredit Obama's candidacy by exploiting the nation's long legacy of racism. However, that does not change the fact that it was because of Wright's overt and unadorned challenge to the nation's racism and institutionalized white-skin color privilege that Wright became fair game for whatever vitriol the press and pundits chose to hurl at him.

The Obama camp responded quickly to the demonization of Wright with hopes of limiting the damage to the campaign. The day after the *ABC World News* airing, the campaign chose not to address the racial overtones of these attacks. Instead, it hurriedly announced that Wright had been removed as chair of the campaign's African American Leadership Committee, so hurriedly, in fact, that it failed to inform Wright of its decision; like the rest of America, he learned of his removal from a television news announcement. However, the jettisoning of Wright was dismissed as political theater, and Obama's relationship with Wright continued to be used to lambaste Obama's patriotism and racial politics. The onslaught became so strong that it threatened to derail the entire campaign. It became clear that much bolder action had to be taken if his candidacy was to survive. Four days later, on March 18, Barack Obama did what he had tried to avoid: He delivered his now-famous speech on race, primarily in response to charges that he was guilty of the same racial hate-mongering, anti-American demagoguery that Wright was charged with.

Was Obama's characterization of Wright and his remarks in "A More Perfect Union" fair? Was he addressing Wright's actual statements, or was he reacting to the press's characterization of Wright and the press's responses to Wright's words? I believe that these questions must be answered in order to accurately assess the speech's pronouncements on race in America, for the speech does not only reflect Obama's understanding of the racial climate of America; it also gives us a sense of what to expect from his presidency with regard to matters of race.

Before we look at Obama's "A More Perfect Union" address itself, we must put the words, events, and charges to which Obama was responding into fuller context. Because it was Wright's public statements and Obama's affiliation with Wright that most directly necessitated "A More Perfect Union," it is with Wright and his utterances that we must begin.

From the media portrayals of Jeremiah Wright, one would expect him to be a militantly black supremacist hater of America and all that she stands for. The irony is how far these portrayals are from reality. The Reverend Dr. Jeremiah A. Wright Jr. is the son of a highly respected old-line Philadelphia minister and a much-revered local educator. An ex–U.S. Marine who volunteered for the armed forces and served as a trained cardiopulmonary technician, he spent six years in the United States military. On Wright's office wall hangs a framed photograph of him monitoring the vital signs of President Lyndon Johnson during one of Johnson's two surgeries while in the White House. Beside it is a personal post-operation letter from Johnson thanking Wright for his role in Johnson's medical care.

Wright is a well-educated man. He holds four earned degrees, including a doctorate in ministry. He completed all the requirements for the Ph.D. in History of Religions at the Divinity School of the University of Chicago except his dissertation, which he put aside in 1975 to devote all his time to building a new sanctuary to house the rapidly growing congregation of Trinity United Church of Christ on the South Side of Chicago, which had called him as pastor in 1972. Beginning with eighty-seven members, by the time he retired he had built a healthy and viable congregation of some eight thousand members, with over sixty ministries serving the church and its surrounding community, including ministries for HIV/AIDS care, drug and alcohol recovery, hospice care, senior citizen health care and housing (two separate residences), a child care program (federally funded), a reading program for the poor, and twenty-two ministries for youths.

By every ministerial measure, Wright was not a pastor who rested on his laurels, of which there were many; for the full thirty-six years of his pastorate at Trinity, he was to his flock what has been described as a servant-leader. Unlike many pastors at large churches, Wright knew most members of his congregation by name and made himself fully accessible to them, including sharing his personal e-mail address with the entire congregation. After e-mail became widely available, he arose at four A.M. daily to respond to his parishioners' e-mailed questions, concerns, and needs.

From 1975 to 2008, Wright held ministers-in-training classes that met one Saturday a month during the academic year. Topics ranged from biblical exegesis to systematic theology to world history to ethnomusicology to pastoral care and counseling. When he retired from Trinity, there were some one hundred attendees at those classes. For years, it has also been his practice to correspond monthly with thirty incarcerated men and women. One of his prison correspondents was so inspired by Wright that after regaining his freedom, he returned to school, excelled as a student, and is now a practicing physician. Wright's inspiring correspondence was not limited to those in prison. An esteemed professor at an Ivy League university received a letter from him, after meeting him only briefly, that she found so spiritually inspiring that today it hangs in a place of honor on her university office wall.

One of the charges lodged against Wright is that he is a racist and a hate monger. This charge is belied, however, by several seldom-acknowledged facts. The denomination to which he and his church belong, the United Church of Christ (UCC), is a mainstream, predominantly white denomination. Whites were among Trinity's congregants, including the conference minister of the Illinois Conference of the United Church of Christ—a white woman. Wright is held in such high esteem by his UCC ministerial colleagues that the Reverend John Thomas, the UCC's general minister and president, called a press conference to denounce the press's depictions of Wright and his Trinity pulpit. "It has saddened me," he said, "to see news stories reporting such a caricature of a congregation that has been such a blessing." On March 2, 2008, numerous white UCC ministers journeyed to Trinity from around the nation to publicly voice their support for Wright. From Trinity's pulpit, Thomas declared, "Those who sifted through hours of sermons searching for a few lurid phrases and those who have aired them repeatedly have only one intention. It is to wound a presidential candidate. In the process a congregation that does exceptional ministry and a pastor who has given his life to shape those ministries is caricatured and demonized. You don't have to be an Obama supporter to be alarmed at this."

The rapper Common, the son of a retired high school principal, has been a member of Trinity United Church of Christ since childhood. The popular performer, who is lauded for the spirituality and social consciousness in his songs, also took strong umbrage at media portrayals of Wright as a hate-filled racist. He shared in a March interview with *Hip Hop News*: "He never really was against white people or another race. It was more against an establishment that was oppressing people." Indeed, those who know Wright are baffled by the press's portrayal of him as a hateful man. Congregants and colleagues alike praise him as a sensitive, deeply caring, and extremely generous man. In his introduction of Wright as the guest speaker at a New Jersey church revival service in 2008, a longtime ministerial colleague remarked, "Jeremiah Wright will give you the shirt off his back and then give you an IOU for his next one," to which the congregation responded with knowing amens.

In his long career before the press destroyed his national reputation and made a pariah of him, Wright was a much-sought-after speaker at church revivals and conferences and even at academic symposia. He has lectured at seminaries, colleges, and universities throughout the United States too numerous to name, including some of the nation's finest. He has been awarded eight honorary degrees (a ninth was rescinded in the wake of the media furor) and has served as a trustee at several colleges and theological institutions. His four books are regularly found in course syllabi at theological institutions and in liberal arts black studies curricula. So widely respected a religious leader has Jeremiah Wright been that he was the only minister to be invited more than once to President Bill Clinton's annual Interfaith Prayer Breakfast.

Yet all his accomplishments, all his ministerial dedication, all the collegial admiration his ministry and community activism had earned over the years, were totally discounted in the wake of the release of the offending video sound bites. What is it that Wright said that was so offensive that Obama's political foes gleefully seized upon it as a bludgeon to attempt to crush Obama's presidential aspirations and destroy Wright in the process? What did Wright say that eventually forced Obama to deliver the speech he had so strategically tried to avoid?

Jeremiah Wright had been used as a weapon for Obama's destruction for months before the brief sermonic clips were aired. In March 2007, Sean Hannity badgered Wright, then still the pastor of Trinity, for what he called the church's "racist" preoccupation with the needs of black people, particularly its embrace of African and African American culture. By early 2008, the attacks on

Wright and Trinity had escalated because of statements on its supposedly racist official church Web site. A January 25, 2008, article posted by Steve Gilbert on the right-wing blog Sweetness & Light trashed Trinity as "Obama's Afrocentric, America-Hating Church." The Trinity Web site (which has been substantially updated since the Wright uproar) was based upon a document written by a church committee in the early 1980s, at the tail end of the era of America's Black Power movement, and little edited for years after. The church's mission statement reflected the Black Power discourse in use during that period. However, probably the most oft-cited offense on the Web site was its opening declaration: "We are a congregation which is Unashamedly Black and Unapologetically Christian."

No less than Martin E. Marty, the eminent professor emeritus of religious history at the University of Chicago Divinity School—who is white—decried the "naïveté" reflected in the press's attacks, explaining, "For Trinity, being 'unashamedly black' does not mean being 'anti-white,'" but rather is a discursive tactic to address the abiding sense of shame in many African Americans that is a legacy of slavery and Jim Crow segregation. Moreover, Marty argued that the Afrocentrism of Trinity "should not be more offensive than that synagogues should be 'Judeo-centric' or that Chicago's Irish parishes be 'Celtic-centric.'"

Despite Marty's stature, his remarks were little reported by the media. Nor did the media attacks mention that the Web site's opening declaration ended with an affirmation—in boldface—that the church's work is grounded in Christian faith: "We constantly affirm our trust in God through cultural expression of a Black worship service and ministries which address the Black Community."

What made the sentiments expressed on the Web site Afrocentric—and apparently what pundits found so objectionable—was their rejection of American society's definition of black America, its needs, worth, and aspirations. This self-determining sense of agency challenged the primacy of the white supremacist gaze and its inherent ideological legitimation of white privilege as somehow natural.

The Web site also affirmed its commitment to what it called a Black Value System, in a document also drafted in 1981. The document's buzzwords also hark back to the Black Power movement, yet ironically the substance of the sentiments it espouses is virtually the same as that contained in a typical conservative social vision. Obama acknowledged as much. "I would be puzzled," he said, "that they would object or quibble with the bulk of a document that basically espouses profoundly conservative values of self-reliance and self-help . . . If I say to anybody . . . that my church believes in the African American community strengthening families or adhering to the black work ethic or being committed to self-discipline and self-respect and not forgetting where you came from, I don't think that's something anybody would object to. I think I'd get a few amens."

Apparently, however, no explanation of the statements on Trinity's Web site was sufficient. The press had seized upon the idea that Jeremiah Wright was an evil presence that had somehow fatally skewed the moral compass of presidential aspirant Obama, and it would not let go, whatever the evidence to the contrary.

Then on March 13, 2008, after reviewing dozens of Wright's sermons, *ABC World News* brought the minister to wider national attention when it aired his "controversial" statements. From there, his words were subjected to intense and prolonged media scrutiny. The statements were contained in four short video clips composed of 156 words from four separate sermons that Wright had delivered at Trinity United Church of Christ over a period of several years. However, most of the controversial excerpts were taken from two sermons: "The Day of Jerusalem's Fall," delivered on September 16, 2001, and "Confusing God and Government," delivered on April 13, 2003.

What follows are the excerpts from Wright's sermons that seemed to raise the most ire:

1. "Racism is how this country was founded and how it is still run." "No, no, no! Not God bless America. God damn America."
2. "The government lied about the Tuskegee experiment. They purposely infected African American men with syphilis."
3. "The government lied about inventing the HIV virus as a means of genocide against people of color."
4. "The government lied about a connection between Al Qaeda and Saddam Hussein and a connection between 9/11 and Operation Iraqi Freedom."
5. "America's chickens are coming home to roost," in response to the 9/11 World Trade Center bombing.

These statements caused the howls of anger and outrage that obscured from public view every vestige of Wright's humanity except what those behind the onslaught wanted to be seen: his "racist" and "anti-American" challenges to America's political and social status quo.

However, the politicians and pundits who were so outraged by Wright's statements either did not have a good grasp of American history or, as with Sam Hose, were more concerned with swaying public opinion than with truth in reportage. Although not all of Wright's claims are completely accurate, each is at least based in fact. No less than Stephen Mansfield, the conservative commentator and admiring faith biographer of George W. Bush, admitted in his book *The Faith of Barack Obama*, "Wright's suspicions that his government may not have his race's best interests at heart are not fantasy and the compassionate in society should try to understand why." Let us examine Wright's charges.

To verify his contention that America was built on racism, one has only to look to Article 1, Section 2, Paragraph 3 of the U.S. Constitution, which codified the exploitation of and devaluation of the humanity of its enslaved population by counting each of its members as "three-fifths" of a human being. And in Section 9 of Article 1, the Founding Fathers declared that traffickers in human misery could continue the African slave trade unmolested for at least another twenty years. As for the abiding presence of racism in America, political commentator Paul Street observed in *Barack Obama and the Future of American Politics* that for African Americans "there is still a black 'separate and unequal' experience . . . [that] results from . . . race-separatist real-estate and home-lending practices, discriminatory hiring and promotion practices, the systematic underfunding and under-equipping of schools predominately attended by blacks, the imposition of racially separate and inferior curricula and pedagogies, [and] the disproportionate surveillance, arrest, and incarceration of blacks." In other words, every objective social measurement bears out the truth of Wright's statement.

As for Wright's damnation of America, this disembodied phrase, when restored to its sermonic context, is found to be part of a typical biblical jeremiad. Or as Rabbi Sharon Kleinbaum of Congregation Beth Simchat Torah in New York City put it, the complete sermons from which these sound bites were taken were "deeply traditional, carefully composed and structured talks in the Biblical tradition of such venerated sources as Isaiah, Jeremiah, and Deuteronomy . . . They were solidly in the tradition of the ancient prophets, who would catalogue the sins of the people and invoke the Divine litany of curses upon people who [had] wandered from the righteous path prescribed in scripture." Actually, Wright had made it clear that it was a biblical indictment that he was invoking:

When it came to treating her citizens of African descent fairly, America failed. She put them in chains, the government put them in slave quarters, put them on auction blocks, put them in cotton fields, put them in inferior schools, put them in substandard housing, put them in scientific experiments, put them in the low-est paying jobs, put them outside the equal protection of the law, kept them out of their racist bastions of higher education and locked them into positions of hopelessness and helplessness . . . The government gives [young black men] drugs, builds bigger prisons, passes a three-strike law and then wants us to sing "God Bless America." No, no, no! Not God Bless America. God damn America—*that's in the Bible*—for killing innocent people. God damn America for treating our citizens like less than human [the emphasis is mine].

There is no credible evidence that the United States government created HIV/AIDS. However, Wright's suspicions were not far-fetched. Indeed, there is incontrovertible evidence that on numerous occasions officials at the local, state, and federal levels of government have subjected black people to clandestine medical experimentation and outright abuse. Harriet Washington, a former fellow in ethics at the Harvard Medical School, a fellow at the Harvard School of Public Health, and a Knight Fellow at Stanford University, documented many of these abuses in *Medical Apartheid: The Dark History of Medical Experimentation on Black Americans from Colonial Times to the Present* (2006), a 528-page study replete with forty-two pages of scholarly notes and a twenty-page bibliography. President Bill Clinton acknowledged the role of the U.S. government in the horrific Tuskegee Experiment, in which over four hundred black men were tricked into believing that Public Health Service physicians were treating them for syphilis, when in fact they were being given place-bos so government researchers could study how syphilis spreads and kills.

With regard to Wright's charge that our government falsified a connection between Saddam Hussein and Al Qaeda and between 9/11 and the U.S. declaration of war on Iraq, the evidence support-ing him is so voluminous that it needs no further elaboration. Indeed, the number of books detailing President Bush's mendacity in leading the United States to war in Iraq is so great as to constitute a veritable cottage industry.

Wright's "chickens are coming home to roost" remark was part of this fuller statement: "We bombed Hiroshima, we bombed Nagasaki, and we nuked far more than the thousands in New York and The Pentagon, and we never batted an eye . . . and now we are indignant, because the stuff we have done overseas is now brought back into our own front yards. America's chickens are coming home to roost." Bill Leonard, dean of the divinity school and church historian at Wake Forest University, observed that here again Wright "was standing and speaking out of the jeremiad tradition of preaching in the U.S.," which "dates back to the Puritans" and which both "black and white ministers have used since the 1600s in this country . . . The jeremiad tradition [deals] with woe and promise and moral failure not only in the church but in the nation." Thus, when given due consideration, Wright's utterance is seen to be yet another jeremiad, whose purpose is to remind Americans, lest we become self-righteous in our righteous indignation, that we too have engaged in mass destruction of innocents.

Wright explained that his "chickens are coming home to roost" statement actually echoed a remark made on Fox News on September 15, 2001, by Edward Peck, a former U.S. ambassador to Iraq and deputy director of President Ronald Reagan's terrorism task force. In a July 2006 interview on the PBS program *Democracy Now!*, Peck also said, "You can think of a number of countries that have been involved in [terrorist] activities. Ours is one of them."

Thus, when viewed apart from media distortions and false portrayals, Wright's statements are seen to be valid critiques and, for the most part, accurate assessments of the particular actions and events of which he speaks with regard to America's social and political practice and its conduct on the world stage. Stephen Mansfield struck a much-needed tone of humility: "[Americans] should pause to reflect that if half of these charges are true, they ought to be of concern to more than just black ministers. Any citizen who takes American values to heart should be both astonished and ashamed. Any faith that values compassion and holds human life as made in a divine image should be appalled and seek to make amends."

As for the charge that Wright's utterances revealed him to be anti-American, Lawrence Korb, director of national security studies at the Council on Foreign Relations and a former assistant secretary of defense under Reagan, admonished that "in calling [Wright] 'unpatriotic,' let us not forget that this is a man who gave up six of the most productive years of his life to serve his country . . . He has demonstrated his patriotism." Georgetown University professor Michael Eric Dyson explained, "Patriotism is the affirmation of one's country in light of its best values, including the attempt to correct it when it's in error. Wright's words are the tough love of a war-tested patriot speaking his mind."

By mid-March, however, the media had successfully branded Wright as racist and anti-American. A Rasmussen Reports national telephone poll taken during that period found that 66 percent of likely voters polled had read, seen, or heard news stories about Wright's comments. Only 8 percent of likely voters held a favorable opinion of Wright; 58 percent of likely voters had an unfavorable view of him. And 73 percent of likely voters believed that Wright's comments were divisive.

Apparently the media were also making a convincing guilt-by-association case linking Wright and Obama as well. A March 18 Gallup national tracking poll, which reflected voter sentiment prior to Obama's speech, indicated the toll the Wright affair had taken on Obama's public support: After having led in every tracking poll from March 9 to March 16, Obama now trailed Clinton by seven points. This was the political environment Obama faced when he wrote and delivered his speech.

Obama faced a difficult choice: He could continue to publicly speak to the Jeremiah Wright he knew and respected and whose perspectives on racial injustice he largely shared, or at least had accepted for twenty years; or he could respond as if the press's mischaracterization of Wright, and especially his indictments of racism, was for the most part on target. In an essay on the Huffington Post Web site, Obama signaled his choice: "I categorically denounce any statement that disparages our great country . . . In sum, I reject outright the statements by Reverend Wright that are at issue." Posted on March 14, Obama's essay indicated the way he had decided to explain his relationship with Wright and the complaints Wright had lodged against America's treatment of its black citizens.

The setting in which Barack Obama gave his "A More Perfect Union" speech was rife with symbolism. The speech's presentation at the Constitution Center in Philadelphia imbued the moment with nostalgic patriotic significance. Obama added to its patriotic tone by immediately invoking the spirit of the Founding Fathers, having chosen as his opening words the opening words of the U.S. Constitution and Bill of Rights: "We the people, in order to form a more perfect union," which he spoke with the solemnity and reverence usually reserved for sacred scripture.

These were important gestures, given the questions about Obama's patriotism and commitment to America that his political opponents had successfully raised. The symbolic gestures also had another effect: They served to reify America's mythical sense of itself and its past by bringing to mind mythic images of dignified, selfless, visionary men guided by God to lay the groundwork for what the spirit of American exceptionalism unabashedly touts as the most just and free society and government in humanity's history. In so doing, Obama seemed to elevate America beyond the need for prophetic critique of its deeds and serious engagement with its shortcomings.

The speech itself was rife with symbolism; it was also rife with contradictions. Immediately after raising the image of the Founding Fathers by invoking one of the most sacred phrases in American political culture, he acknowledged their collective role in institutionalizing racial oppression by decreeing that enslavers could continue, unhampered, to import African human beings to these shores to be treated inhumanely with legal sanction for decades more. He went on to cite "legalized discrimination" as a root cause of the wealth and income gap between blacks and whites. He contended that "segregated schools were, and are"—that is, and *continue to be*—"inferior schools . . . fifty years after *Brown v. Board of Education*." He chided America, albeit gently, saying, "We do need to remind ourselves that so many of the disparities that exist in the African American community today can be directly traced to inequalities passed on from an earlier generation that suffered under the brutal legacy of slavery and Jim Crow."

Obama's recounting of the thread of racial discrimination running through American history from its beginning was little different from Wright's charge that "racism is how this country was founded and how it is still run." Throughout the speech, Obama chided Wright for recounting that history: "The remarks [by Wright] that have caused this recent firestorm . . . expressed a profoundly distorted view of this country—a view that sees white racism as endemic." Yet this was a point that he himself clearly made with his repeated historical references, though with much more subtlety and political finesse.

That is the major difference between the treatment of race in Obama's "A More Perfect Union" and in Wright's pronouncements: Obama soft-pedaled the full implications of his observations on race, while Wright plumbed the full range of meanings and effects of racism in America. Even as Obama cited the nation's ongoing problems with respect to race, he took pains to avoid acknowledging them as manifestations of a deep social pathology that afflicts us yet.

In Obama's presentation, America's racial problems had never been a manifestation of moral illness. In the historiography of America's exceptionalism that he consciously employed in this speech, they were instead tests of moral mettle that our nation has always passed, and with flying colors; milestones, if you will, blessed indications of the greatness of the American spirit on its inexorable journey to moral and political perfection. The result of Obama's perpetuation of the myth of American moral exceptionalism was that his rhetorical presentation reduced the long and brutal history of systemic and in-stitutionalized racism to mere moral lapses. Thus, on the one hand, he described the systematic mistreatment of black people in Amer-ica, yet on the other, he denied that what he cited is systematic—or endemic.

Although Obama spoke of ongoing systematic racism against black people, he also tried to assuage white fears by consigning it to memory, thus casting righteously indignant responses to it, whether individual (Wright) or collective, as passé. "For the men and women of Reverend Wright's generation, the memories of humiliation and doubt and fear have not gone away; nor has the anger and the bitter-ness of those years." In effect, Obama tried to have it both ways: Rac-ism does exist, he acknowledged, but mostly as a memory. America, you are off the hook.

Obama's characterization of Wright's statements as "incendi-ary language" was quite telling, for it suggests that much of the problem Wright presents for Obama is his rhetorical style: "Rever-end Jeremiah Wright [uses] incendiary language to express views that have the potential not only to widen the racial divide, but views that denigrate both the greatness and the goodness of our nation; that rightly offend white and black alike." After twenty years as a pa-rishioner at Trinity, Obama certainly knew that bombast and hom-iletic hyperbole, used to communicate the gravity of social injustice, are staples of the black prophetic preaching tradition. Yet he knew that this explanation would fall on ears made deaf by the media demonization of Wright and would be used to discredit him as a candidate even more. So although Obama knew that essentially it was Wright's rhetorical style that was at issue and not the substance of his social critiques, he chose to respond to him as the media had: solely to Wright's bold and at times acerbic and combative mode of presentation. Thus Obama never directly addressed any of Wright's offending comments in the speech. In fact, he did not refer to a single word in the video clips at issue. Nor did he ever address the veracity or accuracy of Wright's charges. In effect, he never stated what he specifically disagreed with, because apparently he disagreed with little, as would any reflective person.

In reality, there was little chance that Obama did not know the truth underlying Wright's charges. Obama did not have to spend his childhood in an American inner city or in impoverished rural precincts still stinking of Jim Crow to know of the continuing disparities in health care, education, access to decent housing, treatment by police, and economic opportunity. Even if his voluminous reading and his position as a professor of constitutional law at an illustrious academic institution had never brought to his attention the fact that by every credible statistical measure blacks lag behind whites in every crucial socioeconomic category, and that, in some cases, the disparities are increasing rather than getting smaller, he lived on Chicago's South Side. His time spent as a community organizer in disadvantaged neighborhoods on the South Side would have given him firsthand knowledge of the structural, racial, and institutionalized barriers that still stand between blacks and their full share of the American dream. Thus, it is inconceivable that Obama was unaware of the truths to which Wright pointed.

Moreover, the 2005 report issued in Obama's adopted home town by the local branch of the National Urban League was titled "Still Separate, Unequal: Race, Place, Policy and the State of Black Chicago." It quantified numerous grave and persistent racial disparities in every major aspect of Chicago life, including shocking inequities in the areas of health care, criminal justice, family income, poverty levels, quality of education, and employment opportunities. The only way Obama could possibly have been unaware of the truth underlying Wright's social commentary was if he had studiously avoided the stark realities staring from every corner.

What is very clear is that Obama offered an analysis of racism that was in direct conversation with Wright in that it was meant to convincingly contrast himself with the reverend in order to reassure white Americans. It is as if he was saying to whites that he is not going to hold them accountable for racism, past or present. He even invoked the shibboleth that welfare policies and welfare recipients—inevitably identified in the popular mind with Ronald Reagan's mythical "welfare queens," lazy, calculating, promiscuous black women, and shiftless, irresponsible black men—are virtually as responsible for "the erosion of black families" as lack of economic opportunity and the sense of psychic defeat that results from being unable to adequately provide for one's family. In Obama's formulation, the path to full economic, social, and political equality for black people necessitates no real action by white America; although black people have had no share in erecting the substantial barriers of discrimination that still exist to varying degrees in every aspect of black life, it is the fault of black folks that those barriers still stand: "For the African American community, that path means embracing the burdens of our past without becoming victims of our past . . . And it means taking full responsibility for our own lives—by demanding more from our fathers, and spending more time with our children, and reading to them, and teaching them that while they may face challenges and discrimination in their own lives, they must never succumb to despair or cynicism."

However much Obama proclaimed himself to be in opposition to Wright's positions, he did defend him as a sincere and loving Christian servant of God and humanity and a committed champion of the most vulnerable in society. "The man I met more than twenty years ago is a man who helped introduce me to my Christian faith, a man who spoke to me about our obligations to love one another, to care for the sick and lift up the poor." He explained, "He has been like family to me. He strengthened my faith, officiated my wedding, and baptized my children. Not once in my conversations with him have I heard him talk about any ethnic group in derogatory terms, or treat whites with whom he interacted with anything but courtesy and respect." He went on to say, "I can no more disown him than I can disown the black community."

The Wright he refused to disown is apparently the Wright of the past, "the man I met more than twenty years ago." It is the Wright of the present he disowned by consigning every positive trait of him to the past. He disowned him when he called Wright's social commentary flat-out "wrong," "divisive," "racially charged," and "profoundly distorted." He disowned him when he agreed with the barking media that Wright espoused "views that denigrate both the greatness and the goodness of our nation, that rightly offend white and black alike." In effect, he disowned Wright's prophetic ministry, Wright's incisive social commentary, the sincerity of Wright's struggle against injustice. Even though Obama knew that Wright spewed no hate and no anti-American sentiments, in the end, he disowned who Wright is and what he stands for.

"A More Perfect Union" is the speech of a politically astute man who had been placed in the unenviable position of contributing to the ruination of the reputation of a man he deeply admired, but who seemed to have no other choice if he was to successfully reach the office in which he believed he could make a positive difference for all Americans. It was a choice he should never have had to make. It is to the shame of America that he had been forced to. No public figure should ever be forced by political enemies into having to publicly disavow their pastor, priest, rabbi, or imam for anything less than intentional crimes and actions that are harmful to others or egregious betrayals of public trust. Wright was guilty of none of these.

Despite its distortions and contradictions, Obama's speech achieved its purpose. By March 22, he had regained his lead over Clinton and was up by three points. On March 30, polls showed Obama at 52 percent and Clinton at 42 percent.

Clarence Thomas's claim that he was the victim of a "high-tech" lynching at the 1991 Senate confirmation hearing for his nomination to the Supreme Court has been widely reported. What Thomas was referring to was the media frenzy that surrounded the hearing and the cacophony of voices that opposed his nomination.

In fact, Thomas's treatment had little in common with a lynching. Indeed, his use of the term trivialized the destructive horror of the brutal practice. Lynching is broadly defined as putting a person to death without due process of law, as punishment for a perceived crime. The practical reality, however, is that lynching has overwhelmingly been used as a tool of punishment and deterrence against blacks to protect the status quo: i.e., the perquisites of white-skin color privilege. It has always been brutal and has often involved prolonged torture.

It is true that there was a media feeding frenzy surrounding Thomas's hearing and that there were opponents and detractors bent on derailing his appointment, yet there was no mob seeking to destroy a defenseless person who somehow had challenged the status quo, for his supporters were the keepers of the status quo. As a Bush 41 appointee and professed conservative Republican at a time when conservative Republicans controlled all branches of the federal government, not only did Thomas offer absolutely no challenge to the powers that be, but he was fully aligned with them. Moreover, as the Supreme Court nominee of the president of the United States, he had a national platform from which to defend himself and publicly articulate his version of the truth. Indeed, Thomas was never attacked by the self-anointed protectors of the privilege of the status quo. The most powerful political figures in the nation, including the president himself, fought tirelessly and openly on his behalf. Finally, Thomas was not destroyed; he prevailed. He was solidly confirmed and now sits on the bench of the nation's highest court for life.

Like Sam Hose—and unlike Clarence Thomas—Jeremiah Wright *was* the victim of a lynching. The only major difference between Hose and Wright, other than particularities of historical setting and circumstance, is that the goal of Hose's lynching was *physical* death, while the goal of Wright's lynching was *social* death; and while the instruments of Hose's ordeal were knife and flame, Wright's demise was wrought by visual optics, keyboard, and pen. That is, the immediate purpose of Hose's lynching was the agonizing destruction of his body, while the immediate purpose of Wright's takedown was to destroy his reputation, his ministry, his honor, and his credibility as a responsible member of American society. Carried out and staged by state-of-the-art electronic media, it was truly a high-tech lynching.

Otherwise, Hose and Wright suffered similar fates for similar reasons. Like Hose, Wright was subjected to extreme violence— extreme psychological violence, in this case. Like Hose, Wright challenged the right of whites to determine what he and those like him should think and how they should live. Like Hose, Wright was guilty of no crime except lodging a claim for justice and defending himself (and his own) from exploitation and harm. Like Hose, Wright was demonized and mercilessly assailed without regard for his humanity, his feelings, his family, his friends. As in Hose's case, the media of Wright's day convinced the public that Wright was a dangerous threat to white-skin color privilege and thus worthy of (social) death. Like Hose, Wright was subjected to prolonged torment and torture. As with Hose, the destruction Wright's tormentors sought was successful: Jeremiah Wright has indeed suffered an excruciatingly painful social death.

We know of Hose's suffering on the way to his physical death. The suffering inflicted upon Wright is less well known. Seldom has a nonpolitical figure been subjected to such a concerted public effort to destroy him. Throughout his ordeal, Wright received so many death threats that two police cars were stationed outside his home. He had the misfortune to be on a Caribbean cruise with his wife, children, and grandchildren to celebrate his retirement when the continuous twenty-four-hour-a-day video loop began on CNN and Fox News, which, unfortunately, were the only television channels the cruise ship received. During what should have been a joyful, celebratory family time, Wright was subjected to so many hateful stares and insulting comments by his mostly white fellow passengers that he had to sequester himself in his stateroom to protect himself and his family from the growing animosity. Numerous invitations to preach, teach, and lecture—a major part of his income (his requested salary was very low for the pastor of a mega-church)—were summarily withdrawn. His computer was hacked. Flights for which he was booked received bomb threats. His once well-respected name became a term of derision. Not to be taken lightly are the extraordinary physical stress and emotional distress of the ordeal and the toll they took upon his health: the months of anxiety, fear for the safety and welfare of his family, fear for his future, rage at the incessant mean-spirited, distorted portrayals of his beliefs and his character, and grief at a long, honorable career and carefully cultivated life of peace and comfort torn asunder.

In Barack Obama's attempt to assure America that he was not racist and anti-American like its carefully cultivated mischaracterization of Jeremiah Wright, he offered several defenses of Wright. Yet what he offered was not enough. He should have strongly condemned the press's unfair and un-Christian onslaught on Wright. Why didn't he condemn with equal vigor the media's "incendiary language" that denigrated the demonstrated goodness of Wright?

Unfortunately, the deterrence strategy behind Wright's lynching achieved its purpose: It dissuaded Obama from challenging the racially charged status quo because in all probability the media would have destroyed any chance he had to remain a viable candidate for the presidency; condemning with equal vigor the incendiary language that mercilessly denigrated Wright would have been political suicide. Yet there are abiding consequences of Obama's choice. Because the media onslaught was not condemned, (1) Wright's reputation lies in tatters, and the problems and injustices he has identified that cry out for redress have been successfully dismissed as the crazed imaginings of a hate-filled madman; (2) there is now a paradigm in place for discrediting and destroying any influential black minister who raises a critique of the abiding racism in America, no matter how factually accurate and morally correct his observations; (3) Wright's unaddressed high-tech lynching now presents a fearful deterrent to weaken the willingness and diminish the power of prophetic black ministers to effect progressive social change, let alone give leadership to it; and (4) there stands the implicit but unmistakable declaration that African American ministers, no matter how well informed, will not be allowed to engage in serious public debate about governmental policy without repercussions, unless their stated positions support the status quo.

The high-tech-lynching paradigm that victimized Wright must not be allowed to stand unchallenged. It must be addressed with the same vigor that the media and political pundits employed in its construction, for it is extremely dangerous for such a destructive force to remain unchecked. Not only does the paradigm pose an ever-present danger to prophetic voices; it is still in place to be used against any influential Obama supporter, or anyone else identified as a real threat to white privilege. That is why it must be dismantled. The first step is to forcefully discredit the shameful treatment of Jeremiah Wright. A crucial part of this process is restoring his name and his reputation in the public eye. This is not only politic; it is the morally correct thing to do. Moreover, it will signal that "Yes We Can" reclaim our body politic from the tyranny and terrorism of the press—and we are truly committed to doing so.

It would be easy to condemn Obama's comments about Wright and race as disingenuous, as a betrayal of his former pastor. Yet, Obama has no public record of mendacity. By all appearances, in the public sphere he has acted with the utmost integrity. Even the extremely rigorous scrutiny he was subjected to by his political rivals during his two-year presidential run uncovered nothing to bring his integrity into serious question. Thus it is true that Obama's treatment of Wright does represent a humiliating public betrayal, but it was a betrayal that Obama tried hard to avoid.

The sad American reality is that Barack Obama had little choice. He was forced to write "A More Perfect Union" and to respond to the charges against Jeremiah Wright as he did by the unspoken reality of America's disingenuous racial politics, which throttles and ultimately seeks to destroy those who seriously challenge the social and political primacy of white-skin color privilege. Just ask Jeremiah Wright.

"IT'S BEEN A LONG TIME COMIN, BUT OUR CHANGE DONE COME"

Geneva Smitherman

When the news media broke into the midst of the presidential campaign with sound bites from the Reverend Dr. Jeremiah Wright's passionately eloquent sermons, Barack Hussein Obama made a strategic decision to use that historical moment to talk about race in America. He was confronted with a rhetorical situation in which Black and White perceptions and past and present experiences of race are often at odds. In great measure, this is attributable to a long, brutal history of enslavement, followed by an additional century of neo-enslavement* and today's continuing racial separation—-

---

Shout-out to Professor Austin Jackson, of Michigan State University's Residential College, for his critical reading and suggestions for this essay. Any shortcomings are entirely my own.

* "Neo-enslavement" is a term used by a number of Black activists and intellectuals to indicate that nineteenth-century emancipation did not free America's enslaved African population. Rather, it simply reintroduced slavery in a different form—characterized by segregation laws and policies, employment discrimination, etc. This period lasted from the end of Reconstruction in the late nineteenth century until the mid-twentieth century, with the passage of Civil Rights legislation and Supreme Court decisions such as the 1954 *Brown v. Board of Education* decision, which declared school segregation unconstitutional. However, there remain activists today who use the term "neo-enslavement" to indicate that African slave

e.g., in housing and schooling. Since the landing at Plymouth Rock in the seventeenth century, Whites have generally functioned exclusive of Blacks, as "one nation, under God." Since the inception of slavery in the United States, that "peculiar institution," also in the seventeenth century, African slave descendants have generally functioned within the White nation as "one nation under a groove."

In and of itself, the fact that a Black public figure would seek to deliver a speech about race was nothing new. African descendants in the United States have been engaging in public discourse about racial oppression at least since David Walker, born to a slave father and a free mother in Wilmington, North Carolina, in 1785, issued his *David Walker's Appeal, in Four Articles; Together with a Preamble, to the Coloured Citizens of the World, but in Particular, and Very Expressly, to Those of the United States of America* in 1829. What was new, or at least rare, was a race speech delivered in our time, in what many Americans believe is a "color-blind" society, one in which problems of race and racism no longer exist. The argument is that these issues were addressed and dealt with in the last century, and that owing in great measure to the "success" of the Civil Rights Movement, African Americans have made major advancements on all fronts— educational, economic, social, political. Those who hold this position contend that there is no longer a need for a "Black Movement" and speeches of protest against White oppression. Whether or not one agrees with this interpretation of current Black social reality, it is a fact that except for an occasional public talk by the Reverend Jesse Jackson on corporate responsibility to Blacks, or the Reverend Al Sharpton on the shooting of some hapless young brotha by police, the long-standing genre of Black protest oratory is all but dead in the twenty-first century.

---

descendants are still not free, owing to the continuing existence of racism and discrimination in employment and other areas.

To be sure, today's sociopolitical context is decidedly different from that of nineteenth-century Black leaders such as ex-slave turned abolitionist Frederick Douglass or twentieth-century Civil Rights and Black Power activists such as Dr. Martin Luther King Jr., Malcolm X, and Kwame Ture (born Stokely Carmichael). The blatant symbols of racial oppression—for instance, "Whites Only" access to hotels, theaters, and public facilities; police dogs; and water hoses spraying nonviolent protesters—are no longer with us. There is now a sizable, highly educated Black middle and upper class. The NBA, the NFL, Hip Hop, and other forms of Black Popular Culture have contributed to the development of a bling-bling, livin large Black elite, with Benjamins to burn. Moreover, late-twentieth-century periods of "benign neglect"* and the "Second Reconstruction"† virtually succeeded in the erasure from America's social agenda of Black concerns about social justice, poverty, and educational inequities.

---

* The term "benign neglect," referring to America's racial problem, was a policy formulated by Daniel Patrick Moynihan, chief domestic adviser to President Richard Nixon. In a secret memorandum to Nixon, Moynihan recommended nonenforcement of legislation on voting, laws prohibiting school segregation and discrimination against Blacks and minorities in employment, and various other antidiscrimination laws that the federal government had clear legal powers to enforce. Although Black intellectuals and leaders denounced benign neglect as "criminal negligence," it nonetheless prevailed.

† The first Reconstruction was launched in the late 1870s, with the federal government's abandonment of ex-slaves to Southern governments, which promptly rolled back the freedmen's political gains, ushered in U.S.-style apartheid, and began an era of lynching and brutal assaults against Blacks that would not be redressed until the Black Freedom Struggle of the 1960s. Despite some economic, political, and educational gains in the 1960s and 1970s, the mission was not completed. There followed a treacherous pushback as the country shifted to a conservative climate of stagnation and dreams deferred—a move, according to Ronald Walters and other political theorists, that was solidified in 1980 by the election of President Ronald Reagan and the subsequent Reagan-Bush years (1980–1992) in the White House: the Second Reconstruction.

Thus, the White audience for a speech about race was now a 2008, not a 1968, one.

While the Black audience for such a speech was also a twenty-first-century one, these people who are "darker than blue" have long, painful memories of betrayal by both Black and White politicians and leaders. Moreover, even those who seek to invoke historical amnesia in order to keep on keepin on in their overworked, paper-chasin struggle to survive are forced to bear witness to the historical impact and presentness of the past—for example, the re-segregation of schools, the seemingly intractable poverty in urban wastelands, and the skyrocketing incarceration rates among Black males. For Blacks in the racial binary, the reality of the Black condition could not be swept under the rug; it cried out for acknowledgment and recognition. Indeed, Blacks painfully understood—even if they did not endorse—the good Reverend's fiery, Biblically grounded sermonic exhortations about America's misdeeds and failings. And then there was that nagging question about Obama's "blackness." Is he culturally Black? Is he attuned to the Black intellectual tradition?

Given the demands of these two different—and on some levels, diametrically opposed—audiences, the historical moment called for a race speech that was explicatory, but it could not be condemnatory, as was much of the racial rhetoric of the previous century. While the rhetorical task required a speech crafted by an African American, it had to be an "American," not an "African American," speech. Given his background and upbringing, his "improbable" journey in America, Obama seemed especially suited—dare I say called?—for this task. He is, after all, an American who is neither "White" nor "Black" (in the classical stereotypical American sense). At the same time, paradoxically, he is an American who is and has lived as *both* "Black" and "White," who thus is uniquely positioned to *see and feel* both dimensions of the Black-White binary.

Various responses to the speech demonstrate that Obama clearly stepped to the challenge of the rhetorical situation:

- ". . . the best political speech since John Kennedy talked about his Catholicism in Houston in 1960 . . . It was not a sound bite, but a symphony" (Nicholas D. Kristof, *New York Times*, March 20, 2008).
- "He took Malcolm X's jeremiad and turned it inside out . . . He . . . presented 'America' with an opportunity to act on its best principles" (Robert Hinton, H-AFRO-AM, March 24, 2008).
- "In many ways, Barack Obama's speech on race was momentous and edifying" (Maureen Dowd, *New York Times*, March 19, 2008).
- "It was substantive, and it was eloquent" (Anthony A. Samad, BlackCommentator.com, March 27, 2008).
- "One word . . . WOW!!!! I have always been an admirer and supporter of Sen. Obama, but I was never more proud of him than today . . . He just proved to the nation that he . . . will be an effective and great leader" (Gordon, a blogger on the Huffington Post, March 18, 2008).

As the daughter of a baptized-in-the-fire Baptist preacherman, I have, on many occasions, shouted and clapped to the stirring power and visionary message in a Reverend Jeremiah Wright sermon. As a sociolinguist who teaches courses in African American Language and Culture, I have used Wright's oratorical brilliance—as in his "Demons and Detractors" sermon, excerpted in my *Word from the Mother: Language and African Americans*—to teach the rhetoric of what late linguist Grace Sims Holt referred to as "stylin outta the black pulpit." Stanford University sociolinguist John Russell Rickford uses Wright's "When You Fail in Your Trying" sermon for a similar pedagogical purpose. (See John Russell Rickford and Russell John Rickford's award-winning book *Spoken Soul: The Story of Black English*.) As a member of the generation that came of age in the twentieth-century Black Freedom Struggle, I have, on many occasions, shouted and clapped to the flamboyant speechifying and insightful calls to action in a King, Ture, or H. Rap Brown speech. Curiously, I found myself awed by Obama's speech, despite the fact that it didn't seem to reflect the Black oratorical tradition I intellectually and emotionally knew so well. Millions of others were also awed—audiences all over the country, Black and White, male and female, of different generations and classes. For my part, I was awed that I was awed. I asked myself, How could it be that his speech satisfied the complex psychosocial demands of Whites *and* Blacks *and* others while at the same time it candidly spoke the truth to the people?

The answer lies in the wise rhetorical choices Obama made. Verbal persuasion is both an art and a science. The rhetor must have the ability to discern the most effective means of persuasion at his/her disposal. Accurate audience assessment and analysis are critical, as is skill in appropriating available persuasive strategies. The annals of Black oratory record that in the Nation of Islam, Malcolm X reached heights of dazzling speech-making, while Elijah Muhammad was ho-hum. In the Civil Rights Movement, Martin Luther King scaled the rhetorical mountain, while Ralph Abernathy never got off the ground.

For his "A More Perfect Union" speech, Obama selected a familiar rhetorical paradigm, the jeremiad, a master narrative in both the White and the Black rhetorical traditions. But he didn't tarry there. Rather, he skillfully adapted this centuries-old framework to accommodate a postmodern Black and White audience. Further, while he grounded the structure of his speech within the jeremiad, he relied on fundamental rhetorical principles that Aristotle taught centuries ago, principally *ethos* (persuasion based on a speaker's personal character) and *logos* (persuasive appeal based on reason).

THE OLD: THE (WHITE) AMERICAN
AND AFRICAN AMERICAN JEREMIAD

But if ye will not hear these words, I swear by myself, saith the
Lord, that this house shall become a desolation . . . And many nations
shall pass by this city, and they shall say . . . Wherefore hath the Lord
done thus unto this great city? Then they shall answer, Because they
have forsaken the covenant of the Lord their God.

—JEREMIAH 22: 5–9

The jeremiad is a speech, sermon, or other form of public discourse in
which the speaker critiques the society for its misdeeds and wrongdo-
ings while holding out hope that this fall from Grace can be reversed
if the country corrects its behavior and lives up to its divine mandate.
The term "jeremiad" is derived from Jeremiah, the name of the Old
Testament prophet who accounts for the Israelites' trials and tribulations as punishment for departing from their covenant with God.
However, even as he critiques the Israelites for their wayward, un-
godly behavior, he reminds them of their status as God's chosen
people and foreshadows their return to greatness following repen-
tance. The American jeremiad, which has its roots in the European
jeremiad, began as a political sermon in the Puritan era. Like the
"Children of Israel," seventeenth-century Puritans believed that they
were God's chosen people. They had been delivered out of Europe
and called by God to establish a new order, to create in this New
World a nation that would be a symbol of liberty, freedom, and hope
for peoples around the globe. Up in all of this, however, there is no
acknowledgment of the fate of the Indigenous people who were here
when the colonists arrived. But I digress . . .

Puritan leaders used the rhetorical framework of the American
jeremiad to remind the colonists of God's divine plan for America
and their role in the fulfillment of the new nation's destiny. Cultural
historians such as Sacvan Bercovitch, in *The American Jeremiad*,
track the continuing belief in and discourse of American exception-

alism to their beginnings in the American jeremiad of the Puritan era. Bercovitch contends that the jeremiad has persisted for centuries and has "played a significant role in the development of . . . modern middle-class American culture." He notes that the "prophetic history" and "mission" of America, as a special, unique country, are writ large, not only in sermons and speeches, but also in literature, culture, and core values—"devaluation of aristocracy, opening up of political, educational, and commercial opportunities to a relatively broad spectrum of the population." (Notwithstanding Bercovitch's astute, scholarly account of the "process of Americanization," at points he is surprisingly honest in his assessment of what he calls the "patent fiction" that is the "American mission."*)

Jeremiad speeches and sermons had a set tripartite formula: (1) The speaker intoned America's promise as a beacon of liberty, equality, and social justice; (2) he (or she, but it was almost always "he") detailed and castigated America's misdeeds, its grave departure or "retrogression" from the promise; and (3) he reaffirmed the prophecy that America would complete its mission and redeem the promise. This rhetorical structure helped the speaker to simultaneously chastise and uplift his audience. And David Howard-Pitney suggests in *The African American Jeremiad: Appeals for Justice in America* that "the jeremiad . . . was filled with underlying optimism about America's fate and mission . . . [Its] dark portrayal of current society never questioned America's promise and destiny . . . The unfaltering view is that

---

* Bercovitch writes, "What first attracted me to the study of the jeremiad was my astonishment, as a Canadian immigrant, at learning about the prophetic history of America. Not of North America, for the prophecies stopped short at the Canadian and Mexican borders, but of a country that, despite its arbitrary territorial limits, could read its destiny in its landscape, and a population that, despite its bewildering mixture of race and creed, could believe in something called an American mission, and could invest that patent fiction with all the emotional, spiritual, and intellectual appeal of a religious quest." (Madison: University of Wisconsin Press, 1978), 11.

God will mysteriously use the unhappy present to spur the people to reformation and speedily onward to fulfill their divine destiny."

As an archetype of the American jeremiad, Bercovitch analyzes "Brief Recognition of New England's Errand into the Wilderness," a speech by Samuel Danforth delivered in 1670. He notes that Danforth's speech "condemns the colonists' shortcomings and justifies their afflictions." The charge is that "'we have . . . in a great measure forgotten our errand.'" Danforth "underscores this meaning by comparing New England's 'howling wilderness' with that of Moses and John the Baptist." He goes on to "assure the colonists of success not because of their efforts, but God's: 'the great Physician of Israel hath undertaken the cure . . . he will provide . . . we have the promise.'"

Just as there was a Black nation within the White nation, there was a concomitant Black jeremiad within the White jeremiad. Beginning with the antislavery movement, Black leaders adapted the White jeremiad for the purpose of protest against enslavement and later discrimination and racism. In the Black version, the rhetoric envisioned U.S. descendants of enslaved Africans as also being God's chosen people. God's mandate became a charge to the White nation to live up to its divinely inspired calling and provide equality and social justice for the Black nation. Historian Wilson Jeremiah Moses, who is believed to have coined the term "Black jeremiad," argues in his *Black Messiahs and Uncle Toms: Social and Literary Manipulations of a Religious Myth*, "If the bondage of the Colonies to England was similar to the enslavement of Israel in Egypt, was not the bondage of blacks in America an even more perfect analogy? If Americans, by virtue of the ideals of their revolution, were in fact a covenanted people and entrusted with the mission to safeguard the divine and natural laws of human rights, was there not a danger to the covenant in perpetuating slavery?"

Following the tripartite structure of the American jeremiad, the Black speaker lauded America for its founding principles and promise ("life, liberty, pursuit of happiness"; "all men are created equal"); detailed and denounced the society for its failure to live up to that promise (e.g., enslavement, denial of equal opportunity, Jim Crow); and called upon the country to recommit to its historical mandate and divine promise by alleviating Black oppression. A classic example of the Black jeremiad is Frederick Douglass's oration delivered in Rochester, New York, July 5, 1852, which has come to be known as his "Fourth of July" speech. This ex-slave, who became a powerful force in the abolitionist movement and a revered leader of African slave descendants in his time, acknowledges and celebrates the significance of July 4, but he is ultimately dismissive of the holiday since it is meaningless to those still in bondage.

Douglass employs Biblical metaphors, as in the White jeremiad, to recall America's prophetic mission and promise. "This, to you, is what the Passover was to the emancipated people of God." As he continues, he contrasts the lofty ideals and liberatory promise of America with the capture of Africans, the horrors and brutalities of bondage, and his own personal tribulations during enslavement. Although he frames his argument with overtones of the Biblical narrative, his language is caustic and accusatory, his metaphors bitter and brutal:

> Are the great principles of political freedom and of natural justice, embodied in that Declaration of Independence, extended to us? . . . "By the rivers of Babylon, there we sat down . . . We wept when we remembered Zion . . . They that carried us away captive, required of us a song; and they who wasted us required of us mirth, saying, Sing us one of the songs of Zion. How can we sing the Lord's song in a strange land?" . . . What, to the American slave, is your fourth of July? . . . Your celebration is a sham; your boasted liberty, an unholy license; your national greatness, swelling vanity . . . your denunciation of tyrants, brass fronted impudence; your shouts of liberty and equality, hollow mockery; your

prayers and hymns, your sermons and thanksgivings, with all your religious parade and solemnity, are to him . . . a thin veil to cover up crimes which would disgrace a nation of savages. There is not a nation on the earth guilty of practices more shocking and bloody than are the people of the United States . . . This Fourth of July is *yours,* not *mine. You* may rejoice, *I* must mourn.

Calling the question of America's promise, as embodied in its founding documents, Douglass foreshadows the end of enslavement and expresses his belief that Whites will rise to the greatness in that promise. His tone reflects what Obama, borrowing from Reverend Wright, might have called the "audacity of hope":

Now, take the Constitution according to its plain reading, and I defy the presentation of a single pro-slavery clause in it. On the other hand, it will be found to contain principles and purposes, entirely hostile to the existence of slavery . . . Notwithstanding the dark picture I have this day presented . . . [I] draw . . . encouragement from "the Declaration of Independence," the great principles it contains, and the genius of American Institutions.

Perhaps the quintessential Black jeremiad is Martin Luther King's oft-quoted "I Have a Dream" speech, delivered August 28, 1963, in the nation's capital. Following the well-worn jeremiadic script, King invokes the prophetic vision of America: "When the architects of our Republic wrote the magnificent words of the Constitution and the Declaration of Independence, they were signing a promissory note to which every American was to fall heir . . . a promise that all men—yes, black men as well as white men—would be guaranteed the unalienable rights of life, liberty and the pursuit of happiness." However, he says the society has failed to fulfill its "sacred obligation . . . The Negro is still badly crippled by the manacles of segregation and the chains of discrimination . . . The Negro lives on a lonely island of poverty in the midst of a vast ocean of material prosperity."

Like Jeremiahs before him, King foreshadows doom so long as America fails to address the racism and oppression of Blacks and thus remains unrepentant:

> We can never be satisfied as long as our bodies, heavy with the fatigue of travel, cannot gain lodging in the motels of the highways and the hotels of the cities . . . We can never be satisfied as long as our children are stripped of their adulthood and robbed of their dignity by signs stating "For Whites Only" . . . We cannot be satisfied as long as the Negro in Mississippi cannot vote and the Negro in New York believes he has nothing for which to vote . . . There will be neither rest nor tranquility in America until the Negro is granted his citizenship rights. The whirlwinds of revolt will continue to shake the foundation of our nation until the bright day of justice emerges.

With the "fierce urgency of now," he calls for recommitment to the promise, exhorting America to "rise up, live out the true meaning of its creed: 'We hold these truths to be self-evident, that all men are created equal' . . . This will be the day when all of God's children will be able to sing with new meaning: 'My country, 'tis of thee, sweet land of liberty, of thee I sing. Land where my fathers died, land of the pilgrim's pride, from every mountain side, let freedom ring.'"

THE NEW: BARACK OBAMA'S JEREMIAD

As a powerful and eloquent public discourse on race, Obama's speech is clearly situated in the jeremiadic tradition. The structure of his speech follows the tripartite formula of classical jeremiads.

He opens with an allusion to the promise of America as articulated in its founding documents: "'We the people, in order to form a more perfect union' . . . Our Constitution . . . had at its very core the ideal of equal citizenship under the law; a Constitution that promised its people liberty, and justice, and a union that could be and should be perfected over time." He notes that even at the outset there was a retreat from the promise, making his point about slavery with the use of familiar, shared Biblical language: "original sin."

He expands on the retreat from the promise, detailing a litany of past racial injustices, the continuing impacts of which are felt in Black communities today. He uses deductive reasoning (*logos*), anchoring his major claim in the long history of institutionalized racism and deeply entrenched structures of racial oppression in the United States. Given the constraints of time—this was a campaign speech, not, for instance, a lecture in a university hall—he skillfully paints a portrait of that history with broad strokes. The strength of this major premise is his logical, systematic accounting of historical facts. He establishes his minor claim by laying out the destructive effects of this past on the African American community. He concludes by deducing the impact of this history on the pulpit oratory and public rhetoric of Reverend Wright—and on the consciousness and discourse of Blacks of Wright's generation.

On education: "Segregated schools were, and are, inferior schools; we still haven't fixed them, fifty years after *Brown v. Board of Education*, and the inferior education they provided, then and now, helps explain the pervasive achievement gap between today's black and white students."

On economic discrimination: "Blacks were prevented, often through violence, from owning property . . . Loans were not granted to African American business owners . . . Black home owners could not access FHA mortgages . . . Blacks were excluded from unions, or the police force, or fire departments." The result: "Black families could not amass any meaningful wealth to bequeath to future gen-

erations. That history helps explain the wealth and income gap between black and white, and the concentrated pockets of poverty that
persist in so many of today's urban and rural communities."

On the abandonment of Black neighborhoods: "The lack of basic
services in so many urban black neighborhoods—parks for kids to
play in, police walking the beat, regular garbage pickup, and building code enforcement—all helped create a cycle of violence, blight,
and neglect that continues to haunt us."

On the American dream deferred: "For all those who scratched
and clawed their way to get a piece of the American dream, there were
many who didn't make it—those who were ultimately defeated . . . by
discrimination. That legacy of defeat was passed on to future
generations—those young men and increasingly young women who
we see standing on street corners or languishing in our prisons, without hope or prospects for the future."

On the impact on the Black psyche: "Even for those blacks who
did make it, questions of race, and racism, continue to define their
worldview in fundamental ways. For the men and women of Reverend Wright's generation, the memories of humiliation and doubt
and fear have not gone away; nor has the anger and the bitterness of
those years . . . [The anger] find[s] voice in the barbershop or around
the kitchen table . . . And occasionally it finds voice in the church
on Sunday morning, in the pulpit and in the pews."

In characteristic jeremiadic fashion, Obama reaffirms his audience's belief in the promise of America, calling on both Blacks and
Whites—indeed, all Americans—to rededicate themselves to the
realization of America's destiny and the perfection of the union.
"What we know—what we have seen—is that America can change.
That is the true genius of this nation. What we have already achieved
gives us hope—the audacity to hope—for what we can and must
achieve tomorrow." Further, in keeping with the religious trappings
of both the Black and the White American jeremiad, he links his

call to action to global religious ideology: "What is called for is nothing more, and nothing less, than what all the world's great religions demand—that we do unto others as we would have them do unto us."

While Obama's race speech taps into the basic structure of the Black jeremiad, in several respects it departs from that tradition. To begin with, his rhetoric doesn't convey a sense of impending doom and destruction. Yes, failure to "come together" and talk about the common problems of education, employment, and health care that plague *all* citizens will impede the social change that most Americans are desperately clamoring for. But this line of reasoning evokes a very different emotion than the fear engendered by predictions of imminent destruction and danger. This was the hallmark of the jeremiad in the antislavery movement as well as racialized oratory of the twentieth century in which the jeremiad was often directed at Black audiences, such as Malcolm X's "The Ballot or the Bullet" speech. And even King hinted at gloom and doom in his "I Have a Dream" speech, warning that there would be "neither rest nor tranquility" and "whirlwinds of revolt." None of this should be taken as a critique of this earlier style of Black protest oratory. A Curtis Mayfield people "movin on up" to self-realization after centuries of socially imposed inferiority; a Black nation within the White nation in quest of a newfound sense of pride and self-determination; a society that was blind to Black suffering and lacking in the courage and political will to address that suffering—given these concrete, historical conditions, a bold, caustic, agitational, Black-vernacular-driven rhetoric was called for. The case for and analysis of this twentieth-century Black oratorical style are brilliantly made in a pioneering 1969 work by Arthur Lee Smith (now Molefi Kete Asante), *Rhetoric of Black Revolution*.

Obama's speech departs from more than just the fiery zeal, the emotive language, and the biting-hard candor characteristic of the Black jeremiadic tradition. We also do not hear the rhythmic cadence of syntactical repetition, the Tonal Semantics* emblematic of the Black rhetorical style. In fact, the one African American vernacular trope in the speech is articulated in the formal voice of the Language of Wider Communication (LWC)†: "making a way out of no way," as opposed to the vernacular "makin a way outta no way." What he accomplishes by using this linguistic register is to signal Black identity and Black cultural affinity while simultaneously bridging the linguistic-cultural divide. That is, he selects a Black idiom but gives it a "White" articulation.

In the archetypal African American jeremiad, Whites were told what they needed to do to redress Black grievances and thus revive America's promise. These instructions were often boldly stated, with the force of commanding, guilt-inducing directives. Obama chooses not to go there, leaving the rhetorical *pathos* (appeal to emotion) of earlier Black jeremiads aside. Rather than pulling rhetorical heartstrings, he proceeds with calm, deliberate reasoning, seeking to elicit rational, thoughtful understanding and action that will ultimately benefit the entire nation:

> In the white community, the path to a more perfect union means acknowledging that what ails the African American community does not just exist in the minds of black people; that the legacy of discrimination and current incidents of discrimination, while less overt than in the past, are real and must be addressed.

---

* I coined the term "Tonal Semantics" in *Talkin and Testafyin* (New York: Houghton Mifflin, 1977) to refer to the use of speech rhythm, intonation, and melodious repetition—that is, voice sound—to convey meaning in Black oratorical style. In the hands of a skillful rhetor, the sound becomes as important as and helps to convey the sense of the message.

† Multilingual societies characteristically employ a language that makes communication possible with those who live outside of one's own hood. It's a language that allows a speaker to talk to a wider audience. In this country, the LWC may be loosely equated with the "Standard English" variety of American English.

Not just with words, but with deeds—by investing in our schools and our communities; by enforcing our civil rights laws and ensuring fairness in our criminal justice system; by providing this generation with ladders of opportunity that were unavailable for previous generations.

It is not only Whites but also Blacks who have to do some work if America is to realize the promise and perfect the union. Here is yet another example of Obama making a fundamental departure from the classic Black jeremiad, where the message was directed to Whites and there was no critique of Black people's shortcomings. Or, rather, such critique is usually not done in the public sphere, but is reserved for intimate interactional talks in Black homes, mosques, churches, schools, community centers, and barber and beauty shops.

In this racial-uplift discourse, the speaker might chastise Blacks for everything from lack of Black pride, disrespect of Black women, and adoption of White cultural patterns and values to eating pork and other "impure" foods that defiled the Black body. In Obama's case, airing the race's dingy laundry was a decided rhetorical risk that an earlier generation of Black orators, speaking to a White or racially mixed audience, would not have taken. However, he correctly gauged that this national 2008 Black audience would be receptive. After all, many were living in communities rife with Black-on-Black crime, baby daddies and baby mommas, and an educational achievement gap spiraling out of control. (In any event, Bill Cosby beat Obama to the punch here, calling out Blacks for negative behavior in the many public talks he's given since his 2004 speech in commemoration of *Brown v. Board*.)

Obama instructs Blacks thus:

For the African American community, that path [to the more perfect union] means embracing the burdens of our past without becoming victims of our past . . . And it means taking full responsibility for our own lives—by demanding more from our fathers, and spending more time with our children, and reading to them, and teaching them that while they may face challenges and discrimination in their own lives, they must never succumb to despair or cynicism; they must always believe that they can write their own destiny.

Then he goes one step further, to a place that would never have been approached in the classic African American jeremiad. He calls for Blacks to link our struggle against current economic and social injustices with that of Whites: "It also means binding our particular grievances—for better health care, and better schools, and better jobs—to the larger aspirations of all Americans: the white woman struggling to break the glass ceiling, the white man who's been laid off, the immigrant trying to feed his family." Jarring, but logical in a society where loss of jobs and other social ills pay equal opportunity visits to the country's citizens.

Drawing on his personal character and credibility (*ethos*), Obama connects America's prophetic promise to his life's journey and his family history, establishing his identity and authenticity (again, an element not in the typical Black jeremiad, where the speaker generally eschewed any presentation of his personal biography). Here the rhetorical strategy succeeds not simply in reintroducing him to the (Black and White) American public, but also, more crucially, in displaying the diverse, complex unfolding of the American promise—he "too sings America":

I am the son of a black man from Kenya and a white woman from Kansas. I was raised with the help of a white grandfather who survived a depression to serve in Patton's army during World War II and a white grandmother who worked on a bomber assembly line at Fort Leavenworth while he was overseas. I've gone to some of the best schools in America and lived in one of the world's poorest nations. I am married to a black American who carries within her the blood of slaves and slave owners . . . I have brothers, sisters, nieces, nephews, uncles, and cousins, of every race and every hue, scattered across three continents, and for as long as I live, I will never forget that in no other country on Earth is my story even possible.

The personal disclosure continues in the characterization of his relationship with Reverend Wright. Here Obama uses inductive reasoning (*logos*), citing several specific instances to establish his general argument about the logic of his close association with Wright. He catalogs a wide range of noble actions and services. Wright "helped introduce me to my Christian faith . . . [He] spoke to me about our obligations to love one another, to care for the sick and lift up the poor." He lauds Wright's accomplishments in the Chicago urban community in his role as Pastor of Trinity United Church of Christ as well as his leadership role in the national Black community.

Further, he knows Wright as a man who "not once in my conversations with him have I heard him talk about any ethnic group in derogatory terms, or treat whites with whom he interacted with anything but courtesy and respect." Obama's powerful description of a regular church service at Trinity, combined with a list of Wright's good works, induces the audience to Obama's desired conclusion: Wright is doing "God's work here on Earth," he uplifts the downtrodden, and he has an unfailing commitment to empowering the disempowered. At the same time, Obama's personal ethos demands that he honestly acknowledge Wright's "contradictions—the good and the bad," his "profoundly distorted view of this country," and the divisiveness of his comments in the televised sermonic excerpt.

This forthright characterization of Wright is juxtaposed with the candid portrayal of Obama's White grandmother. He describes her as "a woman who helped raise me, a woman who sacrificed again and again for me, a woman who loves me as much as she loves anything in this world." Yet she displays the very racial prejudices and contradictions assigned to Wright: "a woman who once confessed her fear of black men who passed by her on the street, and who on more than one occasion has uttered racial or ethnic stereotypes that made me cringe." The disclosure enhances his credibility, as the audience is made to understand both Wright and "Toot" (Obama's nickname for his grandmother, from the Hawaiian *kupuna wahine*, or *kŭkŭ/tŭtŭ wahine*).* Both vividly and sadly exemplify the thought patterns of Blacks and Whites from another moment in time, and they provide a snapshot of the "racial stalemate" that prevents society from moving forward.

Symbolizing the unity that's needed in this country, the end of the speech rhetorically returns to its beginning, iterating the charge to perfect the union: "This union may never be perfect, but generation after generation has shown that it can always be perfected . . . As so many generations have come to realize over the course of the two hundred and twenty-one years since a band of patriots signed that document in Philadelphia, that is where the perfection begins."

While the overall arc of Obama's "A More Perfect Union" is that of the Black jeremiad, he made significant departures from this tradition. Speaking from both a Black and a White perspective on race, he displayed a depth of understanding of both racial perspectives and the past in which those perspectives are still mired—appropriately and symbolically quoting Faulkner, that son of the South, whose Yoknapatawpha tales revealed to us that "the past isn't dead and buried. In fact, it isn't even past." The genius of the speech lies in the fact that Obama insightfully analyzed his Black and White

---

* According to Mary Pukui and Samuel Elbert's *Hawaiian Dictionary*, *kŭkŭ* can refer to grandmother, grandfather, grandaunt, or any relative or close friend of a grandparent's generation. It is pronounced with the English "t" sound, *kŭkŭ > tŭtŭ*. They indicate that it is "apparently a new word as it has not been noted in legends and chants." (Honolulu: University of Hawaii Press, 1986), 177.

audiences and selected a familiar cultural touchstone, the jeremiad, and core, shared values embodied in the American dream and Christianity. He framed it all in careful arguments that were both personal (*ethos*) and logical (*logos*). In so doing, he stamped his unique rhetorical imprint on American public-speaking conventions, reinscribing old materials to chart a new and different trajectory for race in the twenty-first century.

BARACK IN THE DIRTY, DIRTY SOUTH

Alice Randall

Call it Dixie, the dirty, dirty South, the Red State Empire, or home, The Speech sounds different down here.

It sounds like breaking ties with the Moses Generation. And it sounds like a lie. Or maybe a wish. It sounds like something you want to be true, but isn't. It sounds like something that will never be true. It sounds like a new kind of sermon. It sounds like hope. It sounds like a definition, followed by a quotation, by a history lesson, winding down with a grown-up bedtime story. It sounds like something that should end not with the word "Amen," but with the words "Don't make me out to be no liar, now."

I write from Nashville, Tennessee. I am situated in the center of a blue island in a red state. Davidson, the county in which Nashville is located, went overwhelmingly for Obama. Tennessee went overwhelmingly for McCain.

I first heard The Speech on a car radio. And so it came to me initially as words in air. It came to me as songs often come to me, as disembodied sound that reaches the body with a kind of anonymity that entices one to believe that the voice one hears is one's own.

* * *

Obama ends his speech with a very interesting story, about a young white girl and an older black man. It's a simple story framed in complexity.

There is a young, twenty-three-year-old white woman named Ashley Baia who organized for our campaign in Florence, South Carolina. She had been working to organize a mostly African American community since the beginning of this campaign, and one day she was at a roundtable discussion where everyone went around telling their story and why they were there.

And Ashley said that when she was nine years old, her mother got cancer. And because she had to miss days of work, she was let go and lost her health care. They had to file for bankruptcy, and that's when Ashley decided that she had to do something to help her mom.

She knew that food was one of their most expensive costs, and so Ashley convinced her mother that what she really liked and really wanted to eat more than anything else was mustard and relish sandwiches. Because that was the cheapest way to eat.

She did this for a year, until her mom got better, and she told everyone at the roundtable that the reason she joined our campaign was so that she could help the millions of other children in the country who want and need to help their parents too.

Now Ashley might have made a different choice. Perhaps somebody told her along the way that the source of her mother's problems were blacks who were on welfare and too lazy to work, or Hispanics who were coming into the country illegally. But she didn't. She sought out allies in her fight against injustice.

Anyway, Ashley finishes her story and then goes around the room and asks everyone else why they're supporting the campaign. They all have different stories and reasons. Many bring up a specific issue. And finally they come to this elderly black man who's been sitting there quietly the entire time. And Ashley asks him why he's there. And he does not bring up a specific issue. He does not say health care or the economy. He does not say education or the war. He does not say that he was there because of Barack Obama. He simply says to everyone in the room, "I am here because of Ashley."

What are we to make of Ashley Baia, dubbed "sandwich girl" by the *Pittsburgh Post-Gazette*? How do we feel about the girl who ate mustard and relish sandwiches to help her sick mother have less to worry about? Is it important that she lied? Did she lie? Or did she let her words shape reality and then make it the truth? Did she come to like mustard and relish sandwiches? Did she get away with it? Did her mother believe her story? Did she lessen her mother's burden?

All we know for sure is that Ashley shared her story of eating a year of mustard and relish sandwiches, and how it led to her wanting to help other children help their sick mothers being the reason she was supporting Obama. And Barack Obama shared it with the nation on two momentous occasions: Dr. Martin Luther King Jr.'s birthday, in January 2008 and March 18 in Philadelphia at the Constitution Center during The Speech. In both places, on both occasions, the story reached the same climax:

It ended with an old black man saying, "I'm here because of Ashley."

There are many useful ways to look at this moment, this alliance between a young white woman and an older black man. Ironically, given the speech's call for an end to racial divisiveness, down here, in Nashville, I have encountered a racial divide when talking to people about the speech. In my experience, black people tend to like the story at the end of the speech a lot less than white people. Which is fine—even in a post-racial America. A post-racial America will not mean "no racial difference." It will mean that racial differences are framed by appropriate neutrality and/or with appreciation for the culture, in the most profound sense, out of which the difference arises.

And some black people I have talked to, particularly younger ones, like the Ashley story fine. I, who am approaching the half-century mark, who was born Negro and liberated into blackness as a girl in the sixties, have thought myself into loving the Ashley story. I especially like the way Obama slides into it:

> There is one story in particular that I'd like to leave you with to-day—a story I told when I had the great honor of speaking on Dr. King's birthday at his home church, Ebenezer Baptist, in Atlanta.

By publicly remembering this earlier speech he gave in Atlanta, Obama signals his connection to his own history. When he describes the great honor of speaking on Dr. King's birthday at his home church, he pronounces his connection to the civil rights era—then he tells the story of Ashley again. It brings to my mind Barack's own young mother, Ann Dunham, and an adult Barack. I hear, embedded in the Ashley story, a claim that Barack Obama is brought to the table of his candidacy by that young woman's optimism, industry, and intelligence. I see Ann standing behind Ashley.

"Your dreams do not have to come at the expense of my dreams." I can imagine this as a shared knowledge between Barack and his mother as they tried to grow up together and succeeded. After Barack, she went to college. After being named Barack and being bounced around the globe, he became president of the *Harvard Law Review* and married a dream come true of a woman. "Your dreams do not have to come at the expense of my dreams."

This is the great coda; this is the extraordinary addition, the genius of The Speech. King said, and these are some of the most famous words in America's history, "I have a dream." On March 18, 2008, Barack Obama addressed the fear and the anxiety that King's dream raised. And he addressed the frustrations of having that dream deferred. He took several thousand words to do it, but it all boiled down to—my dreams don't have to come true at the expense of yours.

If we are reasonable. If we are articulate. If we let go of old injuries. If we work hard. If we master knowledge. Dreams can go real.

I have wondered what the old man's name was. I have wondered why he wasn't called by it. The first time I heard the speech, it troubled me that the old man didn't have a name, as it had troubled me many years before as I began to write *The Wind Done Gone* that Margaret Mitchell hadn't given Mammy a name. Then I let myself hear the story with my father's ears, with the ears of an old dead black man, a man from the Moses era, a man who had lived in Selma when most black people in Dallas County, Alabama, hadn't been able to vote. Listening with George Randall's ears, what I heard loudest was that the man, the black man, was calling the young white woman by her first name—out loud in public and without fear. Out loud in public and without fear, the old man was claiming a cross-racial political connection, and he was being called a man. For my green-eyed black father, who had lived in Selma and hadn't been able to call out loud his own white grandfather's name, the Ashley story sounded like something he hadn't lived to see but had hoped could be so.

After March 2008, I read "A More Perfect Union" many, many times, and I watched the speech many times. In October, there was a day when the speech changed. Another frame, a thin line of peculiar irony, was inset around the Ashley story. A McCain intern, also named Ashley, alleged that she had been robbed and mutilated. By Election Day, there were two Ashleys in The Speech: one in the spoken narrative, one in the evolving historical moment into which the speech was being replayed and replayed, Obama volunteer Ashley and McCain intern Ashley.

Both Ashleys had a black man in their story. Obama's Ashley

had an old black man who attended a political meeting, a modest man, respectful of youth. McCain's Ashley had a young black man—a robber who carved a letter "B" (backward) into her cheek. Senator Obama's Ashley was all about alliances and the present. Senator McCain's Ashley was all about enemies and enmity, paranoia and the past. One Ashley was reaching for the future by helping place a black man in the White House; one Ashley was stuck in the past fantasizing about being a black man's victim.

Martin Luther King's name was spoken only one time in the speech. Obama called another preacher's name nine times. That preacher was the Reverend Jeremiah Wright. Reverend Wright reminds me of Jonathan Edwards. Perhaps you don't remember or know Jonathan Edwards. He entered Yale University at the age of thirteen in 1716. He died in 1758 while serving as president of what would become Princeton University, Michelle Obama's alma mater. Between 1716 and 1758, he wrote what Yale (most of his papers were given by his family to that university and are housed there in the Beinecke Library) estimates to be near to a one hundred thousand very-hard-to-read (Edwards had particularly poor handwriting) pages. He is acclaimed on Yale Web pages dedicated to Edwards as "the most influential religious thinker in American history."

Jonathan Edwards was a genius of the jeremiad. The *Oxford English Dictionary* gives this definition of the term: "a lamentation; a writing or speech in a strain of grief or distress; a doleful complaint, a complaining tirade; a lugubrious effusion." I first encountered the word in the late seventies in Alan Heimert's classroom, when I was an undergraduate at Harvard and Heimert was the feared master of Eliot House, a respected professor of English and American studies, and an authority on all things Puritan.

Heimert was a disciple of Perry Miller. Miller, who was born in 1905 and died in 1963, is considered by many, and certainly by

Heimert, to be the greatest thinker on the Puritans the world has produced. Miller called the jeremiad America's first distinctive literary genre.

Here's an excerpt from a classic, my favorite and Edwards's most widely known jeremiad, the sermon "Sinners in the Hands of an Angry God":

> The bow of God's wrath is bent, and the arrow made ready on the string, and justice bends the arrow at your heart, and strains the bow, and it is nothing but the mere pleasure of God, and that of an angry God, without any promise or obligation at all, that keeps the arrow one moment from being made drunk with your blood . . . How many is it likely will remember this discourse in hell? And it would be a wonder, if some that are now present should not be in hell in a very short time, even before this year is out. And it would be no wonder if some persons, that now sit here, in some seats of this meeting-house, in health, quiet and secure, should be there before tomorrow morning.

"Drunk with your blood," these words spoken by the great Puritan divine Jonathan Edwards on July 8, 1741, at Enfield, Connecticut, are radical words. For over a quarter century, I have understood these lines to be the words of a man willing to risk his soul to save souls. Stating the exaggerated case is a very old habit of American preachers. Miller, according to Heimert, was particularly focused on the idea of the Puritans as radical saints intent on building a city on a hill, a new Jerusalem, where true good was everywhere evident.

According to Miller, the Puritans vented their rage at the difficulties of achieving such a utopia in an "unending monotonous wail." They would take up "some verse of Isaiah or Jeremiah" (Reverend Wright could not have been more appropriately or presciently named), "set up the doctrine that God avenges the iniquities of a chosen people," then bring "the list of iniquities up to date by inserting the new and still more depraved practices an ingenious people kept on devising. I suppose in the whole literature of the world including the satirists of ancient Rome, there is hardly such another uninhibited and unrelenting documentation of a people's descent into corruption."

Edwards was cast out of his congregation for stating and overstating the exaggerated case (among other sins), and yet, this man who spoke lovingly of weapons "drunk with your blood," is still widely, and I think rightly, revered. To date, Yale has published seventy-three volumes of his work—and more are forthcoming. And it is useful to remember Jonathan Edwards when we think on Reverend Wright. Syllable and sound, the man Barack Obama referred to as his "former pastor" in "A More Perfect Union" was working, albeit on the fringes, within a long-established tradition with lily-white roots going back to the second generation of Puritans. According to Miller, an inherent weakness of the jeremiad is that it "could make sense out of existence as long as adversity was to be overcome, but in the moment of victory it was confused."*

Obama is not confused in the moment of victory. At the center of The Speech are three words separating then from now: *Not this time.* These three words are Obama's victory. *Not this time.* Repeating this phrase twice and repeating the phrase *This time* six times, Obama begins to break with the past. With these words, Obama moves beyond the jeremiad. Beyond the version fueled by fear, Edwards's, and beyond the version fueled by anger, Wright's. He moves toward an altogether different engine of discourse, the power of reason, the power of education, the power of affiliation, the lure of an excellent future here on earth, the attraction of a time when everything, to use some old-school black slang, is copacetic.

---

* Donna Campbell, a professor at Washington State University, has created an excellent Web site on the jeremiad that I used to brush up on what Heimert taught me.

Everything has not always been copacetic:

There will be days when the water seems wide and the journey too far, but in those moments, we must remember that throughout our history, there has been a running thread of ideals that have guided our travels and pushed us forward, even when they're just beyond our reach, liberty in the face of tyranny, opportunity where there was none and hope over the most crushing despair. Those ideals and values beckon us still and when we have our doubts and our fears, just like Joshua did, when the road looks too long and it seems like we may lose our way, remember what these people did on that bridge.*

On March 4, 2007, my husband, David Ewing, and I were a part of the crowd that walked across the Edmund Pettus Bridge with Barack Obama. Hillary and Bill Clinton were there too, but we, like most, were walking with Barack. Earlier in the day, I had sat in one of the Brown Chapel pews and heard him talk a lot about the Moses generation and the Joshua generation:

So I just want to talk a little about Moses and Aaron and Joshua, because we are in the presence today of a lot of Moseses. We're in the presence today of giants whose shoulders we stand on, people who battled, not just on behalf of African Americans but on behalf of all of America; that battled for America's soul, that shed blood, that endured taunts and . . . torment and in some cases gave the full measure of their devotion . . .

I'm here because somebody marched . . . I stand on the shoulders of giants. I thank the Moses generation; but we've got to remember, now, that Joshua still had a job to do. As great as

---

* Senator Barack Obama, "Selma Voting Rights March Commemoration," Selma, Alabama, March 4, 2007.

Moses was, despite all that he did, leading a people out of bondage, he didn't cross over the river to see the Promised Land. God told him your job is done . . . We're going to leave it to the Joshua generation to make sure it happens.

I'm here because somebody marched. The Barack Obama making this claim has a complex relationship with the Barack Obama who tells us the story of Ashley and the old black man who came because of her. Some of the more cynical among us will say the change was the venue, that in Selma, Obama was playing to the local black stage and in Philadelphia he was playing to the national stage. I see it differently. I think that somewhere between Selma and Philadelphia, Barack Obama decided to rewrite Faulkner.

Midway through The Speech, Obama calls out the name of the great man of Southern letters: "As William Faulkner once wrote, 'The past isn't dead and buried. In fact, it isn't even past.'" Some say Obama is misquoting Faulkner; I say he has transformed him. This is the original Faulkner: "The past is not dead. It's not even past." These lines of Faulkner, remixed by Obama, and placed inside a speech that breaks with Jonathan Edwards, breaks with Wright, breaks with the Moses generation, are a sublime act of subversion. Everything about the speech says the past is dead. The good past and the bad past. It may or may not be buried, but it is past. In the South, that is a very radical message.

My friend Houston Baker is a brilliant man. He was my friend before he was my colleague on the faculty of Vanderbilt University. And before he was my friend, he was a student of my daughter's great-grandfather Arna Bontemps. Baker published the book, *Betrayal: How Black Intellectuals Have Abandoned the Ideal of the Civil Rights Era.* Baker voted for Obama, but he does not like The Speech. He published a response to it on Salon.com:

Charged at the beginning of a now fateful weekend with being a congregant and faithful supporter of the views of Rev. Jeremiah Wright of Chicago's Trinity United Church, Sen. Barack Obama grabbed his pastor's lapels and pushed him under the bus . . . Sen. Obama's "race speech" at the National Constitution Center, draped in American flags, was reminiscent of the Parthenon concluding scene of Robert Altman's "Nashville" . . . [Wright] has washed the tire tracks off. He shrewdly has magnetically and materialistically affixed himself (like a groomed Greyhound) to the broadside of the Obama bus.

Baker offers us a haunting and surreal image of Reverend Wright plastered to the side of a bus. His piece performs the agony of the break with the recent past. In the piece, the Moses generation has been betrayed. Baker gives a tailored wail, an appropriate and necessary wail, a loud and emotional wail, for all that is lost. *And* then he gives a shout toward all that becomes grotesque, for all that becomes distorted, if we do not face the bloody moment of separation.

Wailing, whining, and singing the blues got harder after The Speech. I only miss the wailing and the singing the blues. It's hard to mourn the heroes of the Moses generation without our sobs.

* * *

When our days become dreary with low hovering clouds of despair, and when our nights become darker than a thousand midnights, let us remember that there is a creative force in this universe, working to pull down the gigantic mountains of evil, a power that is able to make a way out of no way and transform dark yesterdays into bright tomorrows. Let us realize the arc of the moral universe is long but it bends toward justice.

—DR. MARTIN LUTHER KING JR., "Where Do We Go from Here?," Atlanta, Georgia, August 16, 1967

Martin Luther King, who would be assassinated, dared to frame the experience of the crisis period, the Moses period, which included Bloody Sunday in Selma and the Birmingham church bombings, in the territory of justice. If King had the audacity of hope to frame that period in an arc of history bending toward justice, Obama is demanding that we, who are not in the crisis, but who wish to honor the crisis, locate ourselves in that rational geometry, the curve toward justice King claimed as inevitable.

There is often in King's sermons a tone of wizened sorrow. "And I've seen the promised land. I may not get there with you." This triumphant statement is bone-shivering sad. King is not afraid, but we are afraid for him. His tone conveys the sound of present danger. And though he is measured, he is always urgent. His voice at times carries in it the sound of a sob that has been courageously swallowed.

With genius, Barack Obama mitigates his radical message that we must let the past be past with a tone of felt cool. Throughout the thirty-eight minutes it takes him to give The Speech, his tone is part Sam Cooke and part Mister Rogers. Sam Cooke didn't scream or plead or beg. Sam Cooke was smooth. He dressed in an understated, "sharp" style that appealed to black and white audiences. Bob Dylan asked a lot of questions in "Blowin' in the Wind." Sam Cooke answered them.

"A Change Is Gonna Come," a song Cooke wrote in 1963, was reinvented during the course of the Obama campaign. Released after Cooke's death, the song, in 1964, was a promise. By the time Obama was voted president-elect, the song stood as a promise fulfilled.

Obama has moved beyond all the thundering denunciations of all the backsliding people and claimed the capacity to overwrite history, with a new aesthetic of cool. Part of the cool is a Mister Rogers kind of cool. I have only recently developed an appreciation for Mister Rogers. When I was a child and I spent the night at the house of a friend who wanted to watch *Mister Rogers*, I would be bored to the point of fear. In 1968 or 1969, when I was a kid watching him for the first time, I thought Mister Rogers was crazy-making dull and just plain too reasonable.

When I told my daughter, a junior in college, that I was perplexed by the fact that Barack Obama, on occasion (and some of these occasions occurred when I was watching his race speech over and over again on YouTube), reminded me of Mister Rogers, she asked me if I had read the Tom Junod piece on Rogers and his Emmy. I told her I had not. She pulled it up on the Internet and read me the relevant passage, starting with a direct quote from the sweater wearer himself as he accepted his award at the ceremony in 1997: "'All of us have special ones who have loved us into being. Would you just take, along with me, ten seconds to think of the people who have helped you become who you are. Ten seconds of silence.' And then he lifted his wrist, looked at the audience, looked at his watch, and said, 'I'll watch the time.'" There was, at first, a small whoop from the crowd, a giddy, strangled hiccup of laughter, as people realized that he wasn't kidding, that Mister Rogers was not some convenient eunuch, but rather a man, an authority figure who actually expected them to do what he asked. And so they did. One second, two seconds, seven seconds—and now the jaws clenched, and the bosoms heaved, and the mascara ran, and the tears fell upon the beglittered gathering like rain leaking down a crystal chandelier. And Mister Rogers finally looked up from his watch and said softly, "May God be with you," to all his vanquished children.

"I'll watch the time." That phrase has something to do with finding a way to companion someone on a journey you can't go on with them, with finding a way to assist. In The Speech, Obama explicitly invites us to assist one another in our separate, sometimes dissimilar, journeys: "Let us be our brother's keeper, Scripture tells us. Let us be our sister's keeper. Let us find that common stake we all have in one another, and let our politics reflect that spirit as well."

Through the magic of YouTube, I've watched Mister Rogers receive his Emmy. His acceptance speech interestingly parallels The Speech. Both men maturely accept the significance of all of those who, as Mister Rogers puts it, "helped you become who you are." And each man underscores the importance of gratitude while also underscoring the importance of not confusing the identity of our mentors with our own identity.

We are not the people who helped us become who we are; we are the people who we became.

When I was a little girl, the one making the speeches about race was my daddy, George Stanley Randall, a black man who longed for "hair like Jesus, kinky as a lamb." He hated the fact that his hair was a little "too white." My father was a racist. When I was a little girl, he told me the only question he would ask if I decided to date a white boy was whether he should shoot me or the boy first. To be fair, the day I told him I was dating a white boy, the only thing he could say was "I can't help but love who you love." I wrote those words—"We are not the people who helped us become who we are: we are the people who we became"—on the day I voted for Barack Obama to be the forty-fourth president of the United States, on a day my father could not have imagined.

The meanest thing I ever saw my father do in my whole life happened in Washington, D.C., during one of the few times he came to visit me there, in this environment where he was completely a fish out of water, where he said, as were walking down the street and we were approached by a white panhandler, a man I think he gave twenty dollars, "If I was born white like you, I would have been president of the United States."

My father, who was born near Selma in 1929, how would he have heard The Speech? I believe he would have heard the aftermath of silence.

"Speak up, son. You're not down South." Those words, my father so very often repeated to me. They are words he heard on his first trip north. He traveled at about the age of thirteen from Selma to Detroit by way of New York. He was hungry on a sidewalk. He had a few quarters in his pocket. He was a few feet away from a hot dog vendor. He took his coins into his hands, but the words came out of his mouth in stammers and mumbles; then the hot dog vendor, a man he did not know, a man he had never seen and would never see again, a man whose words would ring in my daddy's mind and on into my ears, said, "Speak up, son. You're not down South." Emboldened with his words, I have made a life as a writer in which I have tried to do the other thing my father frequently asked me to do: "Speak for those who cannot speak for themselves."

But before the speaking up, there was silence. The only story my daddy ever told me about his Alabama boyhood was a story about walking with his family to his white neighbor's house, or perhaps it was to a country store, to hear Joe Louis fight Jim J. Braddock for the heavyweight championship of the world. The year was 1937. My father's family gathered in the back of the little crowd knotted around the radio full of hope, and fear, full of silence learned. When Louis won, my father's family did not show emotion. They hung their heads and frowned just a little bit. Someone looking at them could think that these good colored folk knew that Joe Louis should not have beat that white fellow, that Joe Louis would surely and appropriately lose the next matchup. Decades later in Detroit, in Washington, D.C., in Cambridge, Massachusetts, in Nashville, when Daddy would tell me the story wearing a silk suit or a mohair golf sweater, when I would hear it tumbling through my head competing with words from professors from Harvard and Howard and Yale and Hampton and Tennessee State University, he would talk about June

22, 1937, and the walk in the darkness toward his home, fear mingling in the air with excitation. They could feel danger and knew to be silent. Low as my daddy's family hung their heads, even the child of eight that he was then could see and feel that these white neighbors were mighty mad that Louis had won. The stars were shining bright above the Alabama night, shining like their celebrating had already begun, like God's own fireworks. Then the clouds rolled in wrapped in the cloak of God's own darkness, and somebody in my daddy's family began to hoot and holler, "Joe Louis won, Joe Louis won!" My daddy and his daddy added their voices to the cry. They would be silent no longer, danger or not.

We circle back to my beginning, the end of Obama's speech. The story about Ashley and the old black man. "I came because of Ashley." This is the end of the silence. "Speak up, son. You're not down South." And what are we to do if we stay South? If we live in a state where nine of ten white men voted for John McCain? I teach at Vanderbilt University. Two of my colleagues published articles in response to Obama's speech that struck me as particularly interesting and, in some sense, as peculiarly Southern.

We've already taken a look at Houston Baker's. Let's take a moment to look at Volney Gay's.

Gay is the chairman of the Religious Studies Department and the director of the university's Center for the Study of Religion and Culture. He's also a white male psychotherapist. This is how his *Tennessean* op-ed begins:

In his celebrated speech in Philadelphia on March 18, Barack Obama talked about the struggle to fulfill the promises made explicit in the Declaration of Independence and presumed in the Constitution.

Less noted were his comments about the effects of systematic racism:

"Legalized discrimination—where blacks were prevented, often through violence, from owning property, or loans were not granted to African-American business owners, or black homeowners could not access FHA mortgages, or blacks were excluded from unions, or the police force, or fire departments—meant that black families could not amass any meaningful wealth to bequeath to future generations. That history helps explain the wealth and income gap between black and white, and the concentrated pockets of poverty that persist into many of today's urban and rural communities."

Gay concludes, "Systematic racism is woven into American history and still shapes us today. It takes multiple efforts and multiple generations to undo the effects of these massive crimes." I like the phrase "massive crimes." It emphasizes both the significance of certain race-based wrongs and the understanding that the wrongs are transgressive.

In The Speech, Obama labels "a view that sees white racism as endemic" as a distorted view. "Endemic" is arguably the single-most important word in The Speech. The *OED* defines "endemic" as constantly or regularly found among a (specified) people, or in a (specified) country. It goes on to further note that when used in relation to a disease, "endemic" denotes "prevalent in a certain country, and due to permanent local causes." Is racism endemic to America or a massive series of crimes that occurred in America? At its core, The Speech asserts that racism is not endemic to America.

"Massive crimes" tied to a past that can be undone are an opposite of "permanent local causes."

In the South, The Speech sounds different. Even after Gay praises it, he also praises, in a measured tone that resonates with the tone of cool that pervades The Speech, "multiple efforts and multiple generations" working in an effort "to undo the effects of these massive crimes."

The last time I checked, 5,369,141 people—five million, three hundred sixty-nine thousand, one hundred forty-one people—had viewed Barack Obama's speech on race on YouTube. As I have watched The Speech intimately framed on the screen of the little white MacBook where I write my novels, e-mail my daughter, and Google the world, I have been aware of watching the speech in cyberspace rather than in the South. In cyberspace, Obama is always giving the speech now. In cyberspace, my community is very, very large. I can quickly see posts that echo my own thoughts and quickly see posts I could not have imagined, but it all remains a virtual, not visceral, reality. In cyberspace, racism is rampant but never endemic. Cyberspace belongs to the Joshua generation.

The speech asking black Americans to get past their anger and fear and asking white Americans to get past their fear and anger was an invitation to have a fundamentally different, fundamentally less passionate, and fundamentally more powerful discussion of race.

"Don't make me out to be no liar, now." There was the speech. And then there was what we would do with it. A leader's prophecy, it called on the led to make it real. And we did.

With a definition, followed by a quotation, by a history lesson, winding down with a grown-up bedtime story, Senator Obama managed to ward off the bogeyman of irrational racial passions—be they a sense of pervasive injustice or a sense of being burdened by less competent or violent others.

The moment before the speech was different from the moment

after. Obama was able to claim out loud a wish for how things were between the races in America, and many people found his wish to be magnetic. Subtly he pulled us beyond how things are, to how things might be. Presenting his wish as a reality, presenting our future as our present, he revealed a future so compelling that many folks reached out to snatch it into our now.

For me, the ultimate brilliance of Obama's "A More Perfect Union" was how the speech itself altered political reality—what was a wish when the speech began was a reality when it came to a close. And many added their voice to the chorus saying, "Not this time."

And so the truth as he knows it, that we have moved beyond race, moved beyond distracting public passions, starts to become a reality. This is a victory for all the thoughtful, hardworking people willing to disagree without being disagreeable, able to renovate and complete our original errand into the wilderness.

At the end of the dirty South gem of a movie *Hustle and Flow*, the pimp played by Terrence Howard is asked a question he doesn't want to answer. He deflects the question by telling a story about the little black baby girl he will raise as his daughter. "One day she's gonna dream big the way kids do, you know, and she's gonna come to me and ask me, when she grow up can she become president. Now I know that little girl got a ho for a mama and a trick for a daddy and nobody even know where he at, and I tell you something, I'm gonna look her right in the eye and I'm gonna lie 'cause sometimes that's what you gotta do." In the dirty, dirty South, our new president's speech on race sounds like something akin to alchemy, something that could turn that lie into the truth.

THE END

MUTT ON CP TIME,
DISCIPLINE OF MALCOLM

PART III

Derrick Z. Jackson

Though never to be mistaken for Richard Pryor, Barack Obama disarmed the race question by joining studied sincerity to soft, sly humor. He granted white America a critical measure of amnesty from the past while asking African Americans to drop the disbelief that white people could elect a soul brother as the soul of America.

In August 2007, Obama was about twenty minutes late for an appearance before three thousand people at the National Association of Black Journalists convention in Las Vegas. He started off by saying, "I want to apologize for being a little bit late. But you guys keep asking whether I am black enough." He stopped to let a roll of chuckles become a roar of laughter. "So I figured I'd stroll in about ten minutes after deadline."

After more laughter, he said, knowingly, "I've been holding that in my pocket for a while."

Two months later, I asked Obama by cell phone what humor got him through the "black enough" questions. He answered, "The first time somebody asked the question in the newspapers about whether I'm black enough, my barber helpfully pointed out, 'Compared to who?' As he pointed out, it's not like I'm running against Malcolm X."

A year later, Obama stood before reporters in a Chicago ballroom at his first press conference as president-elect. He was asked about the White House dog he had promised his daughters. His face deadpanned all the seriousness of discussing the economic crisis.

"With respect to the dog, this is a major issue," Obama said. ". . . We have two criteria that have to be reconciled. One is that Malia is allergic, so it has to be hypoallergenic. There are a number of breeds that are hypoallergenic. On the other hand, our preference would be to get a shelter dog. But obviously, a lot of shelter dogs are mutts, like me."

The mutt on colored people's time still became president. Behind the drollness was in fact the discipline of a Malcolm X. I observed in a *Boston Globe* column that Obama had to be serious without being angry. He had to relate without being a clown. He had to be the soul for the nation without being a singer or preacher. He had to be cool without being cold and, above all, could never lose his cool.

Obama wore Jackie Robinson's and Hank Aaron's mask of calm. He had the focus of the Underground Railroad's Harriet Tubman, who boasted of her nineteen journeys that freed over three hundred slaves, "I never ran my train off the track, and I never lost a passenger."

The Reverend Jeremiah Wright affair did not throw him off track because his "A More Perfect Union" speech was a taut homage to Malcolm and Dr. Martin Luther King Jr., surviving the most slippery tightrope in the American psyche: telling both black and white Americans that they will never understand each other without the context of the racist past and get nowhere by forever resenting it.

My mentor and former *Newsday* columnist Les Payne likens Obama, because of his biracial birth and unconventional upbringing, to an ambassador from the multicultural America that everyone talks about but invariably fights against. The ambassador successfully negotiated a truce.

Three weeks after the speech in April 2008, I interviewed Obama in Philadelphia. He was coming within striking distance of Hillary Clinton in Pennsylvania primary polls, though he would eventually lose. I asked him how much the speech had helped. He said all he knew was that it had been "heartfelt." He added, "I think that people always appreciate those moments where a politician's not talking in sound bites but trying to speak honestly about a question. So I don't know what the political effect of it may be, but I know that as I've been traveling around in Pennsylvania, what people are much more focused on is high gas prices and jobs leaving and the home foreclosure crisis."

I asked him if it was a double standard for him to be forced to address the issue of race. He said, "I'm not sure it's a double standard. My pastor said some very offensive things for a broad cross section of the American people, and I think any candidate for president would have had to deal with that at some level . . . I think that what people want is common sense." He continued,

> They don't appreciate whether it's coming from my former pastor or from talk radio hosts sensationalizing the issue, overstating the issue, using it for political purposes . . . There are obviously some wounds that have to be healed, and there's some concrete issues that have to be dealt with in terms of disparities in health care or income or joblessness, legacies of the past. So we don't want to paper those issues over . . . My speech tried to avoid some of the simplicities that somehow widen division instead of bringing people together.

Six days after the Pennsylvania primary, Wright simplified things for good. He appeared before the National Press Club and reprised "God damn America" and his 9/11 comments with "You cannot do terrorism on other people and not expect it to come back to you." The scorned mentor's sabotage was personal for Obama, coming a week before the May 6 North Carolina and Indiana primaries, and Obama's unfavorable ratings among independents climbed from 27 percent to 36 percent in a *USA Today*/Gallup Poll.

In a final decisive act, Obama told reporters that Wright's appearance was "a show of disrespect to me." He denounced Wright's comments as a "divisive," "destructive" "bunch of rants" that "give comfort to those who prey on hate." Emphatically calling Wright his "former pastor," he said, "There's been great damage . . . I do not see the relationship being the same after this."

Voters must have seen this as a critical degree of separation. A week later, Obama lost Indiana, but only by two percentage points. He captured a stunningly huge fourteen-point victory in North Carolina. The narrow loss coupled with the big win widened Obama's lead in delegates. And no one was happier than Harvey Gantt, the former mayor of Charlotte, North Carolina, who had lost his U.S. Senate challenges to Jesse Helms in 1990 and 1996. The tight 1990 race had been infamous for Helms's ad showing white hands crushing a job rejection letter received because of so-called racial quotas.

Gantt had worried that Wright was having the same effect, saying about 1990, "Every time I gave a great speech about this vision we had down the road and the world we were going to have by the year 2000 in education, the environment, how we're going to deal with health care, I'd take the Q&A from the audience, and it always went, 'What did you think of the ad?'" Instead, the cutting off of Wright cut a clean path. "I think it turned out that the Reverend Wright thing, I think people are getting away from it," Gantt told me in an interview. "One of the most satisfying things about this election is that he was able to get back on message. I believe that the gas-tax issue [Clinton and Republican John McCain supported a gas-tax holiday, while Obama did not] allowed Obama to get back to talking about the big picture, showing how silly some of the stuff was out there and that he was not always going to tell people what they wanted to hear. There was lots of admiration in the barbershops for that."

And respect well beyond the barbershops. Just before those primaries, I went to an Obama speech in Hickory, a small city built on furniture and textiles and located in Catawba County, which had twice voted for George W. Bush by two-to-one margins. Bush had won North Carolina in 2004 with 56 percent of the vote. But the economy had fallen hard there, and the city had lost thirteen thousand jobs, most of them during the Bush years. Hickory mayor Rudy Wright, a registered Republican; Councilwomen Sally Fox and Jill Patton; and Tommy Shores, a leather chair manufacturer, all said the Wright controversy was almost off the radar compared with jobs and gasoline headed to four dollars a gallon.

They all expected that Obama would cut into conservative margins in a general election (Obama did win North Carolina in November). Patton, chief operating officer of a cycling-sock company, said that a Republican friend who had seen all the Republican presidents since Nixon, had attended Obama's speech and remarked "how eloquent Obama was." What I heard in Hickory I heard in suburban Grand Rapids, Michigan, from Scott Laskey, a forty-two-year-old regional manager for a compressed-gas company. Talking in between frames, Laskey and his six bowling-league buddies said Wright was a nonfactor. Referring to the Iraq War and the economy, Laskey said, "What was I thinking? How many times do I have to be hit over the head?"

Fellow bowler Gerry Wojtaszek, forty-nine, a district manager for a furniture and appliance rental center, had voted for Bush in both 2000 and 2004. He said he was voting for Obama. "The first time, I felt that the economy would step up under him," Wojtaszek said of Bush. "The second time, I was supportive of the war. But the economy's a hell in a handbasket. The war is still going on. I thought about voting for McCain on experience, but with all the time he's been in office, what has he done?"

In Green Bay, Wisconsin, one of the most heavily contested battleground cities in the nation in 2004, machinist Mark Muchowski, fifty-four, a Bush voter, said that the "Wright Effect" had had no effect on his switching parties to Obama. "You go back to anybody's life, their friends and the things they do. You can't control them. Nobody cared back when Kennedy was catting around." Ron Nikolai, a thirty-eight-year-old customer service representative, who had voted for Bush, said, "It was blown way out of proportion. How could Obama be held accountable for what his *former* pastor had to say? . . . I believe Barack Obama to be an honorable man."

This was the ultimate verdict: that "A More Perfect Union" had a credibility that discredited anyone who beat the dying horse. In a nationally televised debate in April, ABC News moderators George Stephanopoulos and Charles Gibson spent some sixteen hundred words' worth of time hammering Obama about Wright. Obama was asked more in one night about Wright than had been asked in prior presidential debates of all the Republican candidates about their support of, or sympathy toward, states' rights, apartheid, and Bob Jones University. Stephanopoulos's patronizing questioning of Obama's patriotism—"Do you think Reverend Wright loves America as much as you do?"—was broadly panned.

Clinton stopped beating up on Obama's place in the pews, and McCain, for the most part, did not try. In the North Carolina primary, McCain condemned a state Republican ad saying that Obama was "too extreme" because of Wright. McCain said, "There is no place for that kind of campaigning—and the American people don't want it." In the general election, McCain banned his ad staff from using Wright to assault Obama's character—though surrogates and running mate Sarah Palin occasionally talked about Wright.

In the final month of the campaign, as the polls increasingly signaled an Obama victory, the McCain campaign swerved briefly into "Willie Horton" territory. Instead of painting Obama as soft on crime as the senior George Bush had successfully done with Michael Dukakis by invoking the convicted Massachusetts murderer who had escaped while on furlough and committed armed robbery and rape, the McCain campaign insinuated that Obama was soft on patriotism. It tried to tar him with his thin associations with 1960s radical Bill

Ayers. In her most red-meat moment on the campaign trail, Palin told a crowd, regarding Obama, "I am just so fearful that this is not a man who sees America the way that you and I see America." Expanding on what she meant, she said, "Our opponent is someone who sees America as imperfect enough to pal around with terrorists who targeted their own country." At another event, in a variation on that rhetoric, Palin said that Obama "is someone who sees America, it seems, as being so imperfect, imperfect enough, that he's palling around with terrorists who would target their own country."

The red-meat moment was brief, but it was fiery enough to heat up a supporter in Florida to scream, "Kill him!" Another supporter screamed a racial epithet at an African American soundman in the press corps. It was not completely clear who the "Kill him!" remark was meant for. But the incident had the stench of when supporters of the segregationist former Alabama governor George Wallace, who ran for president in 1968, surrounded some black protesters at a Madison Square Garden event and screamed, "Kill 'em, kill 'em, kill 'em!"

Eleventh-hour innuendo came from other corners. Seeing that Virginia was threatening to go from red state to blue (which it did), McCain's brother Joe declared the suburbs of Virginia near Washington, D.C., to be "communist country." Even though Obama had volunteered in his memoir that he had used cocaine in his youth, McCain campaign cochairman Frank Keating, the former governor of Oklahoma, said, as if it were news, that Obama ought to tell Americans, "I've got to be honest with you. I was a guy of the street. I was way to the left. I used cocaine." And of course, there was the attempt to paint Obama as a socialist for his tax plan that would make the ultrarich pay more than they would under McCain's tax plan. In speeches in October, McCain was saying, "We don't need government spreading the wealth," while Palin was outright calling Obama "Barack the wealth spreader."

Americans did not rise to the red-bait in the days before Obama won the election 365 electoral votes to McCain's 173. It had been forty years since Richard Nixon's "law and order" campaign and twenty years since the Horton ad and eighteen years since the Helms ad against Gantt. Appeals to racial bias and right-wing notions of patriotism certainly work when people have too much time on their hands. But by the campaign's end, America was facing the worst economy since the Great Depression. Obama turned out to have been right when he told me in Philadelphia a few weeks after his speech on race that he thought that people appreciated honesty from a politician, and that voters were much more focused on the economy than on race. The political effect of his speech was that it established him as an honest broker on race.

To be sure, Obama did not win the white vote. He lost the white vote, 55 percent to 43 percent. He won the white vote outright in only sixteen states, according to the Joint Center of Political and Economic Studies, the nation's leading black political think tank. But he carried the day with a rainbow explosion, winning vast majorities of voters of color, young voters, and gay and lesbian voters, and 60 percent of moderate voters. In the process, the Obama campaign redefined patriotism, or at least unleashed an image of it never expressed in modern times.

The single-most memorable moment from election night in Chicago's Grant Park for me was not Obama's actual speech. It was before the speech, when the crowd of 125,000 people said the Pledge of Allegiance. In my fifty-three years, as I wrote for the *Boston Globe*, "I have never heard such a multicultural throng recite the pledge with such determined enunciation, expelling it from the heart in a treble soaring to the skies and a bass drumming through the soil to vibrate my feet. The treble and bass met in my spine, where 'liberty and justice for all' evoked neither clank of chains nor cackle of cruelty, but a warm tickle of Jeffersonian slave-owning irony: Justice cannot sleep forever."

Two weeks after the election, I interviewed University of

Washington political scientist Christopher Parker, who had measured an actual spike in feelings of patriotism among African Americans in Washington State. He also said it was true for him as a
ten-year U.S. Navy veteran. He told me about how his spine had also
tingled when he'd stood for the unfurling of a giant flag at midfield
and the playing of the national anthem at a Washington-UCLA foot-
ball game. "In the navy, we were conditioned to revere the flag, but
knowing what it often stood for, it was a tortured feeling," Parker said.
"I've often had a hard time saying the words. But as I watched the flag
being unfurled, time kind of slowed down. I thought of the race
speech, the Democratic National Convention, and the crowd in Den-
ver. I thought about him at Grant Park. I felt free to be proud, free not
to be angry. I can actually say the words. I'm thinking, 'Oh, I guess
it's OK to be an American now.'"

This was a long way from 1887, when Frederick Douglass said,
"I have no patriotism" for a nation that does "not recognize me as a
man."

Only time will tell how much Obama's "A More Perfect Union"
and his presidency will inspire the nation to recognize all people of
color as full citizens. One thing is certain. I interviewed Obama's
senior adviser, David Axelrod, six days before the inauguration. I
asked him if Obama would have been elected if he had faltered in
the least in that speech in Philadelphia.

Axelrod said, "Maybe not."

The thing Axelrod remembered most about the speech was
how Obama took direct charge of it when the looping video clips of
Wright's comments migrated from conservative cable shows to the
networks. A few days before the speech, Obama had to fly back from
Washington to Chicago for back-to-back interviews with the editorial boards of the *Chicago Tribune* and the *Chicago Sun-Times*.

Axelrod said that Obama "was in the Senate to one in the
morning, flew back to Chicago, and came to the headquarters. He
was supposed to brief for the editorial boards. Instead, he wrote a

statement [about Wright] out himself." He didn't like what the campaign had written about Reverend Wright. "He went off to the editorial boards, three hours of editorial boards of both papers. Did two or three cable shows on Reverend Wright and called [campaign manager David] and me at ten or eleven and said, 'I want to do this speech on race. I want to put this thing in its proper perspective.' He said, 'I think this is an important moment, and people may accept what I have to say or not, but it's an important moment in terms of dealing with the elephant in the room.'"

Obama wrote in the middle of the night for the two nights before the speech. At two A.M. on the day of the speech, Axelrod woke up to see that Obama had sent it to him on his BlackBerry. Axelrod read it and e-mailed Obama back to say, "This is why you should be president."

The speech was given in Philadelphia with all the trappings and gravitas of a presidential speech. It bore out what Obama's friend Marty Nesbitt had told him—as reported by *Newsweek*—to the disbelieving laughter of close friends: that the whole episode was a "blessing in disguise." Axelrod told me, "It was the first time in the campaign where he got a chance to speak to the nation on something of real significance under great pressure, and I think what people saw that day was what they came to see over the course of the rest of the campaign. And what I think they see now is a guy with extraordinary depth and leadership qualities, who's willing to step out and say things that need to be said. He looked like a president that day."

More important, with presidential gravitas, he gave the discussion of race a human element that no one could run from. Asked what he thought was the most difficult part of the speech, Axelrod said he thought it was the section in which Obama talked about his grandmother and her fear of "black men who passed her by on the street."

Axelrod said, "I think that was a very personal revelation . . . such a personal observation." It was so personal, essentially asking

Americans to take this personally, that Axelrod remembered seeing people of all colors choking up and tears running down the cheeks of Michelle Obama, Nesbitt, and Obama's close friend and adviser Valerie Jarrett during the speech.

"When it was over," Axelrod said, "we went into an anteroom, and everybody was in tears. All I remember is Barack saying, 'I think that was solid.'"

"A More Perfect Union" turned out to be as solid as the stone of the White House.

THE SPEECH

A MORE PERFECT UNION

Senator Barack Obama
Constitution Center
Philadelphia, Pennsylvania
Tuesday, March 18, 2008

We the people, in order to form a more perfect union."
Two hundred and twenty-one years ago, in a hall that still stands across the street, a group of men gathered and, with these simple words, launched America's improbable experiment in democracy. Farmers and scholars, statesmen and patriots, who had traveled across an ocean to escape tyranny and persecution, finally made real their declaration of independence at a Philadelphia convention that lasted through the spring of 1787.

The document they produced was eventually signed but ultimately unfinished. It was stained by this nation's original sin of slavery, a question that divided the colonies and brought the convention to a stalemate until the founders chose to allow the slave trade to continue for at least twenty more years, and to leave any final resolution to future generations.

Of course, the answer to the slavery question was already embedded within our Constitution—a Constitution that had at its very core the ideal of equal citizenship under the law; a Constitution that promised its people liberty, and justice, and a union that could be and should be perfected over time.

And yet words on a parchment would not be enough to deliver slaves from bondage, or provide men and women of every color and creed their full rights and obligations as citizens of the United

States. What would be needed were Americans in successive generations who were willing to do their part—through protests and struggle, on the streets and in the courts, through a civil war and civil disobedience and always at great risk—to narrow that gap between the promise of our ideals and the reality of their time.

This was one of the tasks we set forth at the beginning of this campaign—to continue the long march of those who came before us, a march for a more just, more equal, more free, more caring, and more prosperous America. I chose to run for the presidency at this moment in history because I believe deeply that we cannot solve the challenges of our time unless we solve them together, unless we perfect our union by understanding that we may have different stories, but we hold common hopes; that we may not look the same and we may not have come from the same place, but we all want to move in the same direction—towards a better future for our children and our grandchildren.

This belief comes from my unyielding faith in the decency and generosity of the American people. But it also comes from my own American story.

I am the son of a black man from Kenya and a white woman from Kansas. I was raised with the help of a white grandfather who survived a depression to serve in Patton's army during World War II and a white grandmother who worked on a bomber assembly line at Fort Leavenworth while he was overseas. I've gone to some of the best schools in America and lived in one of the world's poorest nations. I am married to a black American who carries within her the blood of slaves and slave owners—an inheritance we pass on to our two precious daughters. I have brothers, sisters, nieces, nephews, uncles, and cousins, of every race and every hue, scattered across three continents, and for as long as I live, I will never forget that in no other country on Earth is my story even possible.

It's a story that hasn't made me the most conventional candidate. But it is a story that has seared into my genetic makeup the idea that this nation is more than the sum of its parts—that out of many, we are truly one.

Throughout the first year of this campaign, against all predictions to the contrary, we saw how hungry the American people were for this message of unity. Despite the temptation to view my candidacy through a purely racial lens, we won commanding victories in states with some of the whitest populations in the country. In South Carolina, where the Confederate flag still flies, we built a powerful coalition of African Americans and white Americans.

This is not to say that race has not been an issue in the campaign. At various stages in the campaign, some commentators have deemed me either "too black" or "not black enough." We saw racial tensions bubble to the surface during the week before the South Carolina primary. The press has scoured every exit poll for the latest evidence of racial polarization, not just in terms of white and black, but black and brown as well.

And yet, it has only been in the last couple of weeks that the discussion of race in this campaign has taken a particularly divisive turn.

On one end of the spectrum, we've heard the implication that my candidacy is somehow an exercise in affirmative action, that it's based solely on the desire of wide-eyed liberals to purchase racial reconciliation on the cheap. On the other end, we've heard my former pastor, Reverend Jeremiah Wright, use incendiary language to express views that have the potential not only to widen the racial divide, but views that denigrate both the greatness and the goodness of our nation, that rightly offend white and black alike.

I have already condemned, in unequivocal terms, the statements of Reverend Wright that have caused such controversy. For some, nagging questions remain. Did I know him to be an occasionally fierce critic of American domestic and foreign policy? Of course. Did I ever hear him make remarks that could be considered controversial while I sat in church? Yes. Did I strongly disagree with many of his political views? Absolutely—just as I'm sure many of you have heard remarks from your pastors, priests, or rabbis with which you strongly disagreed.

But the remarks that have caused this recent firestorm weren't simply controversial. They weren't simply a religious leader's effort to speak out against perceived injustice. Instead, they expressed a profoundly distorted view of this country—a view that sees white racism as endemic, and that elevates what is wrong with America above all that we know is right with America; a view that sees the conflicts in the Middle East as rooted primarily in the actions of stalwart allies like Israel, instead of emanating from the perverse and hateful ideologies of radical Islam.

As such, Reverend Wright's comments were not only wrong but divisive, divisive at a time when we need unity, racially charged at a time when we need to come together to solve a set of monumental problems—two wars, a terrorist threat, a falling economy, a chronic health care crisis, and potentially devastating climate change, problems that are neither black or white or Latino or Asian, but rather, problems that confront us all.

Given my background, my politics, and my professed values and ideals, there will no doubt be those for whom my statements of condemnation are not enough. Why associate myself with Reverend Wright in the first place? they may ask. Why not join another church? And I confess that if all that I knew of Reverend Wright were the snippets of those sermons that have run in an endless loop on the television and YouTube, or if Trinity United Church of Christ conformed to the caricatures being peddled by some commentators, there is no doubt that I would react in much the same way.

But the truth is, that isn't all that I know of the man. The man I met more than twenty years ago is a man who helped introduce me to my Christian faith, a man who spoke to me about our obligations to love one another, to care for the sick and lift up the poor. He is a man who served his country as a U.S. Marine; who has studied and lectured at some of the finest universities and seminaries in the country; and who for over thirty years led a church that serves the community by doing God's work here on Earth—by housing the homeless, ministering to the needy, providing day care services and scholarships and prison ministries, and reaching out to those suffering from HIV/AIDS.

In my first book, *Dreams from My Father*, I described the experience of my first service at Trinity:

> People began to shout, to rise from their seats and clap and cry out, a forceful wind carrying the reverend's voice up into the rafters . . . And in that single note—hope!—I heard something else; at the foot of that cross, inside the thousands of churches across the city, I imagined the stories of ordinary black people merging with the stories of David and Goliath, Moses and Pharaoh, the Christians in the lion's den, Ezekiel's field of dry bones. Those stories—of survival, and freedom, and hope—became our story, my story; the blood that had spilled was our blood, the tears our tears; until this black church, on this bright day, seemed once more a vessel carrying the story of a people into future generations and into a larger world. Our trials and triumphs became at once unique and universal, black and more than black; in chronicling our journey, the stories and songs gave us a means to reclaim memories that we didn't need to feel shame about . . . memories that all people might study and cherish—and with which we could start to rebuild.

That has been my experience at Trinity. Like other predominantly black churches across the country, Trinity embodies the black community in its entirety—the doctor and the welfare mom, the model student and the former gangbanger. Like other black churches', Trinity's services are full of raucous laughter and sometimes bawdy humor. They are full of dancing, clapping, screaming, and shouting that may seem jarring to the untrained ear. The church contains in full the kindness and cruelty, the fierce intelligence and the shocking ignorance, the struggles and successes, the love and, yes, the bitterness and bias, that make up the black experience in America.

And this helps explain, perhaps, my relationship with Reverend Wright. As imperfect as he may be, he has been like family to me. He strengthened my faith, officiated my wedding, and baptized my children. Not once in my conversations with him have I heard him talk about any ethnic group in derogatory terms, or treat whites with whom he interacted with anything but courtesy and respect. He contains within him the contradictions—the good and the bad—of the community that he has served diligently for so many years.

I can no more disown him than I can disown the black community. I can no more disown him than I can my white grandmother—a woman who helped raise me, a woman who sacrificed again and again for me, a woman who loves me as much as she loves anything in this world, but a woman who once confessed her fear of black men who passed by her on the street, and who on more than one occasion has uttered racial or ethnic stereotypes that made me cringe.

These people are a part of me. And they are a part of America, this country that I love.

Some will see this as an attempt to justify or excuse comments that are simply inexcusable. I can assure you it is not. I suppose the politically safe thing would be to move on from this episode and just hope that it fades into the woodwork. We can dismiss Reverend Wright as a crank or a demagogue, just as some have dismissed Geraldine Ferraro, in the aftermath of her recent statements, as harboring some deep-seated racial bias.

But race is an issue that I believe this nation cannot afford to ignore right now. We would be making the same mistake that Reverend Wright made in his offending sermons about America—to simplify and stereotype and amplify the negative to the point that it distorts reality.

The fact is that the comments that have been made and the issues that have surfaced over the last few weeks reflect the complexities of race in this country that we've never really worked through—a part of our union that we have yet to perfect. And if we walk away now, if we simply retreat into our respective corners, we will never be able to come together and solve challenges like health care, or education, or the need to find good jobs for every American.

Understanding this reality requires a reminder of how we arrived at this point. As William Faulkner once wrote, "The past isn't dead and buried. In fact, it isn't even past." We do not need to recite here the history of racial injustice in this country. But we do need to remind ourselves that so many of the disparities that exist in the African American community today can be directly traced to inequalities passed on from an earlier generation that suffered under the brutal legacy of slavery and Jim Crow.

Segregated schools were, and are, inferior schools; we still haven't fixed them, fifty years after *Brown v. Board of Education*, and the inferior education they provided, then and now, helps explain the pervasive achievement gap between today's black and white students.

Legalized discrimination—where blacks were prevented, often through violence, from owning property, or loans were not granted to African American business owners, or black home owners could not access FHA mortgages, or blacks were excluded from unions, or the police force, or fire departments—meant that black families could not amass any meaningful wealth to bequeath to future generations. That history helps explain the wealth and income gap between black and white, and the concentrated pockets of poverty that persist in so many of today's urban and rural communities.

A lack of economic opportunity among black men, and the

shame and frustration that came from not being able to provide for one's family, contributed to the erosion of black families—a problem that welfare policies for many years may have worsened. And the lack of basic services in so many urban black neighborhoods—parks for kids to play in, police walking the beat, regular garbage pickup, and building code enforcement—all helped create a cycle of violence, blight, and neglect that continues to haunt us.

This is the reality in which Reverend Wright and other African Americans of his generation grew up. They came of age in the late fifties and early sixties, a time when segregation was still the law of the land and opportunity was systematically constricted. What's remarkable is not how many failed in the face of discrimination, but rather, how many men and women overcame the odds, how many were able to make a way out of no way for those like me who would come after them.

But for all those who scratched and clawed their way to get a piece of the American dream, there were many who didn't make it—those who were ultimately defeated, in one way or another, by discrimination. That legacy of defeat was passed on to future generations—those young men and increasingly young women who we see standing on street corners or languishing in our prisons, without hope or prospects for the future. Even for those blacks who did make it, questions of race, and racism, continue to define their worldview in fundamental ways. For the men and women of Reverend Wright's generation, the memories of humiliation and doubt and fear have not gone away; nor has the anger and the bitterness of those years. That anger may not get expressed in public, in front of white co-workers or white friends. But it does find voice in the barbershop or around the kitchen table. At times, that anger is exploited by politicians, to gin up votes along racial lines, or to make up for a politician's own failings.

And occasionally it finds voice in the church on Sunday morning, in the pulpit and in the pews. The fact that so many people are surprised to hear that anger in some of Reverend Wright's sermons simply reminds us of the old truism that the most segregated hour in American life occurs on Sunday morning. That anger is not always productive; indeed, all too often it distracts attention from solving real problems; it keeps us from squarely facing our own complicity in our condition, and prevents the African American community from forging the alliances it needs to bring about real change. But the anger is real; it is powerful; and to simply wish it away, to condemn it without understanding its roots, only serves to widen the chasm of misunderstanding that exists between the races.

In fact, a similar anger exists within segments of the white community. Most working- and middle-class white Americans don't feel that they have been particularly privileged by their race. Their experience is the immigrant experience—as far as they're concerned, no one's handed them anything; they've built it from scratch. They've worked hard all their lives, many times only to see their jobs shipped overseas or their pension dumped after a lifetime of labor. They are anxious about their futures, and feel their dreams slipping away; in an era of stagnant wages and global competition, opportunity comes to be seen as a zero-sum game, in which your dreams come at my expense. So when they are told to bus their children to a school across town; when they hear that an African American is getting an advantage in landing a good job or a spot in a good college because of an injustice that they themselves never committed; when they're told that their fears about crime in urban neighborhoods are somehow prejudiced, resentment builds over time.

Like the anger within the black community, these resentments aren't always expressed in polite company. But they have helped shape the political landscape for at least a generation. Anger over welfare and affirmative action helped forge the Reagan Coalition. Politicians routinely exploited fears of crime for their own electoral ends. Talk show hosts and conservative commentators built entire careers unmasking bogus claims of racism while dismissing legitimate discussions of racial injustice and inequality as mere political correctness or reverse racism.

Just as black anger often proved counterproductive, so have these white resentments distracted attention from the real culprits of the middle-class squeeze—a corporate culture rife with inside dealing, questionable accounting practices, and short-term greed; a Washington dominated by lobbyists and special interests; economic policies that favor the few over the many. And yet, to wish away the resentments of white Americans, to label them as misguided or even racist, without recognizing they are grounded in legitimate concerns—this too widens the racial divide, and blocks the path to understanding.

This is where we are right now. It's a racial stalemate we've been stuck in for years. Contrary to the claims of some of my critics, black and white, I have never been so naive as to believe that we can get beyond our racial divisions in a single election cycle, or with a single candidacy—particularly a candidacy as imperfect as my own.

But I have asserted a firm conviction—a conviction rooted in my faith in God and my faith in the American people—that working together we can move beyond some of our old racial wounds, and that in fact we have no choice if we are to continue on the path of a more perfect union.

For the African American community, that path means embracing the burdens of our past without becoming victims of our past. It means continuing to insist on a full measure of justice in every aspect of American life. But it also means binding our particular grievances—for better health care, and better schools, and better jobs—to the larger aspirations of all Americans: the white woman struggling to break the glass ceiling, the white man who's been laid off, the immigrant trying to feed his family. And it means taking full responsibility for our own lives—by demanding more from our fathers, and spending more time with our children, and reading to them, and teaching them that while they may face challenges and discrimination in their own lives, they must never succumb to despair or cynicism; they must always believe that they can write their own destiny.

Ironically, this quintessentially American—and yes, conservative—notion of self-help found frequent expression in Reverend Wright's sermons. But what my former pastor too often failed to understand is that embarking on a program of self-help also requires a belief that society can change.

The profound mistake of Reverend Wright's sermons is not that he spoke about racism in our society. It's that he spoke as if our society was static; as if no progress has been made; as if this country—a country that has made it possible for one of his own members to run for the highest office in the land and build a coalition of white and black, Latino and Asian, rich and poor, young and old—is still irrevocably bound to a tragic past. But what we know—what we have seen—is that America can change. That is the true genius of this nation. What we have already achieved gives us hope—the audacity to hope—for what we can and must achieve tomorrow.

In the white community, the path to a more perfect union means acknowledging that what ails the African American community does not just exist in the minds of black people; that the legacy of discrimination and current incidents of discrimination, while less overt than in the past, are real and must be addressed. Not just with words, but with deeds—by investing in our schools and our communities; by enforcing our civil rights laws and ensuring fairness in our criminal justice system; by providing this generation with ladders of opportunity that were unavailable for previous generations. It requires all Americans to realize that your dreams do not have to come at the expense of my dreams; that investing in the health, welfare, and education of black and brown and white children will ultimately help all of America prosper.

In the end, then, what is called for is nothing more, and nothing less, than what all the world's great religions demand—that we do unto others as we would have them do unto us. Let us be our brother's keeper, Scripture tells us. Let us be our sister's keeper. Let us find that common stake we all have in one another, and let our politics reflect that spirit as well.

For we have a choice in this country. We can accept a politics that breeds division, and conflict, and cynicism. We can tackle race only as spectacle, as we did in the O. J. trial, or in the wake of tragedy, as we did in the aftermath of Katrina, or as fodder for the nightly news. We can play Reverend Wright's sermons on every channel, every day, and talk about them from now until the election, and make the only question in this campaign whether or not the American people think that I somehow believe or sympathize with his most offensive words. We can pounce on some gaffe by a Hillary supporter as evidence that she's playing the race card, or we can speculate on whether white men will all flock to John McCain in the general election regardless of his policies.

We can do that.

But if we do, I can tell you that in the next election, we'll be talking about some other distraction. And then another one. And then another one. And nothing will change.

That is one option. Or, at this moment, in this election, we can come together and say, "Not this time." This time we want to talk about the crumbling schools that are stealing the future of black children and white children and Asian children and Hispanic children and Native American children. This time we want to reject the cynicism that tells us that these kids can't learn, that those kids who don't look like us are somebody else's problem. The children of America are not those kids, they are our kids, and we will not let them fall behind in a twenty-first-century economy. Not this time.

This time we want to talk about how the lines in the emergency room are filled with whites and blacks and Hispanics who do not have health care; who don't have the power on their own to overcome the special interests in Washington, but who can take them on if we do it together.

This time we want to talk about the shuttered mills that once provided a decent life for men and women of every race, and the homes for sale that once belonged to Americans from every religion, every region, every walk of life. This time we want to talk about the fact that the real problem is not that someone who doesn't look like you might take your job; it's that the corporation you work for will ship it overseas for nothing more than a profit.

This time we want to talk about the men and women of every color and creed who serve together, and fight together, and bleed together under the same proud flag. We want to talk about how to bring them home from a war that never should've been authorized and never should've been waged, and we want to talk about how we'll show our patriotism by caring for them, and their families, and giving them the benefits they have earned.

I would not be running for president if I didn't believe with all my heart that this is what the vast majority of Americans want for this country. This union may never be perfect, but generation after generation has shown that it can always be perfected. And today, whenever I find myself feeling doubtful or cynical about this possibility, what gives me the most hope is the next generation—the young people whose attitudes and beliefs and openness to change have already made history in this election.

There is one story in particular that I'd like to leave you with today—a story I told when I had the great honor of speaking on Dr. King's birthday at his home church, Ebenezer Baptist, in Atlanta.

There is a young, twenty-three-year-old white woman named Ashley Baia who organized for our campaign in Florence, South Carolina. She had been working to organize a mostly African

American community since the beginning of this campaign, and one day she was at a roundtable discussion where everyone went around telling their story and why they were there.

And Ashley said that when she was nine years old, her mother got cancer. And because she had to miss days of work, she was let go and lost her health care. They had to file for bankruptcy, and that's when Ashley decided that she had to do something to help her mom.

She knew that food was one of their most expensive costs, and so Ashley convinced her mother that what she really liked and really wanted to eat more than anything else was mustard and relish sandwiches. Because that was the cheapest way to eat.

She did this for a year, until her mom got better, and she told everyone at the roundtable that the reason she joined our campaign was so that she could help the millions of other children in the country who want and need to help their parents too.

Now Ashley might have made a different choice. Perhaps somebody told her along the way that the source of her mother's problems were blacks who were on welfare and too lazy to work, or Hispanics who were coming into the country illegally. But she didn't. She sought out allies in her fight against injustice.

Anyway, Ashley finishes her story and then goes around the room and asks everyone else why they're supporting the campaign. They all have different stories and reasons. Many bring up a specific issue. And finally they come to this elderly black man who's been sitting there quietly the entire time. And Ashley asks him why he's there. And he does not bring up a specific issue. He does not say health care or the economy. He does not say education or the war. He does not say that he was there because of Barack Obama. He simply says to everyone in the room, "I am here because of Ashley."

"I'm here because of Ashley." By itself, that single moment of recognition between that young white girl and that old black man is not enough. It is not enough to give health care to the sick, or jobs to the jobless, or education to our children.

But it is where we start. It is where our union grows stronger. And as so many generations have come to realize over the course of the two hundred and twenty-one years since a band of patriots signed that document in Philadelphia, that is where the perfection begins.

ABOUT THE CONTRIBUTORS

OMAR H. ALI is an assistant professor of history at Towson University and is the author of *In the Balance of Power: Independent Black Politics and Third Party Movements in the United States* (2008). He frequently lectures on independent politics in the United States and has been a commentator on Public Broadcasting Service, National Public Radio, Al Jazeera English, CBS News, ABC News, Telemundo, WLIB, WAOK, BlogTalkRadio, and IndependentVoting.org, discussing the diversification of the black electorate.

KELI GOFF is an expert on youth and minority voters. She emerged as one of the most recognizable political pundits of the 2008 presidential election cycle. She has appeared on numerous national programs including *The CBS Early Show*, CNN's *Anderson Cooper 360*, MSNBC's *Verdict with Dan Abrams*, and BET's *The Truth with Jeff Johnson*, for which she served as a regular contributor. She is the author of the critically acclaimed book *Party Crashing: How the Hip-Hop Generation Declared Political Independence* (2008). One of the first books to explore the rise of Generation Obama, *Party Crashing* has been the subject of coverage in a host of media outlets, including *Vanity Fair* and *Ebony*. Goff holds a B.A. from New York University and a master's degree in strategic communications from Columbia University. A native of Texas, she now resides in New York City.

OBERY M. HENDRICKS JR. is Professor of Biblical Interpretation at New York Theological Seminary and Visiting Professor of Religion and African American Studies at Columbia University. He is also past president of Payne Theological Seminary, the oldest African American theological institution. Hendricks holds a Ph.D in religion from Princeton University. He is one of the most widely read academic biblical scholars in America, and his most recent book is the award-winning *The Politics of Jesus: Rediscovering the True Revolutionary Nature of Jesus' Teachings and How They Have Been Corrupted* (2006).

DERRICK Z. JACKSON was a 2001 finalist for the Pulitzer Prize for commentary. A *Boston Globe* columnist since 1988, he is a two-time winner of and three-time finalist for commentary awards from the National Education Writers Association and a six-time winner of and thirteen-time finalist for political and sports commentary awards from the National Association of Black Journalists. He was the 2003 recipient of Columbia University's "Let's Do It Better" commentary award and a 2004 winner of the National Lesbian and Gay Journalists Association's commentary award. Jackson is also a three-time winner of the Sword of Hope commentary award from the New England Division of the American Cancer Society and a five-time winner of Unity journalism awards from Lincoln University in Missouri. Prior to writing for the *Globe*, he won several awards at *Newsday*, including the 1985 Columbia University Meyer Berger Award for coverage of New York City and the 1979 award for feature writing from the Professional Basketball Writers Association. Jackson, born in 1955, is a native of Milwaukee, Wisconsin, and is a 1976 graduate of the University of Wisconsin at Milwaukee. He was a Nieman Fellow in Journalism at Harvard University in 1984. He holds honorary degrees from the Episcopal Divinity School in Cambridge, Massachusetts, and Salem State College in Salem, Massachusetts, and a human rights award from Curry College in Milton, Massachusetts. Throughout the primary and general elections, Jackson conducted several one-on-one interviews with Barack Obama. He has produced an online photo essay on the candidate's discipline and the changing nature of patriotism.

BAKARI KITWANA is a journalist, activist, and author whose 2002 groundbreaking book *The Hip-Hop Generation: Young Blacks and the Crisis in African American Culture* was called the definitive book on the culture by the *New York Times*. Senior editor at Newsone.com, the Internet news presence of Radio One, he hosts the site's video blog UnderGround Current. Kitwana is also the founder and CEO of Rap Sessions, which tours the nation conducting town hall meetings on difficult dialogues facing young Americans. The 2009 tour, like his contribution to this volume, raises the question "Is America Really Post-Racial?" The former executive editor of the *Source*—the nation's top-selling music magazine—he cofounded the first-ever National Hip-Hop Political Convention, which brought over four thousand young people to Newark, New Jersey, in 2004 to create and endorse a political agenda for the hip-hop generation. He was the 2007–2008 artist-in-residence at the Center for the Study of Race, Politics and Culture at the University of Chicago, and his essays have appeared in the *New York Times*, the *Village Voice*, and the *Progressive*. He is currently at work on *Hip-Hop Political Activism in the Obama Era*.

As poet, publisher, editor, and educator, **HAKI R. MADHUBUTI** has been a pivotal figure in the development of a strong Black literary tradition, emerging from the Civil Rights and Black Arts era of the 1960s and continuing to the present. Over the years, he has published more than twenty-eight books (some under his former name, Don L. Lee) and is one of the world's bestselling authors of poetry and nonfiction, with books in print in excess of three million copies. His *Black Men: Obsolete, Single, Dangerous?: The African American Family in Transition* (1990) has sold more than one million copies. Madhubuti is a proponent of independent Black institutions. He founded Third World Press in 1967. He is also a founder of the Institute of Positive Education/New Concept School (1969) and cofounder of Betty Shabazz International Charter School (1998), Barbara A. Sizemore Middle School (2005), and DuSable Leadership Academy (2005), all of which are in Chicago.

An award-winning poet and recipient of the National Endowment for the Arts and National Endowment for the Humanities fellowships, American Book Award, the Studs Terkel Humanities Service Award, and others, Madhubuti received his third honorary Doctor of Letters from Spelman College in 2006. In 2007, he was named Chicagoan of the Year by *Chicago* magazine. In May of 2008, Madhubuti was honored with a Lifetime Achievement Award from Art Sanctuary of Philadelphia. In 2009, he was named one of the *Ebony* Power 150: Most Influential Blacks in America for education.

Currently he is the University Distinguished Professor and professor of English, founder, and director-emeritus of the Gwendolyn Brooks Center and director of the Master of Fine Arts in Creative Writing Program at Chicago State University.

ADAM MANSBACH's most recent novel, *The End of the Jews*, was published in March 2008. His previous novel, *Angry Black White Boy, or The Miscegenation of Macon Detornay*, was a *San Francisco Chronicle* Best Book of 2005 and is taught at more than fifty universities. His previous books include the novel *Shackling Water* (2002), the poetry collection *genius b-boy cynics getting weeded in the garden of delights* (2002), and the short story anthology *A Fictional History of the United States with Huge Chunks Missing* (2006), which he co-edited. A grantee of the Future Aesthetics Artist Regrant (FAAR)

Program, funded by the Ford Foundation, he is the 2009–2010 New Voices Professor of Fiction at Rutgers University.

JOAN MORGAN is an award-winning journalist and author and a provocative cultural critic. She began her professional writing career freelancing for the *Village Voice* before having her work published by *Vibe*, *Madison*, *Interview*, *Ms.* magazine, *More*, *Spin*, and numerous others. Formerly the executive editor of *Essence*, Morgan coined the term "hip-hop feminism" in 1999, when she published the groundbreaking book *When Chickenheads Come Home to Roost*. Her book has been used in college courses across the country. Morgan has made numerous television and radio appearances on national media outlets—among them MTV, BET, VH-1, *Like It Is*, and CNN.

ALICE RANDALL is writer-in-residence at Vanderbilt University. She is the author of three novels: *The Wind Done Gone* (2001), *Pushkin and the Queen of Spades* (2004), and *Rebel Yell* (2009). The only black woman in history to write a number-one country song, she lives in Tennessee with her husband.

CONNIE SCHULTZ is a nationally syndicated columnist for the Cleveland *Plain Dealer* and Creators Syndicate. She won the 2005 Pulitzer Prize for Commentary for columns that judges praised for providing "a voice for the underdog and the underprivileged." Also in 2005, Schultz won the Scripps Howard National Journalism Award for Commentary and the National Headliner Award for Commentary. She was a 2003 Pulitzer Prize finalist in feature writing for her series "The Burden of Innocence," which chronicled the ordeal of Michael Green, who was imprisoned for thirteen years for a rape he did not commit. The week after her series ran, the real rapist turned himself in after reading her stories. The series won the Robert F. Kennedy Award for Social Justice Reporting, the National Headliner Award's Best of Show, and journalism awards from

Harvard and Columbia universities. In 2004, Schultz won the Batten Medal, which honors "a body of journalistic work that reflects compassion, courage, humanity and a deep concern for the underdog." Recently, the Urban League of Greater Cleveland awarded Schultz the Whitney M. Young Humanitarian Award.

During the 2008 presidential race, Schultz was a frequent guest on *The Charlie Rose Show*, and she has also offered her midwesterner's perspective on MSNBC's *Rachel Maddow Show*, HBO's *Real Time with Bill Maher*, and C-SPAN's *Washington Journal*. Schultz is the author of two books published by Random House: *Life Happens— And Other Unavoidable Truths* (2006), a collection of essays, and . . . *and His Lovely Wife* (2007), a memoir about the successful 2006 race for the U.S. Senate of her husband, Sherrod Brown.

GENEVA SMITHERMAN is University Distinguished Professor of English and the Director of the African American Language and Literacy Program at Michigan State University. She has an international reputation for her work on African American Language and Culture. She is nationally recognized as a pioneer in African American Studies, having begun her work in the vineyards of Black Studies in the early 1970s at Harvard University in what was then called the AfroAmerican Studies Department. Smitherman has lectured and conducted workshops throughout the United States and abroad. Her current work focuses on language and politics in South Africa, where she has worked with scholars and activists since 1995. From 1977 to 1979, she was the chief advocate and expert witness for the children in the federal court case *Martin Luther King Junior Elementary School Children et al. v. Ann Arbor School District Board* (known internationally as the "Black English" case), and she subsequently convened a Rockefeller Foundation–funded national symposium on *King* and edited a publication, *Black English and the Education of Black Children and Youth* (1981), on the court case.

She is the author of several books and monographs, among

them, the award-winning classic *Talkin and Testifyin: The Language of Black America* (1977; 1986), *Black Talk: Words and Phrases from the Hood to the Amen Corner* (1994; 2000), and *Talkin That Talk: Language, Culture and Education in African America* (2000). Her most recent book is *Word from the Mother: Language and African Americans* (2006). She is the editor or coeditor of eight books on language, including *Black Linguistics: Language, Society, and Politics in Africa and the Americas* (2003) and *Language Diversity in the Classroom: From Intention to Practice* (2003).

Universities, school districts, and the media often call upon Smitherman for her expertise. Recently, these have included the Los Angeles Unified School District, Syracuse University, the National Center for Culturally Responsive Educational Systems, Emory University, the University of California, Los Angeles, the Detroit Public Schools, and *New York Times* language columnist William Safire. She has appeared in numerous local and national media venues, seeking to raise public awareness, including National Public Radio, the *Today* show, *The Oprah Winfrey Show*, CNN, *The Phil Donahue Show*, and *CBS Reports*.

DOMINIC THOMAS is the chair of the French and Francophone Studies and Italian departments at the University of California, Los Angeles. He is also a professor of Comparative Literature, French and Francophone Studies, and Italian. He is the author of *Nation-Building, Propaganda and Literature in Francophone Africa* (2002) and *Black France: Colonialism, Immigration and Transnationalism* (2007).

GILMAN W. WHITING is an assistant professor of African American and Diaspora Studies and the director of Undergraduate Studies in the African American and Diaspora Studies Program at Vanderbilt University. He also teaches in the Peabody College of Education in the Department of Human Organizational Development. His areas of research include work on young black fathers, low-income minorities, welfare reform and fatherhood initiatives, education reform, special needs populations (gifted students, at-risk learners, young black men, and scholar identities), and health in the black community. Whiting is the author of over thirty scholarly articles relating to minority populations, especially males, in such diverse publications as *Exceptional Children*, *Urban Education*, the *Willamette Journal: Special on African American Studies*, *Gifted Education Press Quarterly*, *Roeper Review*, *Journal for Secondary Gifted Education*, *Gifted Child Today*, and the *Midwestern Educational Research Journal*. He is the coeditor of *On Manliness: Black American Masculinities* (2008) and the author of a book-in-progress titled *Fathering from the Margins: Young African American Fathers and Presidential Politics and Policies*. He consults with school districts nationally on various issues related to psychosocial behavior and motivation among young students. Whiting is the creator of the Scholar Identity Model and codirects the Scholar Identity Institute for young black males at Vanderbilt.

WILLIAM JULIUS WILSON is the Lewis P. and Linda L. Geyser University Professor at Harvard University. He is a recipient of the 1998 National Medal of Science, the highest scientific honor in the United States, and was awarded the Talcott Parsons Prize in the Social Sciences by the American Academy of Arts and Sciences in 2003. Past president of the American Sociological Association, Wilson has received forty-one honorary degrees, including honorary doctorates from Princeton University, Columbia University, the University of Pennsylvania, Northwestern University, Johns Hopkins University, Dartmouth College, and the University of Amsterdam in the Netherlands. A MacArthur Fellow from 1987 to 1992, Wilson has been elected to the National Academy of Sciences, the American Academy of Arts and Sciences, the American Philosophical Society, the National Academy of Education, the Institute of Medicine, and the British Academy.

His publications include three award-winning and bestselling books: *The Declining Significance of Race* (1980), winner of the American Sociological Association's Sydney Spivack Award; *The Truly Disadvantaged* (1987), which was selected by the editors of the *New York Times Book Review* as one of the sixteen best books of 1987 and received the *Washington Monthly* Annual Book Award and the Society for the Study of Social Problems' C. Wright Mills Award; and *When Work Disappears* (1996), which was chosen as one of the notable books of 1996 by the editors of the *New York Times Book Review* and received the Sidney Hillman Foundation Award. His more recent publications include *The Bridge over the Racial Divide* (1999); a coauthored book (with Richard Taub), *There Goes the Neighborhood* (2006); and the book upon which this essay is based, *More than Just Race: Being Black and Poor in the Inner City* (2009).

A NOTE ON THE EDITOR

T. DENEAN SHARPLEY-WHITING is Professor of African American and Diaspora Studies and French and Italian at Vanderbilt University, where she is also the director of the African American and Diaspora Studies Program as well as the W. T. Bandy Center for Baudelaire and Modern French Studies. She is the author/editor of ten books. Her latest, the award-winning *Pimps Up, Ho's Down: Hip Hop's Hold on Young Black Women*, received the American Cultural Association/Popular Culture Association's 2007 Emily Toth Award for the Best Single Work by One or More Authors in Women's Issues in Popular and American Culture. The book was also recognized by *Ebony* as an April 2007 top nonfiction work. It has been praised in such venues as *Ms.* magazine, the *Source*, the *Philadelphia Inquirer*, and the *Washington Post*. Sharpley-Whiting testified before the 110th Congress in 2007 on degrading images of women in media and popular culture in the wake of the Don Imus controversy. She lectures widely in the United States and abroad and has offered commentary on a range of issues for Fox, MSNBC, NPR, and CBS News. She was the 2006 winner of Brown University's Horace Mann Medal.